Therapies for
Psychosomatic
Disorders
in Children

Charles E. Schaefer
Howard L. Millman
Gary F. Levine

THERAPIES FOR PSYCHOSOMATIC DISORDERS IN CHILDREN

Jossey-Bass Publishers

San Francisco • Washington • London • 1984

THERAPIES FOR PSYCHOSOMATIC DISORDERS IN CHILDREN
by Charles E. Schaefer, Howard L. Millman, and Gary F. Levine

Copyright © 1979 by: Jossey-Bass, Inc., Publishers
433 California Street
San Francisco, California 94104
&
Jossey-Bass Limited
28 Banner Street
London EC1Y 8QE

Library of Congress Cataloging in Publication Data

Schaefer, Charles E
    Therapies for psychosomatic disorders in children.

    Includes bibliographies and indexes.
    1. Pediatrics—Psychosomatic aspects—Addresses,
essays, lectures. 2. Child psychotherapy—Addresses,
essays, lectures. I. Millman, Howard L., joint author.
II. Levine, Gary F., joint author. III. Title.
[DNLM: 1. Psychophysiologic disorders—In infancy and
childhood. 2. Psychophysiologic disorders—Therapy.
WM90.3 T398]
RJ47.5.S32   618.9'2'008   79-88111
ISBN 0-87589-417-8

Manufactured in the United States of America

JACKET DESIGN BY WILLI BAUM

FIRST EDITION
    First printing: September 1979
    Second printing: May 1984

Code 7921

The Jossey-Bass
Social and Behavioral Science Series

GUIDEBOOKS FOR THERAPEUTIC PRACTICE
Charles E. Schaefer and Howard L. Millman
Consulting Editors

Therapies for Children: A Handbook of Effective
Treatments for Problem Behaviors
Charles E. Schaefer and Howard L. Millman
1977

Therapies for Psychosomatic Disorders in Children
Charles E. Schaefer, Howard L. Millman,
and Gary F. Levine
1979

Preface

In recent years there has been a marked upsurge of interest in psychosomatic disorders in children and adolescents. Accompanying this interest has been an expanded awareness of the relationship between psychosocial factors and physical disorders. The term *psychosomatic disorders* refers to any physical conditions that can be initiated, exacerbated, or prolonged by psychosocial factors. Since the emotions influence all bodily processes by means of the nervous and humoral systems, any physical disorder is possibly psychosomatic in nature.

Psychosomatic disorders abound in childhood. In fact, psychosomatic dysfunction occurs so frequently among school-age children that it is among the commonest causes of repeated absence from school. Asthma alone, for example, is estimated to be responsible for nearly one quarter of the days reported lost from school because of chronic illness, and from 2 to 5 percent of schoolchildren suffer from this one illness. Despite the prevalence of such disorders, however, practitioners were until recently ill equipped to deal with many of them because of a lack of basic knowledge about their psychological bases and about useful therapeutic techniques. And children with psychosomatic problems remain difficult to treat despite some advances in the field. We hope this compendium will contribute to the dissemination and advancement of more effective therapeutic practices.

Although the field of psychosomatic medicine continues to develop at a rapid rate, there has been, unfortunately, some lack of communication and carry-over between the specialists in this field and other personnel who work with children. All too often the busy physician has too little time to devote to developing an intensive social and emotional case history of the child and may treat some of the somatic problems without a thorough awareness of related psychological problems. We hope this book will be read by specialists and general practitioners as well and thus serve to improve communication among all those who treat children.

Designed to be representative rather than exhaustive in coverage, this book includes effective treatments for the more classical psychosomatic disorders of the major systems—the cardiovascular, gastrointestinal, neuromuscular, nervous, respiratory, and urinary systems—as well as for skin disorders and conversion reactions. Beyond the scope of this book are disorders that have been termed "somatopsychic," that is, physical illnesses which create secondary psychological disturbances. An example of the latter is provided by the child who has come to relish the "secondary gains" of being attended to because of a physical ailment. Also omitted from coverage are such problems as infant colic and adolescent acne, because this volume focuses on psychosomatic disorders common to the preschool and grade school years, roughly ages three to thirteen.

Within these limitations, however, this practical volume is far ranging and detailed in its treatment. It should prove valuable as a daily reference for professionals and as a resource for students in such fields as pediatric medicine, psychiatry, psychology, social work, nursing, and human development.

Using the digest format of our previous book (C. E. Schaefer and H. L. Millman, *Therapies for Children: A Handbook of Effective Treatments for Problem Behaviors,* San Francisco: Jossey-Bass, 1977), this volume condenses more than eighty widely varied professional articles from the world literature. By eliminating technical research data and lengthy discussion, the digests enable the reader to quickly locate and assimilate clinically relevant information. Since research and practice on childhood psychosomatic disorders have rapidly expanded of late, the condensation format seems especially practical. Of course, readers are encouraged to go to the original sources from which the digests have been abstracted and to read the authors' articles in their entirety.

The space devoted to each disorder in this book is to a large extent related to the amount of research that has been conducted to date. Since asthma, for instance, has been extensively studied in the past, we have treated it in more detail so as to reflect the wide range of treatment options currently available. Whenever possible, we have emphasized studies involving children, although supplementary material from the adolescent or adult literature is occasionally cited.

We have also tried to include in this volume all the recent innovations in the treatment of psychosomatic disorders. Thus the reader will find a large number of behavior therapy approaches, most of which treat specific disorders (vomiting, asthma attacks, headaches) using such techniques as desensitization, stimulus control, and operant reinforcement. The reader will also find recent developments in the self-regulation of internal states (physiological and psychological) by such means as biofeedback, relaxation training, meditation, and self-hypnosis. In addition, family therapy methods as well as more traditional treatments involving the use of psychopharmacological or psychodynamic practices are included, in keeping with a broad eclectic orientation. Finally, the use of parents as therapists for their own children, so as to encourage generalization of treatment effects, is highlighted in this book.

It should be noted that we have not attempted to give a critical review of the theoretical or experimental bases for the therapeutic techniques presented. As previously mentioned, our intent is to describe the practice or specific application aspect of the theory, research, and practice triad. The reader who seeks to fully evaluate the soundness of a particular technique should consult the original article in its entirety, as well as the many excellent books on psychotherapy theory and research. The student, in particular, is cautioned to avoid accepting any method on its face validity.

We wish to thank the many authors and researchers whose work is cited in this volume. Permission to digest each article was given by the authors, except in a few cases where the author could not be located. We would also like to thank Phyllis Saccone for her invaluable assistance during all phases of manuscript preparation.

July 1979   Charles E. Schaefer
                                               Dobbs Ferry, New York

                                               Howard L. Millman
                                               Dobbs Ferry, New York

                                               Gary F. Levine
                                               New York, New York

Contents

Contents

The Authors

Charles E. Schaefer is supervising psychologist at The Children's Village, a residential treatment center for emotionally disturbed children in Dobbs Ferry, New York, and also maintains a private practice for children and their families. In 1967 he received the Ph.D. in clinical psychology from Fordham University, where he remained for another three years conducting research with Anne Anastasi on the identification and development of creative thinking in children and youth.

In addition to numerous psychological tests and articles in professional journals, Charles Schaefer is the author or editor of five books related to children: *How to Influence Children: A*

Handbook of Practical Parenting Skills (1978); *Therapeutic Use of Child's Play* (1976); *Developing Creativity in Children* (1973); *Becoming Somebody: Creative Activities for Preschool and Primary Grade Children* (1973); and *Young Voices: An Anthology of Poetry by Children* (1971).

Apart from clinical practice, his current professional interest concerns the identification and development of more effective ways for parents and teachers to influence children; that is, better ways for adults to promote the personal and social development of children. His affiliations include fellow to the American Orthopsychiatric Association and member of the American Educational Research Association, American Psychological Association, and Psychologists in Private Practice.

Howard L. Millman received the Ph.D. in clinical psychology from Adelphi University in 1964, after having majored in psychology at the City College of New York. He completed a clinical psychology internship at the Neuropsychiatric Institute at the University of California at Los Angeles, where he first became interested in the effects and treatment of brain dysfunctioning. He later became chief psychologist at the Middlesex County Mental Health Clinic in New Jersey. Currently he is director of Psychological Services and Research at the Children's Village and director of Psychological and Educational Services of Westchester. He has taught and supervised doctoral psychology students at Rutgers—the State University and at the City College of New York. At present, he teaches courses on interviewing and counseling and group psychodynamics to graduate students at Manhattanville College in Purchase, New York. He is a member of the Council for Exceptional Children and the Division of Psychotherapy of the American Psychological Association.

Howard Millman has published numerous articles in professional journals on psychotherapy, behavior and learning problems in children, brain dysfunction, and research concerning evaluation of programs designed to treat emotionally disturbed children. His training and interest in adolescents and adults resulted in *Goals and Behavior in Psychotherapy and Counseling* (with J. T. Huber, 1972), a book widely used in training mental health professionals.

Gary F. Levine is the Director of Primary Care Pediatric Resident Training at the New York Medical College. He received his M.D. degree from New York Medical College in 1974. After serving as resident in pediatrics at the Metropolitan Hospital Center in New York City from 1974-1976, he was appointed chief resident. During the period of his postgraduate education he developed an interest in the principles of holistic medicine and their application to pediatric practice and acquired additional training in meditation and relaxation techniques, hypnosis, and acupuncture.

In 1977 Gary Levine was appointed to the full-time faculty of the Department of Pediatrics, New York Medical College, where he has developed a course for medical students that emphasizes the importance of a humanistic approach to patients. He is currently working with a multidisciplinary team of physicians, social workers, and child psychologists to implement a Pediatric Psychosomatics Clinic at the Metropolitan Hospital Center.

*To the advancement
of an effective interdisciplinary approach
for psychosomatic disorders in children*

Therapies for Psychosomatic Disorders in Children

Introduction: Current Trends in Treatment of Children's Psychosomatic Disorders

In general, psychosomatic problems seem to arise when a child develops a pattern of continually responding physiologically to stress. A recent study of twenty-five children with asthma disclosed that in 50 percent of the cases emotional stress or parental behavior or both appeared to have strongly influenced the onset of attacks. In the remaining cases such a correlation was not evident (but could have existed). The particular form the disorder takes seems to depend on a number of variables, including genetic predisposition and personality type.

It has become increasingly apparent that psychological factors play an important role in the precipitation or exacerbation of most physical disorders. Psychological influences may make a person more susceptible to infection by lowering adaptive resources or may prolong an illness as in the case of a person who has negative reactions to being sick. Thus, almost every physical symptom not directly attributable to mechanical trauma can be considered psychosomatic insofar as a person's emotional or psychic life cannot be divorced from the body.

According to the *Diagnostic and Statistical Manual* of the American Psychiatric Association (Washington, D.C., 1968, p. 46), psychophysiological reactions are a "group of disorders characterized by physical symptoms that are caused by emotional factors and involve a single organ system, usually under autonomic nervous system innervation." It is generally recognized today, however, that there is no simple, direct, causative relationship between emotions (or their physiological components) and physical illness. Indeed, the interrelationship of *soma* and *psyche* is quite complex, and most theoreticians agree that several elements are involved in the etiology of psychosomatic disorders. And so although individuals' genetic inheritance may predispose them to certain kinds of disease or illness, environmental influences, to varying degrees, must come into operation to bring out the phenotype.

Beyond this area of general agreement, however, diverse opinions are held about the validity of particular etiological hypotheses. Some investigators have proposed that individuals who are predisposed to psychosomatic disorders are unable to express their emotions and are, in fact, unfamiliar with the subjective experience of their emotions. The word *alexithymia* has been used to describe the condition in which persons systematically avoid expressing emotions. Other theoreticians espouse a specificity hypothesis, asserting that specific conflicts or stresses, personality characteristics, and emotional states lead to specific psychosomatic disorders.

Still another view is expressed by supporters of social learning theory, who propose that individuals unconsciously learn to adopt a sick role because it is shaped by one or more of the following social influences: (a) vicarious learning through models, especially in childhood; (b) direct social reinforcement of illness behavior by family, friends, and physicians; and (c) avoidance learning. This last is demonstrated by the child who has shown a lack of academic or social competence and then adopts an illness role, which can bring about an exemption from social responsibilities without any additional loss of pride or self-esteem.

The "life changes" concept is also gaining more attention of late; its advocates state that an accumulation of adverse life changes or poor coping mechanisms or both predisposes a person to physical illness or death. And finally, different "trigger mechanisms," such as an increase in anxiety, have been demonstrated to set off a psychosomatic illness.

The traditional approach to understanding and treating somatic disorders has been based on a medical model, characterized by an emphasis on the etiology and pathogenesis of physical disease. According to this approach, all overt physical disorders are the result of some underlying organic disease or dysfunctional physiological process. As a result, the treatment of choice is to chemically or surgically cure the diseased state of the organism. An alternate model that is gaining favor in medicine and clinical psychology is the concept of holism—namely, that all biological disorders have psychological elements and all psychological disorders have biological elements which must be considered in both diagnosis and treatment. In short, the organism is a *biopsychosocial* unit. Psychosomatic disorders represent a class of physiological symptoms that are primarily a response to stressful situations or to affective states. And therefore an understanding of psychosomatic disorders requires a knowledge not only of the precipitating psychosocial factors but also of the biological processes resulting in disordered function.

A holistic, integrated, or total approach, then, takes into consideration the initial condition of the child, as well as the physical, emotional, and interactional aspects. People who hold this view often employ a combination of therapeutic techniques, such as drugs, behavior therapy, and family counseling, because they believe the most effective treatment for a number of psychosomatic disorders requires intervention on more than one level of dysfunction. At the same time it is clear that some childhood somatic disorders are entirely physical in origin, such as disorders resulting from physical trauma or poisons, and are best treated according to the medical model alone. Unfortunately, the medical literature has long focused on the biological and physical correlates of psychosomatic disorders and largely ignored the psychological elements. We have therefore focused in this book on the psychosocial factors, in an attempt to balance the literature.

Several recent developments should help advance a holistic or biopsychosocial approach to psychosomatic disorders. First, there is increasing interest in the teaching of medical behavioral science in medical schools. A major goal of introducing behavioral (psychological, social, cultural) sciences into the biomedical curriculum is to increase the doctors' ability to deal with the psychological and social aspects of illness and medical care. A recent publication (L. Van Egeren and H. Fabrega, "Behavioral Science and Medical Education: A Biobehavioral Perspective," *Social Science and Medicine,* 1976, *10,* 535-539), suggests a model for teaching.

In another development, scientists from different fields have proposed a new biopsychosocial model that can encompass all health and disease. A basic premise of this approach is that all physical and psychological illnesses can be considered psychosomatic in that comprehensive understanding and care cannot be achieved without considering the three interrelated systems (biological, psychological, and social). The term *behavioral medicine* is being used to describe this interdisciplinary mode. In contrast to the etiological approach of the "old" psychosomatic medicine, behavioral medicine stresses the prevention and treatment of physical disorders. As defined by a distinguished group of behavioral and biomedical scientists, behavioral medicine is the field concerned with the development of behavioral-science knowledge and techniques relevant to the understanding of physical health and illness and the application of this knowledge and these techniques to diagnosis, prevention, treatment, and rehabilitation (G. G. Schwartz and S. M. Weiss, "What Is Behavioral Medicine?" *Psychosomatic Medicine,* 1977, *39,* 377-381). The present handbook reflects this behavioral medicine approach to the treatment of psychosomatic disorders. We feel that effective therapies for such disorders can thrive only on interdisciplinary research and cooperation.

In recent years there has been a remarkable burgeoning of therapeutic practices for psychosomatic disorders. This new array is challenging professionals to become versatile and skilled in a wide variety of treatments. Some practitioners respond to this challenge by continuing to apply a limited repertoire of techniques to all problems and patients in the belief that one method is as good as another. Other professionals who are more open are attempting to gain proficiency in many treatments in order to match, as closely as possible, the individual child or family and their disturbance with the most appropriate specific therapy. In other words they are trying to base the choice of treatment more on patient variables than on clinician variables.

Underlying their efforts is the concept of prescriptive eclecticism, which integrates the ideas and techniques of many therapists into a broad framework that permits and facilitates the development of individual-specific treatment strategies (see R. E. Dimond, R. A. Havens, and A. C. Jones, "A Conceptual Framework for the Practice of Prescriptive Eclecticism in Psychotherapy," *American Psychologist,* 1978, *33,* 239-248). With this basic theoretical orientation, the therapist's task is to construct an individualized treatment plan that matches the client's needs and situation and thereby maximizes the possibility of therapeutic gain. To achieve such a plan, therapists must draw on a vast array of theory and technique and not be bound by any single approach to therapy. Again, the goal is to fit the treatment to the needs of the particular case, not to fit the client to a favorite theory or technique.

When one is truly adept at different treatment modes, then

a prescriptive eclectic approach is possible. Unfortunately, when many treatments for a given disorder are available, the therapist usually knows something about all of them but is not truly skilled at any (S. I. Harrison, "Therapeutic Choice in Child Psychiatry," *Journal of Child Psychiatry,* 1978, *17,* 165-172). This condition could be prevented first of all by giving professionals educational programs that are in fact multidimensional and that provide basic training in a variety of biological, psychological, and social treatments. A second preventive measure would be greater use of the team approach wherein experts from different disciplines share their knowledge in treating a particular case.

At present, practitioners do not agree about which therapeutic techniques are most effective with specific psychosomatic disorders. No technique has been found to be universally successful with all types of disorders or all types of children. One needs to be flexible, then, and to apply therapeutic methods in accord with the needs of the individual child. In recognition of this need, this book adopts the eclectic approach to childhood psychosomatic problems. For each disorder we have tried to present several different therapies. Our main criteria of selection were the specificity of a particular technique and its success with children in the early and middle childhood years.

1

Cardiovascular System Disorders

The vast majority of studies that have been published on the psychological nature and treatment of cardiovascular diseases have appeared since 1970. Essentially the literature reflects five general areas of concern: hypertension, vascular (specifically migraine) headaches, coronary artery disease, cardiac arrhythmias, and peripheral vascular disease. The incidence of the last three is exceedingly low in the childhood years. However, migraine headache has been a recognized pediatric illness for many years, and recently physicians have been changing their ideas about hypertension in this age group.

Hypertension as a consequence of specific diseases and ab-

7

normal conditions in other organs and systems has been well recognized for a long time. In fact most pediatricians used to limit blood pressure measurements to patients who exhibited signs and symptoms suggestive of problems in the kidneys, adrenal gland, or heart. In 1971, however, an article appeared that reported the presence of blood pressures consistently above the known norms in seventy-four asymptomatic children between the ages of four and eighteen years (S. Londe and others, "Hypertension in Apparently Normal Children," *Journal of Pediatrics,* 1971, *78,* 569-577). Pediatricians began taking blood pressures in children three years of age and older and found a significant number of children who had no evidence of a health problem but were clearly hypertensive. (The incidence of sustained hypertension in the twenty-and-under age group has been conservatively estimated at 1 to 2 percent. See J. Loggie, "Hypertension in Children and Adolescents," *Hospital Practice,* June 1975, pp. 81-92.) Confusion arose among professionals about exactly what standards to apply to children's blood pressures, and no one had any real idea of the significance of blood pressure elevation in this age group as it pertained to long-term prognosis.

The medical community's lack of information led to the formation of a Task Force on Blood Pressure Control in Children set up by the National Heart, Lung, and Blood Institute. In May 1977 it reported its findings in *Pediatrics,* the official journal of the American Academy of Pediatrics. Guidelines were set forth regarding the proper technique for obtaining blood pressure readings in children, data were collated and reported, charts of the distribution curves of arterial pressures by age, sex, and race were prepared, and suggestions for treatment and long-term follow-up were offered.

Today physicians feel that this early form of hypertension may well be a precursor of adult essential hypertension—what the media refer to as "the silent killer." It is the fact that the disease is silent—it does not cause any symptoms at first—which leads to so much difficulty in identifying those who are afflicted. Adult hypertensives are estimated to number close to twenty-five million. The incidence is particularly high in the black population in this country. Hypertension is a leading cause of strokes and adult cardiac disease and is therefore responsible for well over two hundred thousand deaths annually in the United States.

The treatment for essential hypertension is commonly drug-oriented. Unfortunately, however, many of the medications used have potentially dangerous or complicating side effects, and often, even in combination, they do not control blood pressure adequately. The damage caused by elevated blood pressure is directly proportional to its level.

The recognition of the relative inadequacy of drug therapy for many patients with hypertension, coupled with a new understanding of the role of environmental stress in the propagation of the condition, has triggered interest in alternative means of therapy. As the articles in this section reveal, studies on the effectiveness of behavior therapies in treating essential hypertension have been limited to adult subjects, with a few individuals under twenty years of age included in some reports. The methods cited, however, were chosen as representatives applicable to older children and adolescents. The newly raised concerns about childhood hypertension will, we hope, stimulate additional studies directed specifically to the treatment of hypertensive children.

A vascular disorder that is not as physically damaging, but which unfortunately is never "silent," is migraine headache. Unlike essential hypertension, migraine has been noted in children for many years. Infants and children under the age of four usually manifest the condition as cyclical vomiting. Older children and adolescents usually present with the same type of severe throbbing pain as adults. Migraine is one of the most commonly reported psychosomatic disorders, with an estimated incidence across all age groups of 5 percent. Estimates limited to the pediatric age group vary from 2 to 5 percent; the higher incidence is associated with advancing age.

Though some headaches are secondary manifestations of significant pathology (infectious diseases, sinusitis, hypertension, intracerebral hemorrhage or tumor), the vast majority are due to tension. Traditionally theoreticians have stated that migraine and tension headaches differ radically in their pathogenesis. Migraine is thought to be exclusively a vascular phenomenon, whereas tension headaches are considered to be due to muscle tension in the scalp, neck, and back. But a recent review calls the latter assumption into question and argues, on the basis of the existing literature, that all headaches "fit a continuum model in which headaches gain an increasing number of vascular components as they become more severe" (C. Phillips, "Tension Headache: Theoretical Problems," *Behavior Research and Therapy*, 1978, *16*, 249-261). There is no question, however, that migraine is at the top of the scale in terms of severity; nor is there any doubt that its severe pain is due to dilitation of the cerebral vessels. Before the onset of vasodilitation, many patients experience a prodromal attack owing to an initial vasoconstriction during which they may experience nausea, vomiting, abdominal pain, dizziness, or sensory phenomena. Infrared photographs taken of migraine patients' heads between and during attacks clearly show the changing temperature patterns corresponding to shifts in blood flow.

Traditional medical therapy includes vasoconstrictors, such as ergotamine, which, when taken before vascular dilitation begins, are reasonably effective in controlling migraine attacks. However, they are associated with a number of undesirable side-effects. Other medications used are potent analgesics, some of which have a significant potential for abuse. Because many migraine patients do not obtain relief sufficient to live a normal existence, they generally develop increased anxiety, which can then trigger further attacks in a vicious cycle.

The studies of the usefulness of behavior therapies for migraine come basically from the adult literature. It is interesting to note that the vast majority of the case histories presented describe an onset during the subject's early or middle childhood years. It is sad that the same methods were not applied at an earlier age. If successful even as an adjunctive therapy, these techniques can help the child reduce the use of a medication that at best carries with it adverse side-effects and at worst is capable of fostering dependence.

Migraine Headaches

Migraine headache is associated with vasodilitation of the cerebral vessels. Classically it is preceded by a period of somatic and sensory abnormalities owing to a vasoconstrictive phase. There is a definite familial pattern in most patients' histories. The incidence reaches 5 percent in adolescence. It has been found to be particularly amenable to autogenic training methods that effect blood flow to the involved vessels.

Treatment of Stress-Induced Migraine Headaches

AUTHOR: Lloyd K. Daniels

PRECIS: Treating migraine headaches triggered by stress with a combination of behavior therapy and hypnosis

INTRODUCTION: The throbbing and pulsating pain of migraine headaches is due to dilitation and distension of cranial arteries. This phase follows an initial prodromal phase during which there is vasoconstriction of blood vessels supplying the cerebrum, a constriction that often results in visual, motor, and sensory abnormalities—the aura of the impending headache. Many researchers feel that this initial vasoconstrictive phase is due to the patient's overreaction to stress and that it is possible to break the cycle leading to the headache by using relaxation training to modify the stress-induced reaction.

CASE STUDY: The patient was a thirty-eight-year-old woman who had suffered with migraine headaches since the age of nine and who was having them at the rate of one every ten to fourteen days. She described herself as very compulsive and competitive and as a perfectionist who was easily upset when her children's behavior was not up to her standards or when other adults were excessively demanding. In addition to her headaches she also suffered from such stress-related problems as chronic bruxism (teeth grinding) during sleep and various muscle aches in her shoulders and back. She had been treated with a number of different medications including diazapam (Valium), propoxyphene napsylate (Darvon), and ergotamine tartrate with caffeine (Cafergot, a vasoconstrictor) without significant relief.

Her past history revealed that early circumstances had led to a significant amount of secondary gain whenever she suffered with a headache. If the headache occurred at school, the nurse would have her lie down and would then call her parents, who came right over and took her home to go to bed. Later in life her husband also would react with a great deal of concern whenever she had an episode.

Treatment was aimed at reducing the stress response that often led to headache formation. In addition she was instructed to avoid eating substances known to be associated with migraine, such as nuts and chocolate.

Initially she was given muscle relaxation training, during which she was taught to tense and then relax different muscle groups sequentially. She continued with this training and practiced at home until she was capable of reaching a totally relaxed state. Following this, she was taught how to use a subvocal cue in order to more quickly achieve the relaxed state (cue-controlled relaxation). At the end of each exhalation, the subject used a word such as *calm* or *relax* subvocally while concentrating on the overall sensations of relaxation. Training was given by the therapist, who would softly say the cue word at the appropriate time while the patient relaxed. Twenty-five trials with sixty-second intervals between them were used in each training session, and the patient was told to practice at home as well. In a short time the patient was able to achieve the relaxation state solely with the utterance of the cue word.

The patient was also supplied with a hypnotic induction that involved instructions to warm the hands and cool the forehead. This was tape-recorded so she could practice at home. The patient reported practicing all three modalities four times a day for eighteen days. After that she suffered a severe migraine that was triggered by a stress reaction resulting from her son's staying out too late. In response to that the therapist taught her a rational-cognitive approach to dealing with her unrealistic expectations. Essentially she was taught to analyze events in a logical, stepwise fashion:

A. The fact or event
B. Her belief
C. Her feeling or emotional response
D. Analysis (which, when illogical, resulted in a stress reaction)

She was supplied with more logical analyses that involved understanding why the other person—in this case her son—behaved as he did so that she did not have to respond with feelings of tension and anger. To give herself the time to work out the logic, she was taught how to abort the stress response by counting from ten to one, breathing deeply, using cue-controlled relaxation, shifting to a more pleasurable scene, and relaxing.

Within five weeks and after three sessions she was doing much better. Her overall tension feelings were reduced and at the twelve-month follow-up she was totally symptomless and needed no medication. The entire therapy required only six hourly sessions.

COMMENTARY: The author presents a great deal of useful information about how he incorporated a number of different stress-reduction techniques, which resulted in an excellent response in a patient whose migraine headaches were closely related to inner tension and an overreaction to stress. The therapy was designed to respond to her particular needs but was relatively easy to implement and required very little time and few therapist-patient contacts. Reducing secondary gain may play a greater role in the treatment of childhood migraine than it did in this case, but any or all of these methods could be useful in an overall therapeutic plan.

SOURCE: Daniels L. K. "Treatment of Migraine Headache by Hypnosis and Behavior Therapy: A Case Study." *The American Journal of Clinical Hypnosis*, 1977, *19*, 241-244.

Learned Vasoconstriction for Migraine Headache

AUTHORS: Linda R. Friar and Jackson Beatty

PRECIS: Decreasing migraine headache symptoms with operant training

INTRODUCTION: Migraine headache is a rather common disorder with an incidence estimated at 5 percent. The headache itself is due to dilitation of arteries supplying the brain and scalp. A number of studies have been conducted in which attempts were made to affect the flow of blood so that it would be reduced in the extracranial arteries involved. The current report describes how the authors trained individuals to constrict those arteries using an autogenic feedback technique.

METHOD: Nineteen adult migraine headache patients were selected after an initial screening process assured the diagnosis in each case. All of them were suffering from at least five headaches each month and were regular users of many of the medications currently available for treating migraine.

The study was designed to train those in the experimental group to control the tone of their temporal (forehead) arteries to cause vasoconstriction. Those in the control group were trained to cause vasoconstriction in the hand, a result that should only lead to a nonspecific placebo effect.

Pulse waves were recorded from the skin surface with pressure-transducing plethysmographs (Biocom 1010). One plethysmograph was held by an elastic headband over the temporal artery while the other was taped onto the ventral side of the index finger. A simultaneous electrocardiogram was also recorded, and skin temperature adjacent to the pressure sensors was recorded using surface thermistors. The pulse pressure from the temporal artery of the experimentals and finger artery of the controls and the electrocardiogram readings were fed into a computer, which then produced a stable pulse-pressure waveform on a storage oscilloscope. The waveform was used as a visual feedback for the subject. In addition, the computer produced an auditory signal when pulse amplitudes were less than the average of the twenty preceding amplitudes.

Each subject kept a headache log for a one-month baseline period before training and continued making entries until a month after training was completed. Over a three-week period the subjects received a total of eight training sessions and a ninth no-feedback session. During training the subject reclined in a comfortable chair in a quiet room. Detailed instructions were given to patients in each group. All instructions were identical except for the following differentiation. Those in the experimental group were told: "We will train you to decrease pulse amplitude in the extracranial artery most frequently affected during your attacks. We expect the training will be generalized to other parts of your vasculature." The control subjects were told: "Some of our research shows that learning to decrease pulse amplitude in the hand is easier than in the forehead. Training effects are generalized, and training in the hand is expected to affect your extracranial arteries."

The results demonstrated that the experimental subjects were able to voluntarily reduce the pulse amplitude in their temporal arteries, but the control subjects, though able to reduce the pulse amplitude in the periferal artery, did not affect the blood flow through their temporal arteries. The experimental subjects experienced a significant decrease in the total number of headaches and an even greater decrease in the number of fully established migraine headaches. The controls experienced small but insignificant decreases in each of these measures. There was no effect noted in either group in regard to the intensity of headache pain once a migraine was established. Interestingly enough, there was a significant decrease in both groups in the amount of medication being used to control their headaches.

COMMENTARY: The results of this study are quite interesting in that they clearly demonstrate the effectiveness of autogenic feedback training applied to extracranial arterial blood flow in reducing the number of migraine headache attacks. Though migraine was not cured, the fact that the subjects could eliminate a significant portion of the medication previously needed to exercise a lesser level of control is most heartening. Many of the medications used are strong analgesics and sedatives with significant potentials for abuse. The greatest drawback is the need for rather sophisticated equipment to conduct the training as outlined. If available, however, the method could certainly be applied to adolescents, who are all at risk for abuse of potentially addictive medications.

SOURCE: Friar, L. R., and Beatty, J. "Migraine: Management by Trained Control of Vasoconstriction." *Journal of Consulting and Clinical Psychology,* 1976, *44,* 46-53.

Treatment of Migraine Headaches
with Directive Therapy

AUTHOR: Darryl L. Gentry

PRECIS: Treating a headache patient who used her symptoms to gain control over others

INTRODUCTION: Directive therapy is a communication-oriented approach useful for treating patients whose psychopathology is based on their attempts to gain control of interpersonal relationships. In the course of treatment the therapist must gain control of the patient's symptoms so that they no longer serve their original purpose. The therapy does not require an exploration of the effects of childhood experiences on the adult, and it can be applied to older children with equally good results. In the case presented the therapist felt that a goal-oriented directive approach would be useful in the treatment of a patient who appeared to be using the symptoms of severe headaches to gain control over the definition of a relationship with another person.

CASE STUDY: Melody was a twenty-six-year-old woman who had suffered with severe headaches since the age of thirteen. Initially they had occurred once a month and caused her to be confined to bed for several hours. At the time she was seen, she was having three to four each day. A number of extensive medical work-ups had been performed with negative results, and she had been told her headaches were due to stress. Medications such as Stelazine (a tranquilizer) and Darvon (an analgesic) had not relieved her symptoms.

The therapist noted that she seemed very compulsive, over-inhibited, and filled with self-doubts. She had a strong feeling of obligation to her family and to people in general. She was a perfectionist who had difficulty performing housework under pressure. During the first years of her marriage, her husband often socialized with friends while she remained home; she voiced fears that he might resume that behavior and expressed the desire for more affection from him. She was obsessively concerned about the cause of her headaches and described having death thoughts with them.

Therapy was conducted during eleven weekly one-hour sessions. A contract was made between Melody and the therapist in which they agreed to work together on the problem of the headaches and to terminate treatment once the headaches were gone.

During the first session Melody was told that many questions would be asked but she could withhold any information she wanted to. The circumstances of her headaches were explored, and she was told to keep a regular written record of such information. She brought this record with her to the initial sessions. During the next two visits she discussed in detail the written notes she had made. In addition she was asked to bring to the fourth session a list of activities she enjoyed and disliked. She reported that she disliked making out the family budget each week. The therapist pointed out that she might be punishing herself with the headaches and then suggested that she could make the punishment beneficial to her by doing the budget whenever she had a headache. She was instructed to do so and to substitute this activity for the maintenance of the written record of circumstances.

At the fifth session Melody happily reported a reduction in headaches to only four in the week. Before the next visit she spent a week in the hospital at her own request undergoing further neurological tests, which were again essentially negative. This had caused her to stop doing the budget, but she was told to resume the activity. During the next two visits she joyfully reported having had only two headaches during the preceding weeks. However, she mentioned that she had altered her activity slightly and was now finishing whatever task she was involved with at the onset of the headache and was only starting work on the budget once the original task was completed. The therapist, in response to this controlling action, suggested to her that she would have a relapse but that she should not be concerned and should follow instructions exactly as had been previously stated. At the ninth session she reported her relapse. The therapist, who had reclaimed control, gave her much support and reaffirmed the importance of following the budget instructions exactly.

At the tenth session Melody reported having had no headaches. The therapist told her her treatment would soon be terminated, and it was ended at the following session when she again reported having had no headaches. She was told she could resume her "normal" activity pattern. She expressed fears that the headaches might return but was reassured and told she could call for another appointment if she needed to. In addition she was told to institute the budgeting activity if another headache occurred. At a twelve-month follow-up she was reportedly doing well, with no further headaches.

COMMENTARY: The author points out the essential need for the therapist to maintain control over the therapeutic relationship for directive therapy to be effective. When Melody showed resistance, the therapist was careful to encourage her so that the resistance came under his control. When he suggested to her that she would have a relapse, it became "a cooperative endeavor rather than a form of resistance by the patient." Directive therapy may be applied to adolescents who are using headaches in a manipulative manner and would also be applicable to patients using other symptoms for the same purpose.

SOURCE: Gentry, D. L. "Directive Therapy Techniques in the Treatment of Migraine Headaches: A Case Study." *Psychotherapy: Theory, Research and Practice*, 1973, *10*, 308-311.

Treatment of Migraine Headaches
with Autogenic Feedback

AUTHORS: Joseph D. Sargent, Elmer E. Green, and E. Dale Walters

PRECIS: Teaching migraine headache sufferers to control their symptoms by shunting blood flow to their hands

INTRODUCTION: The symptoms of migraine headaches appear to be mediated via the autonomic nervous system and are associated with an increased flow of blood to the head. The authors learned of a research subject who, during the course of an unrelated experiment, recovered spontaneously from a migraine headache, noting at the same time a rapid temperature rise and flushing in her hands. They concluded that it might be possible to ameliorate the symptoms of migraine headaches by training sufferers to control blood flow so it increased to the hands while it decreased to the head. The approach they chose was autogenic feedback training, which involves the concurrent regulation of mental and somatic functions.

PROCEDURE: Some twenty-five headache sufferers, most with migraine headaches and a smaller number with tension headaches, were included in the study. Their ages ranged from twenty-one to sixty-three. After a period of baseline measurements, including daily recording of the severity of the pain, the sum of the potency of the analgesics used, and the number of the analgesics used, the subjects received training in autogenic feedback. The initial training and examination sessions were held weekly or biweekly, and each subject practiced daily.

Participants were taught to use the "temperature trainer," a device that displayed a readout of the temperature differential between the midforehead and the right index finger. Absolute temperatures were not noted. The subjects also received a sheet of paper with certain phrases to be memorized and then concentrated on while simultaneously watching the temperature trainer and feeling for subjective evidence of warmth or throbbing in the hands.

An initial set of phrases was used to achieve a generally relaxed state:

> I feel quite quiet. . . I am beginning to feel quite relaxed. . . My feet feel heavy and relaxed. . . My ankles, my knees, and my hips feel heavy, relaxed, and comfortable. . . My solar plexus, and the whole central portion of my body, feels relaxed and quiet . . . My hands, my arms, and my shoulders feel heavy, relaxed and comfortable. . . My neck, my jaw, and my forehead feel relaxed. . . They feel comfortable and smooth. . . My whole body feels quiet, heavy, comfortable and relaxed.

A second group of phrases was used to achieve the more specific response of increasing blood flow to the hands:

> I feel quite relaxed. . . My arms and hands are heavy and warm. . . I feel quite quiet. . . My whole body is relaxed and my hands are warm, relaxed and warm. . . My hands are warm. . . Warmth is flowing into my hands, they are warm. . . Warm.

After a subject mastered the technique—the time needed to achieve this varied from one to eight weeks—the temperature trainer was only employed on alternate days and was finally withdrawn. The subjects were instructed to continue daily practice and to use the technique to help relieve headache symptoms whenever they occurred. After two to four months, office visits were reduced to once a month. At the time of data processing, follow-up periods for participants varied from one to twenty-two months.

Of the nineteen migraine headache sufferers, twelve were felt to be improved, three were not, and four showed equivocal responses. Of the six tension headache sufferers, two were improved, two unimproved, and two were not decisively changed.

COMMENTARY: The fact that 63 percent of the migraine sufferers improved whereas only 33 percent of tension headache sufferers improved is probably due to the differing etiologies involved. Since tension headaches are associated with muscle contraction in the scalp and neck and do not seem to involve to any significant extent a change in blood flow, a treatment aimed at altering blood flow should not, theoretically, alter symptoms. Unfortunately the authors did not include further details of the actual device used for training (temperature trainer), but it should not be a difficult device to have constructed. It may well be that the patient can learn to sense the subjective feeling of increased flow of blood to the hands without the need for a trainer; if so, this would simplify the procedure for the physician or therapist.

SOURCE: Sargent, J. D., Green, E. E., and Walters, E. D. "Preliminary Report on the Use of Autogenic Feedback Training in the Treatment of Migraine and Tension Headaches." *Psychosomatic Medicine*, 1973, *35*, 129-135.

Additional Readings

Daniels, L. K. "The Effects of Automated Hypnosis and Hand Warming on Migraine: A Pilot Study." *The American Journal of Clinical Hypnosis,* 1976, *19,* 91-94.

Three subjects with migraine headache were treated using a prerecorded taped hypnotic induction with specific instructions to warm the hands and cool the forehead. The tape lasted twenty minutes and was played for the subjects in six different training sessions during which the investigator was not present. The results indicated that each of the subjects experienced a decrease in the frequency, duration, and intensity of his or her headaches. While none experienced a total cure, all were satisfied with the therapy.

Diamond, S., and Franklin, M. "Biofeedback—Choice of Treatment in Childhood Migraine." Paper presented at the seventh annual meeting of the Biofeedback Research Society, Colorado Springs, Colorado, February 1976.

The authors treated thirty-two children with migraine headaches with autogenic training augmented with EMG feedback and temperature-training feedback. All but two of the children required continued medication because of the severity of their conditions. In addition to their laboratory sessions they practiced at home, keeping daily records without parental help or interference. Emphasis was placed on the child's responsibility for his or her own treatment. The results showed a good response (decrease in frequency and severity of headaches) in twenty-six cases, a fair response (decrease in either frequency or severity) in three cases, and no response in two. One patient was lost to follow-up.

Stambaugh, E. E., and House, A. E. "Multimodality Treatment of Migraine Headache: A Case Study Utilizing Biofeedback, Relaxation, Autogenic and Hypnotic Treatments." *The American Journal of Clinical Hypnosis,* 1977, *19,* 235-240.

An adult male migraine headache patient had exhausted most avenues of therapy, including medication and EMG feedback, and was still incapacitated by the pain. His treatment was then conducted in phases and included relaxation therapy, hypnosis-relaxation therapy, heterohypnosis, autogenic therapy (heat transfer from left temple to left hand), and, finally, auto-hypnosis with instructions for posthypnotic anesthesia. This final form of therapy was successful in controlling his symptoms. The authors outline each phase of therapy.

Kudrow, L. "Current Aspects of Migraine Headache," *Psychosomatics,* 1978, *19,* 48-57.

The author reviews the current understanding of migraine headaches with particular attention to the role of biogenic amines in pain production. The psychological aspects of the condition are discussed, and the difficulty in dealing with stress and adapting to new situations is highlighted. Present information leads to the conclusion that migraine appears to be "a strongly familial disorder characterized by psychophysiological, biochemical, and vasomotor dysfunction causing difficulty in adaptation to environmental changes."

Hypertension

Essential hypertension (also called primary or idiopathic hypertension) is hypertension without discoverable organic cause. It is being recognized more frequently in children and is currently estimated to be present in at least 2 percent of the pediatric population. Black adolescents, particularly males, have a somewhat higher incidence.

Meditation and Hypertension

AUTHOR: Herbert Benson

PRECIS: Daily meditation used to reduce blood pressure in a number of hypertensive individuals

INTRODUCTION: Certain physiologic changes occur when an individual successfully uses a meditation technique aimed at promoting a generally relaxed state. These changes include a decrease in oxygen consumption, lowered heart and respiratory rates, reduced arterial blood lactate, slightly increased skeletal muscle blood flow, and greater production of alpha (slow) waves on an EEG. A number of meditation techniques have been advanced over the ages—more in recent years—that often have religious or mystical origins or overtones. The author reviewed many such techniques and reduced them to four basic elements: a repetitive mental device, a passive attitude toward external distractions, decreased muscle tone, and a quiet environment. Using these elements, he and his colleagues developed a simple "noncultic" method for eliciting the "relaxation response." It has been noted for some time that humans living and working in stressful environments that frequently trigger anxiety are more likely to develop sustained elevations of blood pressure than those living with less stress. Benson studied a group of hypertensive adults to determine whether the inclusion of regular meditation in their daily routines would have a beneficial effect.

METHOD: A group of thirty-six adult hypertensive patients were used for statistical purposes. Fourteen required some medication during the study, while twenty-two did not. Weekly blood pressures were taken for a six-week period before the start of meditation training to serve as a baseline control. During this time blood pressures in both medicated and nonmedicated subjects remained unchanged. The average pressures were 145.6/91.9 (mm. of mercury) in the medicated group and 146.5/94.6 (mm. of mercury) in the nonmedicated. Following the control period, the subjects were taught to elicit the relaxation response with the following technique as stated by the author:

Sit quietly in a comfortable position. Close your eyes. Deeply relax all your muscles, beginning at your feet and progressing up to your face. Keep them deeply relaxed.

Breathe through your nose. Become aware of your breathing. As you breathe out, say the word "one" silently to yourself. Continue for twenty minutes. You may open your eyes to check the time but do not use an alarm. When you have finished, sit quietly for several minutes, at first with closed eyes and later with opened eyes.

Do not worry about whether you are successful in achieving a deep level of relaxation. Maintain a passive attitude and permit relaxation to occur at its own pace. Expect distracting thoughts. When these distracting thoughts occur, ignore them and continue repeating "one."

Practice the technique once or twice daily, but not within two hours after a meal, since the digestive processes seem to interfere with elicitation of anticipated changes.

After the subjects were using this technique twice daily for at least two weeks, their pressures were measured approximately every other week over six months. These measurements were taken randomly during the day but never during or immediately following meditation. During this experimental period, pressures in the medicated group averaged 135.0/87.0 (mm. of mercury) and those in the nonmedicated group averaged 139.5/90.8 (mm. of mercury). It was noted that the blood pressures of those subjects from either group who stopped meditating regularly increased to initial levels within a month.

COMMENTARY: Benson cites statistics gathered from a number of different studies conducted by him and other investigators that tend to confirm the successful results demonstrated in the present one. A program of regular periods of evoked relaxation apparently can serve as an adjunctive therapy for many hypertensives. Though this work was done with adults, the method is a relatively straightforward one and could well be adapted to an adolescent population. The incidence of borderline and true hypertension in children and young adults has increased in recent years, most probably as a result of more frequent and regular screening by physicians. Many of these individuals never develop significantly sustained elevated pressures, but a fair percentage does. Some physicians are recommending reductions in the salt content of foods as a simple preventive and control method. Meditation could prove to be an equally valuable approach.

SOURCE: Benson, H. "Systemic Hypertension and the Relaxation Response." *New England Journal of Medicine*, 1977, *296*, 1152-1155.

Treating Essential Hypertension
with Operant Conditioning

AUTHORS: Herbert Benson, David Shapiro, Bernard Tursky, and Gary E. Schwartz

PRECIS: Using a biofeedback exercise to treat adult hypertensives

INTRODUCTION: The authors note that various animal and human studies have demonstrated that blood pressure can be influenced using operant conditioning techniques. In work done with human subjects, this approach has often been combined with other methods. In this particular study the researchers used operant conditioning alone, and in order to isolate the usefulness of the technique for the treatment of hypertension, they maintained the patients' existing levels of medication.

METHOD: Seven adult hypertensives, all but one of whom had been medically diagnosed as having essential hypertension, were studied. All had moderate to severe elevations of blood pressure, and six were taking antihypertensive medications.

The feedback instrumentation measured blood pressure directly, using a standard cuff attached to a constant cuff-pressure system. The cuff could be inflated to a constant pressure using a regulated low-pressure compressed-air source. The cuff was connected by plastic tubing to a Statham P23Db strain gauge pressure transducer. The electrical output of the gauge was recorded on one channel of a Beckman-type RH polygraph. A crystal microphone placed over the brachial artery recorded Korotkoff sounds (the sound of irregular blood flow through a partially compressed vessel) on a second channel. When cuff pressure was greater than systolic (maximum) blood pressure, no blood passed through the artery and consequently no sound was noted. When cuff pressure dropped below systolic pressure, a sound was picked up as blood began to flow again.

Each trial covered fifty heartbeats, after which the cuff was deflated for thirty to forty-five seconds to minimize discomfort. Median blood pressure equaled cuff pressure if a

Korotkoff sound was present for from fourteen to thirty-six heartbeats. If less than fourteen sounds per trial were noted, cuff pressure was decreased by four mm. of mercury. If more than thirty-six sounds were produced, cuff pressure was increased by 4 mm. of mercury.

Sessions were held each weekday and consisted of thirty measured trials. The initial control sessions were conducted five to sixteen times and involved no feedback or reinforcement. In the following conditioning sessions, the first five trials offered no reinforcement, but in the twenty-five subsequent trials a flash of light and a brief audio signal were instantaneously fed back to the patient if relatively lowered pressure was noted (no Korotkoff sound). The patient was instructed to try to make the light and sound appear, and as further reinforcement, he was rewarded with a photographic slide consisting of a pleasant scene and a notation that he had earned five cents for every twenty presentations of the light and tone. These conditioning sessions continued until there was no further reduction in pressure in five consecutive sessions.

The results of the study revealed that there had been improvement in five of the seven subjects. Of the two who did not improve, one did not have any elevation of systolic pressure to begin with, and the other had renal artery stenosis. The mean decrease in systolic pressure for all seven subjects was 16.5 mm. of mercury.

COMMENTARY: The authors are careful to point out that the results were obtained in a laboratory setting and that the usefulness of the technique described as a therapeutic mode needs further exploration. Additional studies have generalized the findings, and the addition of other stress-reducing modalities such as relaxation and meditation exercises has been shown to supplement the benefits. Adolescent patients should be able to learn the technique and are likely to find it as useful as adult subjects.

SOURCE: Benson, H., Shapiro, D., Tursky, B., and Schwartz, G. E. "Decreased Systolic Blood Pressure Through Operant Conditioning Techniques in Patients with Essential Hypertension." *Science*, 1971, *173*, 740-742.

Hypertension Treated with Relaxation and Hypnosis

AUTHORS: Herdis L. Deabler, Edward Fidel, Robert L. Dillenkoffer, and S. Thomas Elder

PRECIS: Aiding medicated and nonmedicated hypertensives with progressive relaxation and self-hypnosis

INTRODUCTION: The drug therapies available for hypertension are frequently effective in controlling significant elevations of pressures, but most of these medications are associated with troublesome, and at times dangerous, side-effects. The approaches that have been examined in order to identify alternative or ancillary treatments for hypertension have included such behavioral techniques as autogenic training, progressive relaxation, verbal feedback, and meditation. The present study examined the usefulness of progressive relaxation with the addition of hypnosis.

STUDY: Two small groups of subjects (medicated and nonmedicated) received training in the techniques studied. For the purposes of the study, blood pressure was measured using the Model 1900 London Pressurometer (Avionics Research Products, Los Angeles, California). All training and blood pressure readings were performed with the subject sitting in a comfortable reclining chair. Eight or nine sessions were conducted at half-day intervals.

Initially in each session skeletal muscle relaxation was achieved by instructing the subject to sequentially tense and then relax the major muscle groups of the body, starting with the extremities and working centrally to the trunk. Once the subject verified that he was feeling completely relaxed with no discernible muscle tension, blood pressure readings were obtained. Following this, hypnosis was begun with the following statement:

> You have relaxed your muscles. Now we would like to have you relax inwardly—your nerves, and

your mind. Close your eyes and imagine that it is night time, you are on your own bed, in your own room, in your own home. You are relaxing your mind and your nerves and are about to drop off into deep inner relaxation.

Additional suggestions including deeper breathing and visualizing stairs spiraling downward were made, and further statements about inner relaxation, descending deeper and deeper, increasing the weight of limbs, and so on, were supplied. Once it was judged that a trance state had been obtained, additional blood pressure readings were made. Finally, a deepening of the trance state was attempted by suggesting relaxation of internal organs (heart and blood vessels). This was, again, followed by pressure readings.

After three or four sessions the subjects were told that they could use the techniques they were learning at home, and the final sessions were spent observing and helping them to self-induce their relaxation and trance states. Practice at home after sessions and daily use of the techniques once the training program was terminated were strongly encouraged.

At the conclusion of the study period it was noted that although progressive relaxation achieved good results in both medicated and nonmedicated subjects, the effects of hypnosis were even more impressive in terms of lowered systolic and diastolic blood pressures. In addition, many of the subjective complaints noted by participants at the start of the training program had been markedly reduced by the end.

COMMENTARY: An interesting aspect of this study was that the subjects had not been chosen on the basis of their susceptibility to hypnosis, and, in fact, many seemed to be poor subjects. Despite that, there was marked improvement in all subjects after hypnotic induction was performed. This is important to keep in mind, because many practitioners might speculate that unless a subject were very susceptible to hypnosis, the technique would not be a useful therapeutic modality. The training would be applicable to adolescents and, as described, would not take a great deal of time. The special blood pressure instrument used would not be necessary if the purpose of the training were therapeutic. A standard cuff and sphygmomanometer would be all that was necessary to document changes in pressure.

SOURCE: Deabler, H. L., Fidel, E., Dillenkoffer, R. L., and Elder, S. T. "The Use of Relaxation and Hypnosis in Lowering High Blood Pressure." *American Journal of Clinical Hypnosis,* 1973, *16,* 75-83.

Relaxation Training for
Essential Hypertension

AUTHORS: Lewis E. Graham, Irving Beiman, and Anthony R. Ciminero

PRECIS: Progressive relaxation training for a young adult male hypertensive

INTRODUCTION: The fact that everyday stress appears to contribute to the development of essential hypertension has led many researchers to investigate the possible therapeutic benefits of behavioral therapy techniques designed to reduce stress. Such methods have included biofeedback, progressive relaxation training, metronome conditioned relaxation, and meditation. Treatment programs that combine methods have been most successful in controlling blood pressure, but few studies have evaluated the pattern of blood pressure outside the experimental environment. The present study was designed to determine whether any reduction in pressure that could be attributable to progressive relaxation training would be maintained in other settings and would extend over long periods of time without continuous therapist-patient contact.

CASE STUDY: A twenty-three-year-old white male with a twelve-month history of essential hypertension was selected for study. He was receiving no medication and was adhering to a low-sodium diet. His blood pressure was measured in a local clinic (in extra-session readings) every four days for an eighteen-day period both before and during the training. There were seven training sessions in twenty-five days, each one lasting one and a half hours. In the first two sessions the subject was taught to sequentially tense and relax sixteen different muscle groups. During the following two sessions this number was reduced to four. In the fifth and sixth sessions he reviewed the exercise with the four groups by recall only, and in the final session he used recall with counting. Throughout the training he practiced relaxation twice daily (morning and evening) at home. After completing training, he was told to practice relaxation by recall at fixed times and also in different situations, such as during anger, before meals, at traffic lights, or when writing.

The subject's blood pressure was moderately above normal during the baseline period, but after a week of training it had dropped to normal levels, as measured in the extra-session setting. Blood pressure readings after each session were consistently lower than those obtained just before the sessions. Forty weeks after the completion of training he was reevaluated for four weeks, during which time he remained normotensive.

COMMENTARY: It is gratifying to note that the beneficial results obtained with this treatment method remained in effect almost a full year after the subject was no longer in contact with the therapist. This technique, and the other behavioral techniques that have been used in treating hypertension, can be readily incorporated into one's lifestyle. Certainly the adolescent patient can learn these methods.

SOURCE: Graham, L. E., Beiman, I., and Ciminero, A. R. "The Generality of the Therapeutic Effects of Progressive Relaxation Training for Essential Hypertension." *Journal of Behavior Therapy and Experimental Psychiatry,* 1977, *8,* 161-164.

Treatment of Hypertension with Yoga

AUTHOR: C. H. Patel

PRECIS: Treating adult hypertensives with yogic relaxation and meditation, and with simultaneous biofeedback

INTRODUCTION: Although the cause of essential hypertension, as its name implies, is not specifically known, a great deal of experimental work has suggested that increased sympathetic nervous system activity in response to environmental stress is an important factor in the development of essential hypertension. The author explored the use of a stress-reducing activity as a therapeutic approach for a number of hypertensive individuals, many of whom were on antihypertensive medications owing to the severity of their conditions.

METHOD: Each patient was seen individually for a half hour, three times a week, over a three-month period. Blood pressure was measured before and after each session, and medications were reduced or eliminated where appropriate.

The patient lay in a comfortable position on an examination couch and was connected via two finger electrodes to a relaxometer—a device that measures sympathetic nervous system activity indirectly by changes in the electrical resistance of the skin. An audio signal was emitted that rose in pitch with increases in nervous activity and was reduced during relaxation.

Patients were first instructed in physical relaxation with a progressive relaxation technique in which they mentally went over each major muscle group and concentrated on relaxing it. Typewritten instructions and suggestions for useful phrases ("my arms are feeling very heavy and relaxed") were supplied for home practice. After mastering physical relaxation the patients were instructed in mental relaxation using an approach akin to dharna in yoga. They concentrated on the phases of respiration and repeated "relaxed . . . relaxed . . ." with each expiration (a process similar to the use of a yogic mantra). The relaxometer feedback tone helped to reinforce successful relaxation. At the end of each session the patient was told his blood pressure levels before and after the session.

Overall the author found a mean blood pressure drop from 121 mm. to 101 mm. of mercury. There was also a 41 percent reduction in the total medication needs of the patients.

COMMENTARY: One of the most interesting aspects of this particular study was the use of a biofeedback technique that measures general sympathetic tone as a way of reinforcing efforts to reduce blood pressure. Certainly this type of monitoring is far easier than attempting to use direct blood pressure measurements either with an indwelling arterial transducer or an inflated blood pressure cuff that can be quite uncomfortable. The training could be used for the adolescent who is well motivated, and a number of spin-off benefits (such as relief of migraine headache) could well accompany any additional blood pressure control.

SOURCE: Patel, C. H. "Yoga and Bio-Feedback in the Management of Hypertension." *Lancet,* 1973, *2,* 1053-1055.

Additional Readings

Ragland, D. R. "Behavioral Approaches to the Treatment of Hypertension: A Bibliography." Washington, D.C.: DHEW Publication No. (NIH) 77-1219, Superintendent of Documents, U.S. Government Printing Office, 1977.

A thorough collection of references to articles pertinent to the subject, covering such treatment modalities as biofeedback, relaxation, psychotherapy, environmental modification, placebos, sleep, exercise, and acupuncture.

Jacob, R. G., Kraemer, H. C., and Agras, W. S. "Relaxation Therapy in the Treatment of Hypertension: A Review." *Archives of General Psychiatry*, 1977, *34*, 1417-1427.

This article critically reviews the literature on the use of relaxation and similar therapies for the treatment of hypertension. The authors approach their task from the standpoint of examining the type of studies performed—single group outcome research, group studies with a nonrandomly selected control group, and controlled group outcome studies. They conclude that relaxation therapy is significantly more effective than a placebo in lowering blood pressure. They caution, however, that conclusions about whether or not this form of therapy can completely replace drug therapy cannot as yet be reached because of insufficient data on the incidence of long-term complications of the disease when treated solely with relaxation therapy.

Stone, R. A., and DeLeo, J. "Psychotherapeutic Control of Hypertension." *The New England Journal of Medicine*, 1976, *294*, 80-84.

The authors conducted a six-month study of the effectiveness of a Buddhist meditation exercise in controlling elevated blood pressure in a group of young adult males. In addition to measuring blood pressure, the study also examined the relative activity level of the peripheral sympathetic nervous system by assaying levels of a catecholamine-synthesizing enzyme in the plasma (catecholamines are compounds involved in peripheral sympathetic nervous system activity and include adrenalin). They conclude that the meditation technique was significantly effective in reducing blood pressure. A simultaneous reduction in the level of the enzyme was also noted, suggesting a mechanism involved in the process.

2

Gastrointestinal System Disorders

The gastrointestinal (GI) system is a common site for the expression of a wide range of emotional disturbances. The emotions affect all parts of the body, but the digestive system seems to be particularly vulnerable. A noted expert on human stress, Hans Selye, has stated that "the gastrointestinal tract is particularly sensitive to general stress" and that "signs of irritation and upset of the digestive organs may occur in any type of emotional stress" (*The Stress of Life,* rev. ed., New York: McGraw-Hill, 1976, p. 12). Thus any type of discord, trauma, or the accumulated effects of general stress may result in a "nervous" stomach or "nervous" bowels. It is not surprising then that the

41

most common gastrointestinal disorders are those that are "functional" in nature. The term *functional* defines a broad category of disorders for which no organic cause can be found, such as psychophysiological reactions. It has been estimated that emotional factors are the chief cause of at least two thirds of the cases of GI-tract disorders (E. Weiss and O. S. English, *Psychosomatic Medicine,* Philadelphia: W. B. Saunders, 1949).

The GI tract is phylogenetically the oldest system in the body and hence most likely to be used to express an emotion that cannot be released more openly. When needs such as loving or being loved and giving protection or being protected are not successfully met, this oldest system will be called upon in a vain attempt to solve the problem in a primitive way. This has been called "organ language." Since it is not intended for service of this kind, the GI tract is doomed to failure, and its misguided effort to be of service for such psychological purposes causes dysfunction and discomfort which result in illness.

The abdomen has aptly been called the "sounding board of the emotions." It is well known that the student before an examination may get "butterflies" in the stomach, nausea, or diarrhea. The businessman may get indigestion, heartburn, and actual abdominal pain when faced with financial reverses. A worried mother can develop indigestion or constipation when there is trouble with the children or a special dinner to be prepared. The child who is not making a good adjustment in school may have an attack of vomiting in the morning before school time.

The GI tract is characterized by three variable physiologic functions: motility, vascularity, and secretion. These three functions can vary in either an overactive or an underactive direction. Overactivity leads to hypermotility, vascular engorgement, and excessive secretion. It is generally believed that these states are mediated through the rich innervation of the gastrointestinal tract with autonomic nerve fibres, both sympathetic and parasympathetic.

The most significant factors in the variations of motility, vascularity, and secretion appear to be emotional ones (A. H. Chapman and D. G. Loeb, "Psychosomatic Gastrointestinal

Problems," *A.M.A. Journal of Diseases of Children,* 1955, *12,* 717-724). These three functions can change rapidly, depending on the emotional state of the individual. Feelings of marked anxiety, anger, or resentment and frustrated needs for affection may lead to hypermotility, hypervascularity, and hypersecretion. States of depression, loneliness or grief, and apathy may lead to hypomotility, hypovascularity, and hyposecretion.

In the upper GI tract hyperactivity of these three functions may lead to peptic ulcer or to ulcerlike symptoms without ulceration, depending on the intensity and duration of the hyperactivity. In the lower gastrointestinal tract, hyperactivity of the functions leads to diarrhea, mucous colitis, and perhaps ulcerative colitis if the hyperactive processes persist. Hypoactivity of the upper GI tract produces lack of appetite and anorexia, whereas hypoactivity of the lower GI tract leads to constipation.

Although the relationship between psychosocial factors and GI-tract disorders is well known, it is surprising how little attention has traditionally been given to psychological factors in the treatment of these disorders. Apart from paying lip service to the role of the emotions and social elements in producing disorders of the digestive system, many physicians spend very little time trying to deal with the effects of external stress or faulty learning. The psychosomatic approach does not neglect the physical problems involved but tries to give equal consideration to the role of the psychosocial factors. This does not mean one studies the soma less; it does mean one studies the psyche more. This approach emphasizes the multiple factors involved in etiology and pathogenesis and attempts to deal with the resulting composite clinical picture.

Among the psychosomatic disorders of the GI system that are discussed in this chapter are anorexia, abdominal pain, diarrhea, encopresis, ulcerative colitis, and vomiting.

Ulcerative Colitis

Ulcerative colitis is a chronic inflammatory disease of the large intestine characterized by severe abdominal pain, malabsorption and diarrhea, and damage to the lining of the gut leading to bleeding and mucus discharge. Its etiology is probably multi-determined, but family histories suggest a genetic predisposition. Patients frequently suffer the disease's onset and further exacerbations when under emotional stress, and distinct personality patterns are often noted in those afflicted.

Ulcerative Colitis: Psychological Aspects of Management

AUTHOR: George L. Engel

PRECIS: Thoughts on an important aspect of the management of patients with ulcerative colitis

INTRODUCTION: Engel points out that there is considerable controversy over whether ulcerative colitis is a disease with psychosomatic characteristics or a physical ailment that is exacerbated by the emotional turmoil it can trigger in the patient (somatopsychic). The debate becomes less important when one realizes that experimental work has shown directly that changes in one's emotional state can be accompanied by definite alterations in the vascular, motor, and secretory behavior of the colon. Given this information, the physician treating the ulcerative colitis patient must be aware of those approaches and considerations in management that can be most effectively used to foster successful control (or cure) of the gastrointestinal problem. Engel suggests attitudes and behaviors that should be adopted by the attending physician and other professionals who provide care for the patient.

MANAGEMENT CONSIDERATIONS: Engel has found that the root of many ulcerative colitis patients' problems can be traced to a disturbed parent-child relationship in which the parent's demands and needs were often inconsistent and conflicting, making it difficult, if not impossible, for the child to successfully satisfy them. This results in significant feelings of ambivalence and stress within the child that can become somaticized to the gastrointestinal tract. Normally bowel activity is influenced to varying extents by psychologic stimuli. Once the bowel is damaged, it becomes even more sensitive to such stimuli.

The recognition of the patient's underlying insecurity and distrustfulness can aid those caring for the ulcerative colitis patient to adjust their own behavior (and their responses to the patient's behavior) so as to work *with* the patient. The physician should not push the patient into revealing feelings or disturbing psychologic conflicts. Rather the patient should be allowed to talk freely about his or her own concerns and needs in a nondirective manner. If the patient introduces relevant information, however, it should be gently pursued in order to determine whether or not assistance should be obtained from a psychiatrist so that the patient can more effectively work through underlying conflicts.

The physician must be consistent, predictable, and reliable. Engel feels that the physician should use a parent-child kind of relationship as a guide to the type of relationship he or she should develop with the patient. The patient lives in fear of abandonment, especially since self-esteem is often lowered by the regressive aspects of the disease, such as soiling. Consequently, "a doctor should not undertake the care of a colitis patient unless he can be reasonably sure of being able to see the case through."

Attention to details is also very important. The entire management team (physician, nurses, aids, dieticians) must at all times remember the needs of the patient and must be constantly on guard against reacting to excessive demands with anger and insensitivity. Ulcerative colitis patients are handicapped physically and emotionally, and their activity and behavior should be consistently viewed in that context.

The patient's family often faces the same difficulties the hospital staff has in dealing with the person. The physician can help greatly by counseling them so that they have a deeper understanding of the problems the patient is facing.

Finally, the author points out that when the patient becomes angry with a caregiver (either for realistic or neurotic reasons), it is important for the caregiver to continue to actively solicit the trust and cooperation of the patient. If this individual withdraws, then the patient's expectations of abandonment will be seemingly confirmed. This experience might well result in a treatment setback, particularly if the individual involved played a significant role for the patient.

COMMENTARY: Emotional conflict and stress undoubtedly play important roles in the etiology and progression of ulcerative colitis. Although this article does not present a treatment modality per se, the information it provides is important to keep in mind as one attempts to aid the ulcerative colitis patient. The treatment for some psychosomatic disorders can be easily compartmentalized into behavior therapy or psychotherapy. But ulcerative colitis has more causes than these other disorders and consequently requires a broader treatment approach that incorporates medicinal therapy as well as psychotherapy in order to be successfully managed.

SOURCE: Engel, G. L. "Psychologic Aspects of the Management of Patients with Ulcerative Colitis." *New York State Journal of Medicine,* 1952, *52,* 2255-2261.

Children with Ulcerative Colitis

AUTHORS: Stuart M. Finch and John H. Hess

PRECIS: The psychological characteristics of children with ulcerative colitis and suggestions for therapy

INTRODUCTION: The authors initially review the literature on the psychological aspects of the development and progression of ulcerative colitis. There is almost complete agreement that difficulty in the parent-child relationship and a propensity (genetically, congenitally, or otherwise determined) to refer psychic conflict and stress to the gastrointestinal tract are the cornerstones for the development of ulcerative colitis. The authors studied seventeen children with ulcerative colitis and report here cumulative data from the social, psychological, and psychiatric examinations of all the subjects. From their data and practical experience, the authors suggest psychotherapeutic considerations in the management of children with ulcerative colitis that are just as important when considering therapy from a medical standpoint.

TREATMENT SUGGESTIONS: Ulcerative colitis is a multifactorial illness that requires simultaneous interventions on both physiological and psychological levels. Experience teaches that patients must be handled by a cooperative team of specialists—a gastroenterologist, dietician, surgeon, and psychotherapist—each of whom is well trained and competent to handle the various aspects of therapy. In reality, these teams are difficult to establish and maintain, but for best results one should make an effort to use such an approach where possible.

Children with ulcerative colitis should be seen as suffering from severe psychopathology. It is important to recognize the function of the illness itself, which serves as "a problem-solving device for intrapsychic, intrafamilial, and social conflict." The task of eliminating the need for the illness is difficult and time-consuming. The therapist must be prepared to take a very active treatment role, intervening in situations where existing family

dynamics threaten to retard improvement in the child's condition. The problem cannot be handled on a short-term basis.
During the course of therapy with the patient an "intensely
dependent and demanding" transference relationship is likely to
develop. Typically, however, this relationship is quite fragile,
and this fragility makes more difficult the therapist's task of
remaining supportive while simultaneously leading the patient
to accept a less dependent role.

Finally, one must remember that ulcerative colitis patients
suffer from intense feelings of inferiority and often fall into
deep depressive states. In order to enable the patient to more
freely express hostility and aggressive feelings, the therapist
must be able to provide a comfortable and secure relationship
and avoid condemnation.

COMMENTARY: The combination of a severely disabling, potentially devastating physical ailment and a complex psychological disturbance requiring a broad-based and protracted treatment approach makes the successful management of the child
with ulcerative colitis an extremely difficult and demanding
undertaking. The more insight into the factors contributing to
the development and progression of the condition the responsible physician can obtain, the greater the likelihood of achieving
a favorable therapeutic outcome for the patient.

SOURCE: Finch, S. M., and Hess, J. H. "Ulcerative Colitis in
  Children." *American Journal of Psychiatry,* 1962, *118,*
  819-826.

Supportive Psychotherapy in Ulcerative Colitis

AUTHORS: J. Groen and J. Bastiaans

PRECIS: General description of a psychotherapeutic approach to patients with ulcerative colitis

INTRODUCTION: In this early work the authors attempted to determine the usefulness of psychotherapy for patients with ulcerative colitis. In order to more decisively measure the impact of psychotherapy, they withheld all medication from the patients in their study and found results comparable to those of medical therapy (at the time). In addition, a majority of the subjects in the study received their psychotherapy from the attending physician—not a psychiatrist. The results of treatment and a general outline of the therapeutic principles and approach are included.

TREATMENT APPROACH: A supportive form of psychotherapy was employed. Psychoanalysis was not used because the authors found over the years that it was not useful in most cases. The psychotherapy itself was performed at the bedside or other comfortable place by the physician, who adopted the attitude of a "sympathetic listener." As such, the physician allowed the patient to present an outline of his or her life, reacting where appropriate. When topics were introduced that involved personal conflicts the patient had experienced with another person, the physician was quick to sympathize with the patient and offer support for his or her position in the disagreement. At times this expression of support would involve "transferential aggression"—the physician would express the anger and hostility toward the offending person that the patient was unable to. This method was frequently associated with a rapid improvement in physical condition, as if the patient had been the one to act out.

Ulcerative colitis patients have low self-esteem stemming from earlier life experiences and the regressive aspects of their disease. As a result, they frequently have a great deal of difficulty in asserting themselves. The physician should attempt to protect them from any conflicts or further disturbances. Consequently in this study no attempts were made to offer insight into personality deficiencies, and frequent ego-boosting comments were offered and found to be effective in improving the patient's outlook.

Throughout the series of psychotherapeutic interviews every effort was made to assure the patient that the physician considered him or her a worthwhile individual. This was expressed both directly and by the attitude adopted by the physician during the treatment course. Appointments were scheduled at short intervals in order to counteract the patient's frequently noted fear of abandonment. It was found most useful to schedule each subsequent appointment at the conclusion of the preceding visit.

If, during the course of the interviews, the patient revealed the existence of social or marital problems, the physician intervened as much as possible, counseling family members, employers, teachers, and so on, where appropriate, in an attempt to give them a degree of insight into the needs of the patient so that they could deal with him or her in a more understanding fashion.

The authors caution about the tendency of some physicians and other professionals involved in caring for ulcerative colitis patients to feel that excessive coddling will only perpetuate the dependency role most of them have assumed. They strongly argue that any ill patient, but especially a patient with an illness that leads to dysfunction in an organ system one is supposed to be able to control at a very early stage of development, can lead to increased regression and feelings of inadequacy. They point out that the recognition of this regressive tendency as simply another aspect of the disease process has enabled the medical, nursing, and other staff members in the hospital to more effectively regulate their own emotions in response to the patient's actions and demands. As the patient improves, the regressive tendencies diminish as well; in this study almost all patients were able to resume normal or near-normal functioning.

COMMENTARY: A noteworthy aspect of this study was the fact that most of the patients had their psychotherapy performed by the attending physician, who was not a psychiatrist. The authors emphasize that a strong desire to heal is the most important attribute of the physician caring for the ulcerative colitis patient. The kind of psychotherapy described is not complex, nor does it require a great deal of psychological sophistication on the part of the physician. Time might be a factor, but the sessions themselves did not last long, especially when the patients were acutely ill and not feeling much like talking. The physician could incorporate much of the conversation in the time used for physical assessment. However, an inattentive listener would most likely do more harm than good for the patient.

SOURCE: Groen, J., and Bastiaans, J. "Psychotherapy of Ulcerative Colitis." *Gastroenterology*, 1951, *17*, 344-352.

Supportive Psychotherapy in Ulcerative Colitis

AUTHOR: Dane G. Prugh

PRECIS: Important psychotherapeutic considerations in the management of childhood ulcerative colitis

INTRODUCTION: The author is a pediatrician with psychiatric training who managed a number of cases of ulcerative colitis. During the course of psychotherapeutic interviews with patients and parents, and while conducting therapeutic play sessions, he was able to delineate a number of historical points and personality traits that were evident in the vast majority of his patients. Armed with this information, he attempted to incorporate psychological management techniques in the overall medical and surgical care of his patients. Some of his more consistent findings follow.

FINDINGS: The sixteen children in his series ranged in age from four to nineteen. Despite this variation, Prugh was able to reach some conclusions about the underlying personality structure of children with ulcerative colitis. He described them as "ordinarily rather passive, rigid, quite dependent on parent figures (particularly the mother), socially inhibited, often narcissistic and emotionally immature. Compulsive needs to conform exaggeratedly to social dictates, as well as unusual concentration on orderliness and detail, were additional features among most of the children, as was marked inhibition of normally outgoing heterosexual relationships." In particular Prugh was struck by their inability to deal effectively with hostile and aggressive feelings, especially when directed toward parents or other authority figures.

In the majority of his cases, Prugh was able to isolate a preceding triggering event that was closely followed by the first symptoms of the illness. The closer the onset of symptoms to the event itself, the more fulminant was the disease course. The most important factor in determining what type of reaction the particular child would have seemed to be his or her underlying personality structure—the more immature and dependent the child, the worse was the reaction to the precipitating stress.

The author also outlined the child's hospital course and was able to associate changes in the emotional state of the patient with gastrointestinal symptoms.

Psychotherapy was conducted either in a play situation (if the child was preadolescent) or in interviews (if the child was older). When possible, psychotherapy was provided for the parents as well. The goal of the psychotherapy with the patients was to enable them to deal more effectively and appropriately with their intense feelings of anger and aggression toward their parents and other authority figures. Time and again it was noted that as the child was able to express those feelings, the symptoms and objective examination findings of the ulcerative colitis would abate.

COMMENTARY: It is important to keep in mind that the psychotherapy provided for these patients was in addition to the regular medical and surgical management of their illness. The children's improvement as they were able to express previously unacceptable hostility was marked and impressive. Anyone who is managing cases of ulcerative colitis in children should keep this in mind.

SOURCE: Prugh, D. G. "The Influence of Emotional Factors on the Clinical Course of Ulcerative Colitis in Children." *Gastroenterology*, 1951, *18*, 339-354.

Additional Readings

Sperling, M. "Psychoanalytic Study of Ulcerative Colitis in Children." *Psychoanalytic Quarterly,* 1946, *15,* 302-327.

The author presents case discussions from a psychoanalytic viewpoint of two children suffering from ulcerative colitis. Details of the family dynamics that led to the development of a colitis-prone personality structure in each of the children are presented. The symbolic nature of the disease's symptoms and how they relate to the individual child's psychosocial level of functioning are explored. A number of generalizations are offered based on the cases actually presented, as well as on other cases from the author's experience.

Daniels, L. K. "Parental Treatment of Hyperactivity in a Child with Ulcerative Colitis." *Journal of Behavior Therapy and Experimental Psychology,* 1972, *4,* 183-185.

A six-year-old hyperactive boy suffering from ulcerative colitis was treated by his parents, who were taught to condition attending behavior in him. The parents were instructed to modify their own behavior so as not to serve as role models for the problem behavior and were told to ignore all hyperactive behavior in their child while simultaneously praising all attending behaviors he exhibited. Significant improvement in the child's activity and frequency of bowel movements was noted within two weeks, and complete improvement was noted in both areas after ten weeks. Long-term follow-up revealed continued normal functioning.

Crohn, B. B. "Psychosomatic Factors in Ulcerative Colitis in Children." Editorial in *New York State Journal of Medicine,* 1963, *63,* 1456-1457.

The author notes that it is well recognized that violent psychic trauma often immediately precedes the development of ulcerative colitis. In particular he cites the example of a seventeen-year-old girl who developed fulminating ulcerative colitis after doing poorly on a competitive examination in college. He warns that excessive demands to excel, when placed on individuals prone to developing gastrointestinal symptoms under stress, can lead to potentially devastating health problems. A plea is made to reduce some of the pressures on children to perform well in school.

Vandersall, T. A. "Ulcerative Colitis." In B. B. Wolman, J. Egan, and A. O. Ross (Eds.), *Handbook of Treatment of Mental Disorders in Childhood and Adolescence.* Englewood Cliffs, N.J.: Prentice-Hall, 1978.

The role of the psychotherapist in the management of the ulcerative colitis patient is outlined. In particular the author reviews the psychological factors involved in the etiology and course of the illness and then discusses the psychotherapeutic evaluation and treatment of the child and the family. The need for close cooperation with the managing physician (usually a gastroenterologist) and the psychological considerations when surgery is being contemplated are emphasized.

Diarrhea — Irritable Colon

Diarrhea consists of the discharge of undigested food in a fluid state. The outward signs are watery stools that occur several times a day and are often accompanied by abdominal cramps. Constipation often precedes the diarrhea. It is well known that the bowels may be suddenly evacuated during times of intense stress or anxiety. There is a definite pathway whereby external stress can evoke an anxiety reaction that influences the autonomic nervous system and enhances intestinal activity. Because of the increased movement of the bowels, the gastric material is rushed through the GI tract without the time needed for proper digestion and emerges undigested and in a liquid form. When chronic psychogenic diarrhea persists, the source is usually a deep-seated emotional problem. Psychogenic diarrhea can usually be controlled temporarily with drugs and a diet high in fiber content. Long-lasting recovery, however, requires removing the underlying conflict or teaching the child to respond differently to stress.

Drug Treatment of Chronic Nonspecific Diarrhea

AUTHOR: Sidney Q. Cohlan

PRECIS: A success rate of 53 percent with the drug Diodoquin

INTRODUCTION: The author conducted a preliminary study of forty-one consecutive cases of chronic nonspecific diarrhea in children, in which each case served as its own control, and a double-blind placebo-versus-drug study of forty-one subsequent cases. The children ranged in age from six months to three years. The common symptom was diarrhea of varying frequency and consistency. Tenesmus or irritability at stool was a prominent complaint in 44 percent of the cases. Tenesmus is a sensation of the need to evacuate the bowels, without result. Varying degrees of abdominal distension were present in about 50 percent of the children.

The onset of the disorder in most of the children occurred in connection with an infection of the respiratory tract. The diarrhea persisted, however, after this infection passed. Many of the children were classified as having "celiac disease" or "starch intolerance." All the cases had been treated with some form of a "celiac diet" in which bananas were fed and which was high in protein, low in fat, and free of starch and wheat. Such a diet resulted in moderate improvement in the diarrhea, but relapses were common.

TREATMENT: The parents were given a supply of diiodo-hydroxyquinoline (Diodoquin) tablets and were instructed to give one tablet (0.22 gm) to the child twice daily for one to two weeks. If the child's stools became more normal and tenesmus improved, the child was to gradually receive a normal diet. After two weeks of normal stools and a normal diet, the drug treatment was discontinued. It was reinstituted if a relapse continued to occur for three to five days. The medication was easily taken when crushed in food or drink, and it produced no apparent side-effects. About 53 percent of the eighty-two children in the initial and subsequent studies showed a good response to this treatment.

COMMENTARY: The ability of the children who responded to the drug treatment to tolerate foods that previously provoked diarrhea would seem to argue against a food-sensitivity etiology. Furthermore, the author notes that few, if any, of the children in this study meet the criteria for being classified as having the idiopathic celiac disease. Thus, the diagnosis of chronic non-specific diarrhea seems best. The author speculates that Diodoquin may be effective because it reestablishes a more favorable intestinal bacterial activity, although no evidence yet exists on exactly how it operates in these cases.

SOURCE: Cohlan, S. Q. "Chronic Nonspecific Diarrhea in Infants and Children Treated with Diiodohydroxyquinoline." *Pediatrics,* 1956, *18,* 424-431.

ADDENDUM: Subsequent to the publication of Cohlan's study it has been reported that prolonged administration of diiodohydroxyquin (as well as other 8-hydroxyquinoline compounds) has led to severe neurological damage in some patients. Specifically optic atrophy, optic neuritis, and peripheral neuropathy (subacute myclo-optic neuropathy) have occurred. The drug, no longer marketed as Diodoquin but available generically from several manufacturers, is contraindicated for patients with nonspecific chronic diarrhea. There is no specific drug therapy currently recommended for this condition.

SOURCES: Gellis, S., and Kagan, B. *Current Pediatric Therapy 8,* Philadelphia: W. B. Saunders Co., 1978.

Rudolph, A. M. (Ed.), *Pediatrics.* New York: Appleton-Century-Crofts, 1977.

Treating Chronic Diarrhea
by Systematic Desensitization

AUTHOR: Allan G. Hedberg

PRECIS: Case study of chronic diarrhea associated with interpersonal anxiety

INTRODUCTION: The client was a woman with a twenty-two-year history of chronic diarrhea. Previous treatment by psychodynamic therapy and self-help groups had proven ineffective. The problem had originated because of complications due to the birth of her second child. Since the woman had experienced several distressing "accidents" in public places, she was in a constant state of high anxiety. As a result, she restricted herself to situations in which she was within fifteen seconds of a bathroom. Her average number of daily bowel movements was ten, and she was currently averaging three "accidents" a week.

TREATMENT: During the first two treatment sessions the woman was instructed in muscle relaxation and advised to practice this at home. Since interpersonal anxiety was her major problem, three personal hierarchies of anxiety-provoking situations were constructed. An additional hierarchy was developed in which proximity to a bathroom was the variable. During the next six weeks the woman received twelve sessions of systematic desensitization. Two months later she was given four booster sessions to promote overlearning. After the third treatment the woman stopped her medications and reported substantial emotional relief and increased energy. By the eighth session bowel control was achieved and she was becoming active in community affairs once again. Therapy was terminated after twelve sessions. At a two year follow-up she was defecating once a day and able to control her bowels for hours if needed.

COMMENTARY: A psychosomatic problem of long duration was rapidly relieved by the use of a behavior therapy method. The woman in this case learned to associate body relaxation and pleasant mental events with her bowel functions rather than high anxiety. Such a systematic desensitization procedure seems applicable for use with children who have learned to be anxious about their persistent diarrhea.

SOURCE: Hedberg, A. G. "The Treatment of Chronic Diarrhea by Systematic Desensitization: A Case Report." *Journal of Behavior Therapy and Experimental Psychiatry*, 1973, *4*, 67-68.

Additional Readings

Davidson, M., and Wasserman, R. "The Irritable Colon of Childhood (Chronic Nonspecific Diarrhea Syndrome)." *Journal of
Pediatrics*, 1966, *69*, 1027-1038.

The authors studied the case histories of 186 children with
a diagnosis of chronic nonspecific diarrhea. The data indicate
the disorder is not caused by gastrointestinal infection, nor is it
a form of malabsorption that is made worse by the ingestion of
starch. Usually the condition affected children between the ages
of one and three, and in 90 percent of the cases, it cleared up
within thirty-six to thirty-nine months. In the main, only three
to four bowel movements a day occurred during attacks. More
than half the children were constipated both before and after
the diarrhea episode. Respiratory infections and teething episodes were frequently associated with exacerbations of the diarrhea. A special diet did not appear to help the condition. More
specifically, the restriction of starch and vegetable intake in
these children did not alter the underlying process. There appears to be a high familial coincidence of functional bowel
symptoms, such as nervous diarrhea and mucous colitis. Both
adults and children with "irritable colon" have small, loose,
mucus-containing bowel movements mainly in the morning and
tend to have associated constipation problems. The authors suggest that the elimination of chilled beverages helps the disorder,
since cold material in the stomach has a tendency to stimulate
the urge to defecate. The drug Diodoquin has been found to be
of value in treating this condition, but recent evidence indicates that
this drug is not to be used because of adverse side effects.

Davis, W. D. "The Irritable Bowel Syndrome—How to Recognize and Manage It." *Modern Medicine*, 1978, *16*, 62-65.

The irritable bowel syndrome is the most common problem encountered by gastroenterologists, accounting for 50 to 70
percent of their patients. Characterized by abdominal pain and
altered bowel habits—constipation, diarrhea, or both—it is usually directly related to some acute or ongoing life stress. The key
to diagnosis is recognizing the patient's psychological problems,
as well as the characteristic history of intestinal disorders. Management consists of sympathetic support and reassurance, along

with a program of regular exercise, retraining of bowel habits, and administration of hydrophilic colloids, anticholinergenics, and antidepressants, or mild sedatives, as necessary, to relieve symptoms or aid bowel functions. Biofeedback training may also prove to be a useful therapeutic aid.

Wender, E. H., Palmer, F. B., Herbst, J. J., and Wender, P. H. "Behavioral Characteristics of Children with Chronic Non-specific Diarrhea." *American Journal of Psychiatry,* 1976, *133,* 19-25.

The authors note that chronic nonspecific diarrhea is a common syndrome of early childhood. Typically, the diarrhea starts between three months and two years of age, occurs in variable episodes lasting from a few weeks to a few months, and usually subsides spontaneously between the third and fourth years of life. Having investigated sixteen children with this disorder, the authors report that these children demonstrated a significantly higher than normal frequency of sleep problems, crying and irritability, digestive problems excluding diarrhea, overactivity, and resistance to discipline; they also tended to have a family history of gastrointestinal problems. The authors conclude that these behavioral characteristics represent temperamental traits based on physiological factors, perhaps an imbalance of autonomic nervous system function.

Vomiting

Although occasional vomiting is common among children, persistent or recurrent vomiting can result in a rapid breakdown of bodily functions, and immediate intervention is usually required. In psychogenic vomiting there is no discernible medical reason for the act, which seems related to anxiety, tension, or stress. Chronic psychogenic vomiting tends to be cyclical: for periods that may last several weeks, the child may throw up after every meal and then the problem will seem to disappear, only to resume later when the emotions are again upset.

It has long been recognized that vomiting may have psychogenic determinants. Considerable recent research has clarified the precise types of emotional "triggers." Vomiting may, for example, be a rebellious act against parents who are battling the child over feeding. It may also be a symptom of the following: a reaction to the actual or threatened loss of a loved person; a symbolic rejection of parental attempts to impose some attitude or activity on the child; a reaction to the fears and anxieties of youth, particularly those related to school; and a somewhat nonspecific upper-GI-tract reaction to diffuse anxiety about a wide variety of upsetting life situations. And, the

child's vomiting can be a learned habit that is reinforced by increased parental attention or control over the home situation.

Psychogenic vomiting occurs more often in females than in males. Notably, few chronic vomitors show the emaciation that is characteristic of anorexia nervosa; and only rarely is malnutrition a complication, perhaps because the entire meal is seldom expelled. Furthermore, many psychogenic vomitors appear to have the ability to suppress the vomiting. Although children may not be able to control the urge to vomit after each meal, they can usually wait until they reach a bathroom (they almost never vomit in public).

The nature of the vomitus can assist in differentiating organic from psychogenic vomiting. Thus, vomitus containing gastric juice or bile, which produces a distinctly sour or stinging sensation in the throat, can signify a duodenal ulcer or hyperacidity. Signs of mucus, considerable blood, or pus in the vomitus also suggest a physical cause and should result in an immediate referral to a physician.

In regard to treatment, drugs may alleviate acute vomiting, but they seldom get to the root of the problem or forestall the next episode. Contingent use of positive and negative reinforcement has proven quite effective.

Treating Hysterical Vomiting by Modifying Social Contingencies

AUTHORS: Geary S. Alford, Edward B. Blanchard, and T. Michael Buckley

PRECIS: Success with an extinction procedure (withdrawal of attention and social contact)

INTRODUCTION: The client was a seventeen-year-old girl who was admitted to a hospital following a suicide attempt. A major reason for the self-destructive gesture was her inability to control her vomiting. The disorder started when she was seven, and she had vomited after every meal since then. No physical basis for the vomiting had been discovered by physicians. Medications, such as prochlorperazine, had not helped. In the hospital it was noticed that the girl constantly sought the attention of staff members and other patients, sometimes by acting seductively with male staff members. A diagnosis of hysterical neurosis was made.

TREATMENT: First, the girl was given six small-portion meals a day at fixed times. Two staff members sat with her while she ate in her room and timed the latencies and frequencies of vomiting. The staff members chatted casually with the client but avoided discussing her disorder or her problems. During the first phase of treatment the staff actually observed all vomiting behavior. In the second phase, they immediately left the girl's room when she first vomited, and they did not return for the remainder of the meal period. Thus, there was a complete withdrawal of social attention and contact following vomiting behavior. In the final phase of treatment, the staff explained to the girl the progress she had been making and the extinction procedure. She was now allowed to return to a regular three-meal-a-day schedule and permitted to eat in the dining room with the other patients. The staff called a meeting of the other patients and asked for their help in treating Miss X. They were instructed to ignore her (for example, by walking away) whenever she spoke of nausea or vomiting. They were also asked to move to another table if she verbalized anything about vomiting or if she in fact vomited during a meal. For every vomiting episode the girl was now required to spend thirty minutes in the time-out (isolation) room. This program rapidly brought the vomiting to an end. The program was terminated when she did not vomit for twelve consecutive meals. A seven-month follow-up disclosed that she had vomited only once since leaving the hospital.

COMMENTARY: The ease with which this long-standing disorder came under control surprised the authors. The vomiting in this case was clearly a psychosomatic disorder that was very responsive to changes in social attention. When the "secondary gains" (of a social nature) were stopped, the vomiting soon disappeared. By explaining the nature of the "illness" and treatment to the girl, the staff avoided any implication of malingering on her part and thus made it easy for her to give up the sick role. Two days after treatment began the girl began complaining of head and back pains but these complaints (possible symptom substitution) were ignored by the staff and they disappeared as quickly as they started. During the last phase of treatment several discussions were held with the girl to give her guidance in more adaptive ways to gain attention and capitalize on her positive attributes.

SOURCE: Alford, G. S., Blanchard, E. B., and Buckley, T. M. "Treatment of Hysterical Vomiting by Modification of Social Contingencies: A Case Study." *Journal of Behavior Therapy and Experimental Psychiatry,* 1972, *3,* 209-212.

Eliminating Habitual Vomiting by Positive Practice and Self-Correction

AUTHORS: Nathan H. Azrin and Michael D. Wesolowski

PRECIS: Handling psychogenic vomiting with a combination of positive practice and self-correction procedures

INTRODUCTION: The authors treated a profoundly retarded woman who had been vomiting on herself and her bed about twice a day for many years, without any apparent medical reason. The procedures they used seem applicable for use with children. Whenever a misbehavior occurs, the positive-practice procedure requires the person to practice the correct mode of responding. For vomiting, the correct reaction to an urge to vomit is to hurry to a sink or toilet so as to vomit in a nondisruptive manner. The self-correction procedure requires the vomitor to clean up his or her own mess.

TREATMENT: During the six weeks of training, whenever the woman vomited, she was required to clean it up and change her clothes or bed sheets if they had been soiled. After this self-correction procedure, she was required to conduct fifteen practice trials in the correct manner of vomiting (positive practice). For each trial she was escorted to the toilet, where she bent over the bowl for several seconds with her mouth open, and was required to flush the toilet. She was then returned to the site of the vomiting to begin the next trial. Initially, the trainer manually guided her in these activities. It took about forty-five to sixty minutes to complete both these procedures. The woman was also reminded every hour during the day that she should vomit only in the toilet and that she would have to clean up and practice if she vomited elsewhere.

After these procedures had been used for a week, the improper vomiting virtually disappeared; during the next five weeks the woman occasionally vomited in the toilet without the assistance of staff members and flushed the toilet. A follow-up a year later revealed the same pattern. Previous efforts to correct the problem by use of required relaxation or a time-out procedure had proven ineffective.

COMMENTARY: The authors conclude that the self-correction and positive-practice procedures are effective because they are reeducative in nature rather than punitive. They teach an individual not only how to respond correctly to a vomiting urge but also how to handle the mess once vomiting has occurred. They seem appropriate for use with both psychogenic vomiting and vomiting for medical reasons. In contrast, the authors have found other techniques such as required relaxation, time-out, and overcorrection to be interpreted as punitive by all concerned and to elicit negative emotional reactions.

It should be recognized, however, that self-correction and positive practice are both at least mildly aversive to children and may produce signs of emotional upset.

SOURCE: Azrin, N. H., and Wesolowski, M. D. "Eliminating Habitual Vomiting in a Retarded Adult by Positive Practice and Self-Correction." *Journal of Behavior Therapy and Experimental Psychiatry*, 1975, 6, 145-148.

Episodic Vomiting in a Three-Year-Old Child

AUTHOR: I. N. Berlin, Gwen McCullough, E. S. Liska, and S. A. Szurek

PRECIS: Psychoanalytic treatment of intractable vomiting

INTRODUCTION: A basic assumption of psychoanalytic treatment is that the origin of psychogenic vomiting in children is related in part to the attitudes, feelings, and conflicts of the parents. Thus the parents are often treated concomitantly with the child. The present case study highlights eight months of therapy with a hospitalized child, his mother and stepfather. Before the treatment, the child had experienced twenty-two hospitalizations in the preceding twenty months. The child was seen twice a week and the parents once a week during the eight months of treatment.

A detailed history revealed that the mother had felt depressed during her pregnancy, vomited continuously, and lost considerable weight. She stated that she felt this way because her husband was being unfaithful and failing to provide money for food, clothes, or fuel.

From birth, Louie, the patient, vomited his formula until he was started on solid food at ten months. In regard to the twenty-month period of vomiting, his mother could relate his vomiting episodes to events in her relationships with others that intensified her anxiety and tension or to situations in which the child's wishes and demands were not gratified. For example, the mother related the onset of his current vomiting problem to the first prolonged separation she had had with the boy's father. Louie was then 25 months old. Other events, such as the birth of a sister and the brief hospitalization of the mother, had also triggered vomiting episodes in the child. Repeated physical examinations had revealed no abnormalities. On admission for the twenty-third hospitalization, in which this treatment began, the child showed signs of marked dehydration, emaciation, cyanosis, and lack of tissue turgor.

TREATMENT: At the beginning of treatment the boy's mother gave the impression of childlike helplessness. Her own mother had experienced three stormy marriages, which left the boy's mother feeling depressed and unwanted. Seeking to escape home life at age nineteen, she married an irresponsible, improvident, and unfaithful man. She then became overly preoccupied with her son and was unable to refuse him anything. In therapy she expressed her mixed feelings about Louie and her current husband. She stated that she guessed the "stepfather ought to come first, but Louie does." Suggestions or advice by the therapist were met with severe somatic reactions. However she made steady progress when the therapist simply listened attentively to her. A different therapist met regularly with the stepfather, and in these sessions he was able to discuss his jealousy of Louie and the lack of support he received from his wife in disciplining the boy.

By the sixth month of treatment the mother stated that she was developing the ability to do things for herself and was less compulsive about the housework. In the seventh and final month of therapy the stepfather seemed more relaxed and mentioned that he felt more comfortable expressing his angry and tender feeling toward his wife. The mother reacted to Louie's impending discharge from the hospital by exhibiting a variety of physical symptoms, such as chest pains and "dizzy" feelings. She was able to work through her initial panic at the thought of the boy's returning home and was able to cope with the first and most difficult week after his return. Since the boy did not vomit at home after discharge, the parents soon stopped coming for outpatient treatment. They returned six months later when the boy suddenly relapsed and resumed vomiting. They attended one joint session in which they were able to air their differences about managing Louie. At the end of the session the mother agreed with her husband's observation that she needed to be more firm with the boy. The parents seemed to have made significant progress in improving their own relationship. They did not feel the need to return for future visits to the outpatient clinic.

The boy's treatment was equally successful. When first hospitalized he showed dramatic shifts from being a sad, sick, vomiting child to being a vivacious, vigorous, hungry boy. The shifts from well-being to vomiting often occurred when Louie was thwarted in his demands. During the first few months on the ward he vomited intermittently. In the beginning play sessions the boy would readily vomit whenever he became angry at the therapist. But he gradually learned to accept the playroom limits imposed by the therapist and seemed more free and relaxed in his play. By the fourth and fifth month of treatment the boy began to vomit less frequently and for shorter periods while on home visits.

When the boy vomited in the playroom, the therapist pointed out that he needed to learn other ways of expressing his feelings. The therapist remarked that they "both knew that often Louie felt very angry when he vomited." Louie responded to this interpretation by cursing the therapist and pounding vehemently on a peg board. Subsequently Louie decreased his vomiting in the playroom and became more aggressive with toys. When he attempted to scratch the therapist, he was stopped and encouraged to express his feelings in words and in play. Similarly, whenever the boy attempted to break the playroom materials, he was stopped and asked to "say or play out" his feelings.

When the boy was discharged after seven months, he continued the play sessions as an outpatient. He played freely and laughingly called the therapist a "stinker" when limits were set. Since the boy was happy and not vomiting at home now, the outpatient sessions were stopped by the parents.

COMMENTARY: In this case, the mother's unresolved childhood and marital conflicts were clearly an important factor in the etiology of the boy's vomiting behavior. Quite unhappy and dependent, she became overly involved with the boy and unable to set limits. This resulted in the following symptoms in the child which are common in disorders of this nature: early feeding disturbances, exclusive possession of the mother and long periods of sleeping with her, the mother's tendency to give excessive attention to the child, and the child's use of vomiting to control and prolong the dependent relationship with the mother. The authors speculate that vomiting behavior may represent a defense against the strong incorporative tendencies of the mother.

Therapy in this case focused on encouraging an expression of pent-up feelings in both the parents and the child. Such an approach seemed particularly appropriate in light of the mother's comment about her childhood that when she got angry she got slapped for it, held in her rage, and got "sick in the stomach." The therapists in this case were impressed with the ability of the parents and child to freely ventilate their tensions and to work through their difficulties with little need of interpretations. Much of this paper is devoted to understanding the underlying dynamics of the case, particularly the mother's conflictual dependency on her own mother. The need to work with both the parents and the child was clearly indicated in this case, which involved severe family conflict.

SOURCE: Berlin, I. N., McCullough, G., Liska, E. S., and Szurek, S. A. "Intractable Episodic Vomiting in a Three-Year-Old Child." *Psychiatric Quarterly*, 1957, *33*, 228-249.

Treating Persistent Vomiting
by Shaping and Time-Out

AUTHORS: Barbara Ingersoll and Franklin Curry

PRECIS: Case report of the successful treatment of persistent vomiting in a fourteen-year-old female

INTRODUCTION: The present case combined several procedures so as to produce a rapid reduction of the problem behavior. The following techniques were selected because they were the most acceptable to the family: shaping, positive reinforcement, and time-out.

Before the start of treatment, which was twenty-seven days after the onset of vomiting, the girl consistently vomited all food about three minutes after feedings. However, no significant weight loss occurred during this period. A medical exam revealed no physical cause for the persistent vomiting. The onset of vomiting occurred after a twenty-four-hour episode of nausea and malaise. Despite four different hospitalizations for the problem, the vomiting persisted. A diet of small portions of soup, tea, and gelatin at two-hour intervals proved ineffective.

TREATMENT: A shaping procedure was instituted whereby the child was given positive reinforcers for gradually retaining more food. She was fed specified amounts of food at regular intervals, and these time intervals between meals were to be gradually increased from five minutes to the interval required by full meals (about four hours); the type of food was gradually changed from a liquid to a solid diet; and the amount ingested at a feeding gradually expanded from two ounces to a full meal. The girl was informed of the retention goal at the beginning of each feeding. A timer was used to record the time of food retention.

For retaining specified amounts of food, the girl was given social reinforcers (praise and attention from the therapist) and activity reinforcers (games, visits to other hospital patients or to the gift shop). And for each minute of food retention the girl earned one penny. The money earned was given at the end of each retention interval. Points exchangeable for visits and evening television also were given on the same schedule of reinforcement (one point for each minute of retention).

For intervals in which no vomiting occurred, food reinforcers were made available and repeatedly presented if retention occurred. However, if vomiting happened, a fifteen-minute time-out penalty was immediately imposed. Time-out consisted of sitting in a chair in the corner, engaging in no activity and being permitted no access to food. Thus, she could not earn reinforcements during this time-out period. The therapist avoided eye contact and all interactions with the girl during the penalty period. After a time-out, the girl was returned to the feeding area, and food of the same type and amount that was given before the time-out was offered and other reinforcers again became available. Eight therapists rotated this training between 9 A.M. and 6 P.M. After 6 P.M., the girl was returned to the hospital ward and allowed to spend points earned from eating. If vomiting occurred, she was placed in bed for the night.

After the first use of a time-out interval, no further vomiting occurred in that two-hour treatment session. This first session included six successful small feedings. That night no vomiting occurred on the ward. For breakfast the girl requested and retained two doughnuts and a soda. She was then returned to a regular diet, with frequent snacks of candy and soda. Points and money were still awarded for food retention. The girl had no further vomiting episodes after this, and individual office visits were terminated after two days. She continued to earn money and points on the ward and was discharged the fifth day after admission.

COMMENTARY: The combined procedures in this study resulted in a rapid relief of the twenty-seven-day-old persistent vomiting behavior. Noteworthy is the fact that the girl and her family found the procedures acceptable and offered little or no resistance to the treatment. Thus there appear to be effective alternatives to electric shock delivered contingent on emesis.

SOURCE: Ingersoll, B., and Curry, F. "Rapid Treatment of Persistent Vomiting in a Fourteen-Year-Old Female by Shaping and Time-Out." *Journal of Behavior Therapy and Experimental Psychiatry*, 1977, *8*, 305-307.

Treating Compulsive Vomiting by Forcing the Child to Vomit

AUTHOR: Stanley M. Spergel

PRECIS: Five trials of forced vomiting by a ten-year-old boy

INTRODUCTION: The boy in this study, a patient in a children's psychiatric unit, was diagnosed as having both organic brain damage and childhood psychosis. Previous treatments by means of medications and token economies had proven ineffective. The child began vomiting two months after admission. He vomited nine times the first day and eleven times the second. The fact that he would call a staff member and proudly proclaim that the vomitus was his suggested a learned habit.

TREATMENT: In order to induce the child to vomit, a nurse escorted the child to a sink in the bathroom. She explained that since he seemed to enjoy vomiting, the staff would be pleased to help him vomit as much as possible. Wearing a rubber glove, the nurse then tilted the child's head forward and placed her finger down his throat. The boy vomited a small amount into the sink. He announced that he "didn't want to vomit any more." Nevertheless, the nurse repeated the procedure. A smaller amount of vomitus was expelled this time. After the fifth trial, the child proclaimed vigorously that he didn't want to vomit any more. It was then decided to stop the treatment. Vomiting did not recur thereafter and was still absent at a seven-month follow-up.

COMMENTARY: The child was interviewed two months after the treatment, and no residual effects from the forced vomiting were evident. It would seem, then, that this method of extinguishing the undesired behavior by massed practice to build up reactive inhibition can be dramatically successful with children who use vomiting to gain attention or control.

SOURCE: Spergel, S. M. "Induced Vomiting Treatment of Acute Compulsive Vomiting." *Journal of Behavior Therapy and Experimental Psychiatry*, 1975, 6, 85-86.

Additional Readings

Barbero, G. J. "Cyclic Vomiting." *Pediatrics,* 1960, *25,* 740-741.

The author found that cyclic vomiting, or recurring episodes of unexplained vomiting in children, usually terminates by puberty. Barbero also notes that the families of one fourth of the children studied had a history of migraine, and the children experienced recurrent headaches after the recurrent vomiting ceased. This article includes a description of the physiological process of vomiting, and the author concludes that psychological factors are a prime cause of this disorder.

Burgess, E. P. "Elimination of Vomiting Behavior." *Behavior Research and Therapy,* 1969, *7,* 173-176.

The client, a female college freshman, presented the symptom of increased incidents of vomiting attacks. Each attack followed a date the previous evening. The therapeutic task was to eliminate the control exercised over the vomiting response by the date-sleep-vomit sequence. The therapeutic program attempted to restrict the stimulus complex by eliminating such cues as petting, privacy, locale, late hours, and alcohol. The date segment of the sequence was abbreviated in order to create a time interval between date and sleep. The girl was asked to change her dating practices and follow an outlined program of successive approximations leading toward normal dating behavior. She was instructed to date every night for the next two weeks. The time spent on each date was brief, beginning with an hour and gradually increasing by fifteen to thirty minutes. She was advised not to extend the date time more than five minutes, to refrain from alcohol, to date in public places for the first three to five dates, and to avoid heavy petting for two weeks. She was asked to keep a dating log of times and places. If she vomited, the girl was told to proceed with her regular activities and dating schedule as if nothing had happened. This classical conditioning strategy was successful in relieving her discomfort and restoring her to normal pursuits within two weeks. After a year she had experienced no further difficulty and had not acquired a substitute symptom.

Cunningham, C. E., and Linscheid, T. R. "Elimination of Chronic Infant Ruminating by Electric Shock." *Behavior Therapy*, 1976, *7*, 231-234.

Rumination in infancy is the name given to the involuntary regurgitation of previously swallowed food and the rechewing and partial reswallowing of the food. An aversive therapy program was initiated after previous treatments failed to reduce ruminative vomiting in a nine-month-old infant hospitalized for malnutrition and weight loss. Mild electric shocks produced an immediate suppression of ruminating, weight increases, and a general improvement in the infant's social responsiveness. The systematic variation of observers and treatment location ensured generalization. A follow-up after six months revealed continued weight gains, with no recurrence of ruminating.

Flanagan, C. H. "Rumination in Infancy—Past and Present." *Journal of Child Psychiatry*, 1977, *16*, 140-148.

Rumination can be explained on the basis of hyperexcitability of the involuntary muscles. The regurgitation of milk produces satisfaction in the child, whereas failure to do so results in nervous unrest and irritation. Only when a child is alone and in a drowsy, vacant state does the act take place. Many infants who ruminate have been observed to be "spastic, hyperactive types of infants" who respond well to antispasmodic medication. Some investigators have found that both understimulation (neglect by parents) and overstimulation and too much tension are associated with rumination. The infants turn to their own bodies for satisfaction. Vomiting in the first few weeks of life has been found to be related to this disorder. Rumination seems to be a voluntary act of the infant and not associated with any central nervous system dysfunction. Treatment often involves providing an adequate mother substitute while helping the natural mother overcome her problems by watching the substitute. Treatment with aversive stimuli or antispasmodics has also proved effective.

Hammond, J. "The Late Sequelae of Recurrent Vomiting of Childhood." *Developmental Medicine and Child Neurology*, 1974, *16*, 15-22.

The author stresses that recurrent vomiting in childhood is not a benign condition that will completely disappear at puberty. He investigated the longitudinal effects of childhood vomiting by studying twelve adult patients who had experienced vomiting episodes throughout childhood. Hammond concluded that these patients, in the absence of symptom remission, continued to have gastrointestinal symptoms, more frequent psychological disturbances, and an increased risk of migraine headaches through adult life.

Illingworth, R. S. "Vomiting Without Organic Cause." *Clinical Pediatrics,* 1965, *4,* 685-686.

Vomiting in older children is a common feature of the so-called periodic syndrome. In this condition there may be any combination of the symptoms of headache, vomiting, fever, pale stools, and abdominal pain. It is probably a manifestation of migraine. There may be a history of the usual precipitating factors of migraine—emotion, fatigue, or infection. Vomiting can also occur as the result of anxiety or excitement.

Krakowski, J. "Psychophysiologic Gastrointestinal Disorders in Children." *Psychosomatics,* 1967, *8,* 326-330.

The author defines "psychosomatic illness" and offers a classification for consideration of GI disorders based on the observation of seventy-four children and the treatment of forty-nine. Psychogenic vomiting, chronic epigastric pain and gastritis, peptic ulcer, psychogenic diarrhea, psychogenic megacolon, and ulcerative colitis are explored. Common personality characteristics were not found among the subjects. However, disturbed parental influences were evident. Opipramol or Amitriptline, or a combination of psychotherapy with one of these drugs, was used. Satisfactory improvement occurred in 43 percent with psychotherapy, 75 percent with chemotherapy, and 54 percent with a combination of the two.

Mogan, J., and O'Brien, J. S. "The Counterconditioning of a Vomiting Habit by Sips of Ginger Ale." *Journal of Behavior Therapy and Experimental Psychiatry,* 1972, *3,* 135-137.

A sixty-year-old woman had been vomiting for a six-week period following an acute myocardial infarction. A medical exam revealed no organic cause for the vomiting, which, on psychiatric evaluation, was found to be a conditioned response to stimuli from the depression that had started very shortly before the onset of the infarction. The conditioned vomiting was counter-conditioned by the use of small doses of ginger ale, producing forward peristalsis. The depression was treated by the introduction of behavior incompatible with the depression. Ginger ale was chosen because it is not irritating to the stomach and because in small amounts (five cc.) no antiperistaltic gastric response is elicited; rather, there is normal peristaltic activity of the stomach and small intestine in a direction incompatible with vomiting. The patient was instructed to take one sip of ginger ale every fifteen minutes while awake. By the second day she stopped vomiting and started taking larger sips of ginger ale.

Murray, M. E., and Keele, D. K. "Behavioral Treatment of Ruminations." *Clinical Pediatrics,* 1976, *15,* 591-596.

The patient, a small six-month-old boy, was recently hospitalized because of persistent vomiting after every meal since his mother had taken a job outside the home a few weeks before. Physical examinations were negative, and a diagnosis of rumination was made. The treatment program was as follows: (1) The child's formula was thickened with cereal to make the initiation of rumination more difficult (stimulus control). (2) The child was held affectionately during the actual feedings. (3) As soon as he started his emetic behavior by tongue manipulation (deliberately protruded his tongue and making chewing motions with his jaw), he was returned to his crib (punishment). (4) Then, his mouth was opened and two drops of highly seasoned tabasco sauce were put on his tongue (punishment). (5) If the tongue rolling which started the rumination cycle was started again, the tabasco sauce (lemon juice could be substituted) was reapplied. (6) The child was not held or touched while his emetic behavior continued (extinction procedure). And (7) once his tongue manipulation ceased, the child was immediately picked up and attended to (reinforcement of incompatible behavior). During the first day, five or six punishments had to be administered after each feeding in order to stop the ruminating. On the second day only one or two punishments were needed, and by the third day the child initiated no tongue-rolling or emetic behavior after being fed.

Reinhart, J. B., Evans, S. L., and McFadden, D. L. "Cyclic Vomiting in Children: Seen Through the Psychiatrist's Eye." *Pediatrics*, 1977, *59*, 371-377.

These authors define cyclic vomiting as fits of vomiting that recur after intervals of uncertain lengths. The vomiting continues for a few hours or a few days. The cause of this syndrome, though possibly psychogenic, is not known definitely. The authors studied sixteen children hospitalized for this disorder and concluded that cyclic vomiting can truly be considered a psychosomatic syndrome. It is, they believe, a somatic reaction to psychological stress, and attention to psychosocial factors is imperative in all instances. The earlier one can intervene to help parents deal with their anxiety about the problem and their mixed feelings about their children, the more prompt and lasting will be the results. Psychiatric interpretations may have value even for families who do not wish to accept a psychiatric explanation of the syndrome. This is not a benign condition that terminates with puberty but is a syndrome much like peptic ulcer. In the case of a family unable to accept an emotional basis for this disorder, laparoscopy now enables the physician to assure the parents that there is no abnormality in the abdomen to account for the disorder. The authors conclude that a greater awareness of the importance of emotional stress as a precipitating factor in recurrent vomiting in childhood will lead to improved treatment and may also help to prevent migraine in adolescence and adult life.

Parental anxiety about keeping the child alive—anxiety due to past losses (miscarriage, stillbirth, loss of parents, or threatened loss through illness), is a common feature. The typical child with this disorder seems more anxious and immature than normal and may have a biologic predisposition to vomiting, just as others have to abdominal pains. As a result the child is too enmeshed with the parents and has trouble separating. That is, the parent is too involved in controlling the child's behavior beyond the time that the child should have control for herself.

Treatment should be directed toward having the parent give responsibility to the child.

Tasto, D. L., and Chesney, M. A. "The Deconditioning of Nausea and of Crying by Emotive Imagery: A Report of Two Cases." *Journal of Behavior Therapy and Experimental Psychiatry,* 1977, *8,* 139-142.

As a result of past learning, certain stimuli gain the capacity to evoke autonomic responses, and as a result of nonadaptive conditioning, autonomically mediated responses may occur inappropriately and under undesirable circumstances. Although relaxation is an effective counterconditioning procedure for overcoming such autonomic response habits, emotive imagery appears to be a potent alternative. A twenty-five-year-old male was helped to overcome nausea and vomiting triggered by foul-smelling objects or imagined scenes. The patient was asked to describe a pleasant scene which, if he were in it, would prevent the nausea. He stated that a scene on a ski poster in the therapist's office would inhibit nausea. After practicing imagining the scene, he stated that he felt comfortable and refreshed when he did so. He was then instructed to imagine the typical smells that occurred when emptying the trash. He was told to keep this imagery until he felt just the slightest degree of nausea. When nausea was experienced, he was to immediately switch to the ski scene. This switch stopped the feelings of nausea. In subsequent trials the patient was able to imagine the garbage scene longer until he was able to maintain it for two minutes without feeling any nausea. He was then helped to desensitize himself to other scenes such as cow manure and messy diapers. He was told to practice *in vivo* by exposing himself to the problem stimulus until he felt the slightest nausea. He was then to leave immediately and imagine the ski scene until he no longer felt nauseated. Follow-up reports over a one-year period revealed the problem had not returned.

Toister, R. P., Condron, C. J., and Arthur, D. "Faradic Therapy of Chronic Vomiting in Infancy: A Case Study." *Behavior Therapy and Experimental Psychiatry,* 1975, *6,* 55-59.

A seven-month infant hospitalized for four weeks was unsuccessfully treated for vomiting by thickened feeds, upright posturing, parental counseling, and frequent handling by the nursing staff. At this point contingent faradic therapy was instituted and resulted in an immediate suppression of vomiting and rumination with a weight gain of two pounds in seven days. A decrease in withdrawal and stereotyped mannerisms and an increase in social smiling, vocalizations, and attentiveness were observed. The faradic stimuli consisted of an electric shock repeated at half-second intervals until vomiting ceased. The electrodes were taped to the infant's calf.

Wright, D. F., Brown, R. A., and Andrews, M. E. "Remission of Chronic Ruminative Vomiting Through a Reversal of Social Contingencies." *Behavior Research and Therapy*, 1978, *16*, 134-136.

This case study involved a nine-month-old female with a history of ruminative vomiting since the age of three weeks. The mother-child interaction was described by the hospital staff as "distant." The mother would sit holding the child on her knee away from her body. After observing the child for nine days, the hospital staff implemented the following procedure. Immediately after the child started to ruminate, the nurse left the room. The nurse also made certain there were no external stimuli to which the baby had access during this absence. The nurse returned after three minutes to wipe the child's mouth. No other attention was directed to the rumination. The staff members interacted with the child as they would with any other child when she was not ruminating. The child's parents followed the same procedure at home. With this treatment the ruminations gradually decreased during the child's sixty-eight days in the hospital. Subsequent follow-ups indicated continued symptom remission. For cases of rumination that are not considered serious, the authors suggest these procedures in lieu of electric shock.

Wright, L., and Thalassinos, P. "Success with Electroshock in Habitual Vomiting." *Clinical Pediatrics,* 1973, *12*, 594-597.

The authors report the case of a four-year-old retarded girl who was vomiting frequently and becoming dehydrated. She was showing signs of malnutrition as well. She would readily accept food when offered, but then would frequently place her hands in her mouth in such a manner as to stimulate vomiting. On the day of admission she was observed to regurgitate on an average of fifteen times during the first half hour after each feeding. The treatment involved fitting the girl with a shock-providing apparatus before each feeding. The electrodes were attached to the left thigh. Whenever she retched, she received an electroshock of about sixty volts. This resulted in an immediate reduction in the regurgitations, and after twelve sessions she was symptom-free. Similar results were obtained with a second case, a five-year-old girl with leukemia.

Encopresis

Encopresis *denotes persistent fecal soiling in a child over four years of age which is not due to organic factors. Primary or continuous encopresis is soiling behavior that has been constant from birth.* The term secondary *or* discontinuous encopresis *is applied to soiling cases wherein the child had at one time acquired fecal continence but later began to soil. Physical examination of the encopretic child almost invariably reveals no abnormality, although there may be a slight dilation of the lower colon due to chronic fecal retention. Though most children are toilet trained by the age of two and a half, a margin of error is allowed and a child is not considered encopretic until he reaches the age of four. The encopretic child usually soils his underwear from once to several times each day with a moderate amount of feces. For unclear reasons, encopresis is much more common in boys than girls.*

Encopresis may occur in children and families that are relatively well adjusted emotionally but who are going through a period of situational stress; it may also occur in children with

more deep-seated personality problems. The etiology is varied and may be related to toilet-training habits, parent and family orientation and experience, constitutional factors, the low intelligence of the child, poverty and being a member of a large family, psychologically related conflict, stress, insecurity and overprotection, regression, anal fixation, and an expression of aggression or resentment.

Encopresis can cause serious problems for the school-age child. The foul odor of feces may be a major obstacle to attending school, and it often causes much ridicule from siblings, other children, and adults. It may also lead to the exclusion of the child from social activities. Encopresis tends to have a disturbing effect on parent-child relationships as well. The parents' lack of success in teaching their children bowel control leads to frustration, anger, and undesirable behavior on both sides.

The long-term prognosis for encopresis is good, even without treatment, though it may last two or three years before it disappears. With treatment, it often improves in a few weeks or two to three months. The treatment of encopresis is often global, since so many factors may contribute, in greater or lesser degree, to the disorder.

Home-Based Treatment of Childhood Encopresis

AUTHOR: Elaine A. Blechman

PRECIS: Treating chronic constipation by combining the techniques of giving information, emphasizing positive antecedents to toileting, making the child responsible for cleaning, giving rewards for clean pants, and training the child to have appropriate bowel movements

INTRODUCTION: The author treated five children with the diagnosis of acquired megacolon. Four of the five had encopresis. The treatment goal was to relieve the chronic constipation by emphasizing positive antecedents and consequences as opposed to more aversive forms of treatment, such as laxatives, nagging, and punishment.

TREATMENT: After the initial interview the parents were given charts for the daily recording of soiled pants and bowel movements. The parents were to check the child's pants at three set times during the day: before school, after school, and before dinner. The charts were usually kept in the bathroom, and most of the children recorded the incidence of their bowel movements in the toilet. The therapist made occasional phone calls at midweek to check on the recordings and treatment.

The first aspect of treatment involved an orientation session in which the parents were given basic information about encopresis, help in designing a comfortable toileting setting, instruction to make the child responsible for cleaning up after soiling, instruction to praise the child for all relevant successes and to be nonchalant after failures, and advice about laxative use (continue to use mineral oil as needed, if prescribed by the pediatrician).

The second treatment component involved giving the child a predetermined reward for clean pants when the child returned home from school. The child was often given another reward for appropriate bowel movements in the toilet. Once the constipation and soiling were consistently improved for several weeks, the parents were instructed to start fading out the contingent rewards. Among the rewards used were ice cream, play time with father, and twenty-five cents toward a model car. One child received a reward of a special activity with his parents for seven consecutive bowel movements.

COMMENTARY: The author emphasizes the finding that a reward for appropriate bowel movements is an essential aspect of this treatment program, since children do not do as well when this component is missing. The four children whose treatment included this reward showed good short- and long-term results. The child whose treatment did not include such a reward made good short-term progress, but he relapsed and resumed soiling after six months. The author also reports that enemas and laxatives were used before this home-based management program to remove impacted feces. In one of the four successful cases the child did relapse during an illness, but reinstituting the program quickly produced good results.

SOURCE: Blechman, E. A. "Short- and Long-Term Results of Positive Home-Based Treatment of Childhood Chronic Constipation and Encopresis." Unpublished manuscript, 1978, available from author, Department of Psychology, Wesleyan University.

An Eclectic Approach to Treating Encopresis

AUTHOR: Werner I. Halpern

PRECIS: A multilevel intervention that takes into account individual and family differences

INTRODUCTION: The author follows an eclectic approach to childhood encopresis which is based on the belief that more than one technique is needed for effective therapy. In the initial interview the clinician takes a detailed history and offers a sympathetic understanding of the child's plight and the parents' frustration. The treatment of choice for ten encopretic children between the ages of four and fifteen involves the use of a suppository and behavior therapy techniques.

TREATMENT: During the first phase of treatment, the quick-acting suppository bisacodyl (Dulcolax) is inserted once daily for three days according to a predetermined schedule. Since bowel evacuation usually occurs within half an hour after insertion into the rectum, the child can immediately experience success without the more intrusive effect of an enema. Occasionally, this suppository results in abdominal cramping when first used, and reassurance may be needed about the transient nature of this side effect. After three days on the suppository, the child is urged to move his bowels by himself. If fecal retention is again evident for a three-day period when Dulcolax is stopped, the suppository is again used for another three-day cycle.

In addition to the suppository, the author recommends that systematic positive reinforcement be used to promote voluntary defecation. One child, for example, was given small toy cars for bowel movements in the toilet. These rewards were usually unnecessary after four weeks.

The author has found that most children quickly respond to the above combination of physiological therapy (suppositories) and behavior modification techniques. A few children will require additional measures. The child who is fearful of the toilet, for example, will have to be desensitized to this fear before the training can begin. And the child who continues to produce hard, painful stools will need a period of time on a stool softener, such as dioctylsodium sulfasuccinate (Colace).

COMMENTARY: Most of the children in this study could be classified as having a "slow-to-warm-up" temperament, characterized by shyness or a fear of new situations and novel experiences. Also noteworthy is the author's finding that effective treatment of the encopresis tended to result in an improvement in the parent-child relationship. Finally, the author presents a rationale for his multimodal intervention (physiological, psychological), which recognizes both individual and family differences.

SOURCE: Halpern, W. I. "The Treatment of Encopretic Children." *Journal of Child Psychiatry*, 1977, *16*, 478-499.

Treating Encopresis with a Combination of Dietary Control, Bowel Training, and Family Counseling

AUTHORS: Herman A. Hein and Jerold J. Beerends

PRECIS: Practical management techniques employed by pediatricians

INTRODUCTION: The authors, both pediatricians, treated eighteen encopretic children (ages four to twelve) in the following manner. First a physical exam was given to rule out possible physical causes. Then the parents were counseled that the child did not have voluntary control over the bowel and that they should not punish soiling behavior or be punitive in their attitudes. The child and the parents were told that the treatment had worked for many other children and would also work for them.

TREATMENT: First, the child was given a Fleet enema in the evening and another the following morning to clean out the system and restore normal muscle tone to the bowels. The child sat on the stool or potty chair ten minutes after each meal. If the child's feet did not touch the floor when he used the regular toilet, a platform was built for his feet or the child used a potty chair.

The parents encouraged the following foods: prunes or prune juice, bran cereal, vegetables, and extra water. At the same time they were to limit the child's ingestion of bananas, apples, and milk (to sixteen ounces a day). In addition, milk of magnesia was added when the diet alone did not improve the consistency of the stool. Monthly sessions with the parents were held to ensure that they were following the instructions.

The results indicated that fourteen of the eighteen children had stopped soiling completely. The program was usually successful within one month, but a few children required five to six months of treatment. Three of the other children were markedly improved, and the one failure was due to lack of parental cooperation in following the program.

COMMENTARY: In view of the success experienced with this standardized treatment program, the authors conclude that the treatment of possible underlying emotional problems is not needed for most encopretic children. A combined program of dietary control, initial enemas, and parent counseling regarding bowel training would seem to ensure good results with most children. Referral for child therapy is only necessary when severe emotional disturbance is evident in the child. Utilization of knowledge about the normal physiology of the bowel, including the gastroileal reflex (see G. C. Young, "The Treatment of Childhood Encopresis by Conditioned Gastroileal Reflex Training," *Behaviour Research and Therapy*, 1973, *11*, 449), seemed to contribute to the success of this program.

SOURCE: Hein, H. A., and Beerends, J. J. "Who Should Accept Primary Responsibility for the Encopretic Child?" *Clinical Pediatrics*, 1978, *17*, 67-70.

A Pediatric Treatment Program for Encopresis

AUTHORS: Melvin D. Levine and Harry Bakow

PRECIS: A comprehensive treatment program, consisting of counseling and education, initial bowel catharsis, a supportive maintenance program to continue bowel evacuation, retraining, and careful monitoring and follow-up

INTRODUCTION: The authors integrated several forms of intervention in order to treat 127 children. Any child over four years old who regularly passed stools into his underwear or pajamas was considered to have encopresis. Before treatment, a careful history was taken of the disorder, and the child's abdomen was X-rayed to determine the degree of stool retention. The primary goal of intervention was to directly relieve the soiling, not to provide therapy for underlying or associated problems.

MANAGEMENT PROGRAM: During the first visit, the physician provided the parent and child with information about the normal functions of the intestines, possible reasons for the problem, the fact that many other children have the same difficulty, and the need to strengthen bowel muscles that have become weak and thin from distension. Reassurance was offered during this counseling and orientation session to the effect that the child could, with consistent effort, build up his bowel muscles and thus gain control of the bowel functions. It was explained to the parents that it was not the child's fault she had lost muscle tone and that children often become so accustomed to fecal odor that they may not be aware they have soiled. The overall approach was positive and nonaccusatory in nature; no use of punishment was made.

   The next step of the program was to use cathartics to clean out the child's bowels. This was done at home and was organized around three-day treatment cycles. On the first day of a cycle, the parents gave the child two adult Fleet enemas in succession. On the second day, the child was given a biscodyl

(Dulcolax) suppository right after school and again in the early evening. On the third day, the child received a ten-mg. biscodyl tablet right after school and one in the evening. This same treatment cycle was repeated three or four times for each child. For mild cases and in children under seven, half of the above doses was used in each cycle. If the child had particularly severe fecal impaction or if it was not possible for enemas to be given at home, the child was admitted to the hospital, where he was given saline enemas two or three times a day, together with Dulcolax suppositories twice a day. This initial bowel evacuation phase was considered complete when an X-ray film showed evidence of little, if any, fecal retention. Often a child's abdomen can be soft to palpation while the X-rays disclose considerable retained stool. In order to avoid relapses, it was considered essential to have clear evidence of a thoroughly cleaned-out bowel.

After the initial bowel catharsis, a maintenance phase was implemented. Light mineral oil was used in most cases at an average beginning dose (for a seven-year-old) of 30 cc. twice each day. This dosage was raised rapidly for those children who did not have regular movements at least once every two days. The parents and child were told that this laxative would have to be taken for at least six months. The mineral oil was tapered off gradually in successful cases. In conjunction with the mineral oil, the children were advised to take two multiple vitamin pills each day between oil intakes to minimize the possible effects of malabsorption of fat-soluble vitamins. If signs of stool retention continued to appear (large-caliber stools, less frequent defecation, abdominal pain, soiling, or excessive leakage of mineral oil), a supplemental oral laxative was given for one or two weeks. Senokot (one tablet or five cc. of the syrup daily) or Modane (starting dose of 37.5 mg.) was used. The parents were urged not to use enemas or suppositories for relapses so as to avoid a prolonged "anal assault" on the child.

The training component of the program was designed to make the child feel comfortable on a toilet. The children were told they needed to sit on the toilet with adequate foot support for at least ten minutes at a time twice each day at exactly the same time daily in order to establish a bowel rhythm. A kitchen timer was available for timing these periods. These two fixed periods were not to depend on whether the child felt the urge to go or had gone at other times during the day. Children under eight years were given stars on a wall chart to reinforce these two sittings. A certain number of stars earned the child a prize.

The final aspect of the program involved monitoring and support. A physician was available each morning by telephone to give advice. The family was seen three weeks after the initial clean-out, and further sessions were scheduled every four to eight weeks depending on the degree of persistence of the encopresis.

A one-year follow-up of 110 children treated with this program revealed that 51 percent had no soiling incidents for at least six months, another 27 percent showed marked improvement (less than one soiling episode every two weeks), 14 percent showed some improvement but continued to have incontinence, and 8 percent showed no improvement whatsoever during the treatment year. It was found that the degree of parent-child compliance with the program was a major determinant of treatment success. It was also noted that treatment failure was associated with very severe constipation, frequent accidents in school or in pajamas, the presence of learning problems in school, and general behavior problems, such as excessive moodiness, disobedience, and fearlessness.

COMMENTARY: The follow-up evaluation indicated that this pediatric management program was effective with 78 percent of the cases treated. The authors conclude that a broader, interdisciplinary management program might be needed for children who fail to respond to this type of program. Such "hard-to-treat" children include cases of severe incontinence (daily soiling), children with other behavioral, developmental, and academic problems, and families who are disinclined to cooperate with this vigorous management program.

SOURCE: Levine, M. D., and Bakow, H. "Children with Encopresis: A Study of Treatment Outcome." *Pediatrics,* 1976, *58,* 845-852.

An Effective Program
for Psychogenic Encopresis

AUTHORS: Logan Wright and C. Eugene Walker

PRECIS: A standardized treatment for psychogenic encopresis

INTRODUCTION: Fecal retention resulting in chronic constipation is the cause of most cases of childhood encopresis. The
soiling is the result of seepage around the impacted fecal material. Psychotherapy to resolve some possible underlying conflict
resulting in the fecal retention has produced relatively meager
results. In contrast, programs designed to directly manage and
resolve the chronic constipation have generally proved quite
successful. The authors describe a relatively simple program that
is easy to explain and supervise. It differs from most pediatric
programs in that it gives the major responsibility to the child,
less to the parents, and only a supervisory role to the therapist
or physician. It also uses an incentive system of rewards and
penalties.

TREATMENT: After an assessment has been made to rule out
physical illness or severe emotional disturbance, the therapist in-
structs the parents in the details of the treatment program so
they can explain it to the child. The first step in the program is
the parents' administration of one or two Fleet enemas to thoroughly clean out the child's colon. The next morning the child
is to go to the bathroom immediately upon awakening. If the
child produces a reasonable amount of feces, he is praised and
given a reward agreed upon in advance. The reward is used to
motivate the child to try hard to evacuate his colon. If the child
is unable to produce at least one quarter to one half cup of
feces, the parent inserts a glycerin suppository into the rectum
and the child then dresses and has breakfast. After breakfast the
child tries again to defecate, and if successful, he receives a reward. This reward is smaller than what he would have received
if he had been successful without the suppository. If the child is
still unsuccessful, the parent administers an enema. If prolonged
use of enemas seems needed, they may be administered every

second or third day. No reward is given when enemas are needed for the morning movement. This regular evacuation of the bowel ensures that the colon regains its normal shape and muscle tone.

At a specified time later in the day, such as after school, the child's underwear is inspected, and if no soiling is evident, he receives a reward. A mild punishment is given if soiling is evident. The choice of the rewards and the penalties is tailored to the individual child and knowledge of what he finds particularly attractive and aversive. Among the rewards that the authors have found successful are money, candy, small toys, and extra privileges. A particularly effective reward is allotting the children twenty or thirty minutes in which their parents will do anything they ask, such as play, talk, or read a book. Some penalties that have worked well are the restriction of television viewing, a loss of privileges, being kept indoors, monetary fines, and having to do extra chores (especially the chores of siblings). Requiring the child to sit in a chair for a set period of time, such as fifteen minutes, has also proven quite effective.

Since this program must be carried out with 100 percent consistency by the parents, the therapist should motivate the parents by asking them to keep a daily notebook record of exactly what was done. This record is to be mailed to the therapist every week, and the therapist should phone the family after reviewing the record. During the phone conversations the therapist gives support, advises the parents how to handle problems, and gives recommendations on dietary control and stool softeners when these measures seem necessary. These weekly phone calls are very important to keep the parents motivated and the program on track.

After two consecutive weeks of no soiling, the family can begin to phase out the program. This is begun by selecting one day during the week in which no cathartics (enemas, suppositories) will be given. If one more week of no soiling occurs, one more day of no cathartics is added to the schedule. These cathartic-free days should be kept several days apart. This schedule is kept up until the child is completely free of cathartics. At this point the rewards and penalties are also stopped. In the event soiling recurs during this phase-out period, one day of cathartic use is added. If soilings become frequent again, it often helps to give an enema the morning after each soiling.

COMMENTARY: The authors have found that if parents apply this standardized program consistently and rigorously, they will almost invariably be successful in eliminating the encopresis problem within fifteen to twenty weeks. Parents of low socio-economic level or marginal IQ require more prompting and supervision than is normally required. Children who start soiling again after the program is terminated generally respond well to a repeat of the program. The authors have never encountered a child who relapses a second time. In summary, this is a highly specific program that has proven very successful with a wide variety of children. The most difficult parts of the program for parents are the administration of enemas and the 100 percent consistency required.

SOURCE: Wright, L., and Walker, C. E. "Treatment of the Child with Psychogenic Encopresis." *Clinical Pediatrics*, 1977, *16*, 1042-1045.

Additional Readings

Andolfi, M. "A Structural Approach to a Family with an Encopretic Child." *Journal of Marriage and Family Counseling,* 1978, *4,* 25-29.

This article describes brief therapy using a structural approach. During the course of therapy the encopretic behavior of a preadolescent boy was observed in relation to the interaction and structure of the family system. The presenting problem was analyzed as a sign of family dysfunction and of the stress consequent to the parents' separation. The success of the therapy did not consist only of the disappearance of the encopretic behavior, but also of the discovery of different methods of treatment, which produced a liberating effect on the identified child and other family members.

Doleys, D. M., McWhorter, A. Q., Williams, S. C., and Gentry, W. R. "Encopresis: Its Treatment and Relation to Nocturnal Enuresis." *Behavior Therapy,* 1977, *8,* 77-82.

The authors describe a comprehensive treatment approach which involves (a) Full Cleanliness Training (FCT), (b) regular pants-checks and toileting, and (c) reinforcement for appropriate toileting behavior. During FCT, the child is required to correct the results of the soiling by cleaning himself and his clothes. This procedure both teaches responsibility, by having the child correct the detrimental effects of his own behavior, and motivates the child to perform the desirable behavior, because having to clean up serves as a negative consequence of the accident.

Johnson, J. H., and Von Bourgondien, M. E. "Behavior Therapy and Encopresis: A Selective Review of the Literature." *Journal of Clinical Child Psychology,* Spring 1977, pp. 15-19.

This paper considers the general nature of childhood encopresis and reviews published studies to date that have employed behavioral approaches to treatment. Although few controlled studies were found, a number of published case reports suggest that behavioral methods have value in treating the encopretic child. A frequent behavioral approach is to give the child positive reinforcement for appropriate eliminations in the toilet, while ignoring the soiling behavior. Other approaches combine positive reinforcement with punishment for soiling. In general, the studies suggest caution should be used in applying punishment, since this contingency can lead to adverse side-effects, such as increased bowel retention. Punishment should be reserved for cases where fecal smearing accompanies the soiling or where the soiling behavior itself seems reinforcing to the child.

Musicco, N. "Encopresis: A Good Result in a Boy with UTP (uridine-5-triphosphate)." *American Journal of Proctology,* 1977, *28,* 43-46.

This case involved an eight-year-old boy with total incontinence of liquid or soft excreta and incomplete loss of solid waste. The incontinence became complete even with solid excreta when the boy was distracted by something very attractive for him, such as playing football. The administration of a drug containing adenosine and organic phosphoric acid at the beginning of treatment, and later of another product containing UTP, produced very good results. The drug containing adenosine and organic phosphoric acid was designed to stimulate the cortical substance of the brain to control the anal sphincter muscle. This produced only modest improvement after forty days. The author then prescribed uridine-5-triphosphate (one tablet a day for three months, then one tablet on alternate days for another two months). After only one week's treatment the encopresis disappeared. It was only necessary to repeat the administration of the UTP for another three months, after a six-month interval. It seems that UTP increases the contraction tone and activity of the smooth musculature of the lower bowel. It is particularly useful if muscular hypotonia is suspected in the child. In the present case, the incontinence of feces had been present since birth. There appeared to be no fecaloma or mass of feces in the colon in this case, and evacuation of the bowels occurred every day. This led the author to think of muscular hypotonia. Since the mother worked, it was also likely that the boy did not pay more attention to his bowels as an unconscious way of gaining maternal attention.

Plachetta, K. E. "Encopresis: A Case Study Utilizing Contracting, Scheduling, and Self-Charting." *Journal of Behavior
Therapy and Experimental Psychiatry,* 1976, 7, 195-196.

The child and the therapist agreed on a verbal "contract"
that involved the following treatment elements: scheduling,
positive reinforcement, and self-charting. The six-year-old boy
was to go to the toilet four times a day (morning, noon, after
school, and before bed) and attempt to eliminate. Each ten-
minute attempt was rewarded with a penny, and for each "success" he received a nickel. Emphasis was placed on "trusting"
the child to report accurately. During the first week of this behavioral program the child experienced only two accidents,
both the result of forgetting to eliminate at school. A prompt,
consisting of a picture of a commode on his lunchbox, helped
to remind him. For each day free of soiling the child pasted a
star on his chart. His parents paired praise with the financial
reinforcer. After two months the child gradually faded out the
charting and reward system, stating, "I don't have to be paid for
going to the toilet."

Segall, A. "Report of a Constipated Child with Fecal Withhold-
ing." *American Journal of Orthopsychiatry,* 1957, 27,
819-825.

The author reports the case of a two-year-old girl who
would retain her feces for three days and then empty her
bowels in bed. This behavior had persisted for six months. The
girl also exhibited feeding difficulties, stubbornness, and fear of
dirt. The treatment consisted of play therapy wherein the girl
played with sand and water. She liked to smear the mixture of
sand and water with her hands and was reassured by the therapist that it was alright for her to get her hands dirty. A nondirective approach was taken, and the girl enjoyed bossing the
therapist around. The girl soon was going to the toilet in the
playroom and flushing the water by herself. The child's soiling
behavior disappeared after six play sessions. The mother was
also seen individually and these analytic sessions were designed to help her become more accepting and at ease with the
child.

Schaefer, C. E. "Treating Psychogenic Encopresis: A Case Study." *Psychological Reports,* 1978, *42,* 98.

An eight-year-old boy with chronic encopresis was treated with the standardized program developed by Logan Wright. This program involves parental administration of behavior modification principles and cathartics (enemas and suppositories). The use of an adult-sized enema rather than a child-sized enema was crucial for success in this case. The results indicate that severely constipated children must be thoroughly cleaned out before they regain normal sensations and muscle tone in the colon.

Wright, D. F. "Parental Intervention in the Treatment of Chronic Constipation." *Journal of Behavior Therapy and Experimental Psychiatry,* 1977, *8,* 93-95.

Chronic constipation was successfully eliminated in a three-year-old girl through a regimen combining behavioral and medical treatments. The onset of constipation was at birth. The procedures entailed the use of mineral oil to produce reflex defecation, concurrent with a token economy established by the parents in the home. After symptom remission, the behavioral-medical interventions were systematically faded. Long-term follow-up revealed no recurrence of constipation and no symptom substitution.

Recurrent Abdominal Pain

Recurrent abdominal pain is the most common complaint of children ages six to fifteen. The diagnosis of recurrent abdominal pain (psychogenic) usually results from the following signs: (1) a varied and erratic history of recurrent abdominal pain; (2) additional symptoms of facial pallor, dizziness, headaches, and pellet stools; (3) external stress that is associated with the onset or exacerbation of pain; (4) tenderness on deep palpation of the abdomen commonly located over portions of the colon; and (5) negative lab and X-ray examinations. It is estimated that at least one school-age child in ten suffers from this ailment. Unusual before age five, recurrent abdominal pain has its greatest incidence in children ages nine to ten. It is slightly more common in girls than boys. Noteworthy is the finding that similar abdominal complaints in parents and siblings of these children are much more frequent than in children who do not report abdominal pain.

Both physical and psychological etiologic possibilities have to be considered for each case. However, most abdominal pain in children does not seem to have an organic basis. In only about 5 percent of children with this disorder does it have an identifiable physical cause, such as an ulcer. Anxiety in a child is expressed more often as "I have a stomach ache" than as "I feel nervous or edgy." The latter phrase tends to be an adult expression. Apart from expressing anxiety, abdominal pain may yield some secondary gain. Among the psychological gains from this disorder are getting increased attention and solicitude (the child may, for example, be allowed to sleep in the parents' bed) or gaining greater control of a situation, as, for example, by avoiding a stressful event or preventing parents from fighting.

The relationship between recurrent abdominal pain and diarrhea in young children is not clear. About 12 percent of children with recurrent abdominal pain also report diarrhea problems. Some investigators consider both disorders to be manifestations of a more general syndrome entitled "the irritable bowel of childhood."

Treating Psychogenic Recurrent Abdominal Pain

AUTHOR: Morris Green

PRECIS: A standard pediatric approach to both diagnosis and treatment

INTRODUCTION: The author describes the characteristics of psychogenic recurrent abdominal pain as follows: About half the children examined for this complaint will have had the problem for less than a year; the rest, for one to five years. The frequency of the pain will vary from six or seven times a day to once a week or once a month. Usually the disorder is directly related to a stressful event, and a temporal relationship to meals is rare. The pain almost never awakens the child from sleep. The pain attacks usually last from five to thirty minutes but may persist for hours. The attacks typically begin gradually and the pain is mild or moderate rather than severe. The child describes it as "It just hurts," "It feels funny," or "I don't know." The complaint is poorly located in the stomach or intestinal regions, and a few children report that it changes from place to place. Symptoms that may precede or accompany the pain include nausea, pallor, vomiting, dizziness, headache, or faintness. Abdominal tenderness, distention, or muscle spasm are generally not present in a child with psychogenic abdominal pain.

In interviewing the parents the physician should try to relate the onset or recurrence of the pains to important events in the child's life. Most parents will have trouble thinking in this manner because they believe the pain to be organic in nature, such as appendicitis, ulcer, "female trouble," or spastic colitis. Since the child has real pain, they do not see how it could be psychological in origin.

A physical examination of the GI tract should be conducted to rule out such disorders as peptic ulcer, diverticulum, ulcerative colitis, constipation, and parasites. In addition to the absence of organic factors, the diagnosis of "psychogenic abdominal pain" requires evidence of significant psychopathology in the child or home situation.

TREATMENT: When there is no evidence of organic lesion, this finding should be clearly stated to the parents. They should also be told that many children whose pain has a psychogenic etiology do not just "grow out of" the complaint; indeed, many become "pain-prone patients" unless they receive proper treatment.

When the initial interview strongly suggests a psychogenic cause, the parents and child should be given the opportunity to fully discuss their feelings and current problems, such as alcoholism, marital discord, or childrearing difficulties. At times direct advice to the parents is warranted, as, for example, to return the child to school, obtain a tutor for reading, change sleeping arrangements, stop physical punishment, reduce excessive demands or expectations of high achievement, permit expression of angry feelings, reduce parental commitments outside the home, pay more attention to the child, place an aging grandparent in a nursing home, or obtain medical or psychological help for themselves. Family group interviews when the child is older than eight or nine can be helpful in revealing sources of stress on the child.

Because of the parents' concern about a physical cause of the problem, these cases are best treated initially by a pediatrician. Later the physician may wish to collaborate with mental health professionals when severe psychological problems become evident in the family.

Drug therapy is of limited or no usefulness, except for suggestion. Medication not only fails to deal with the underlying problem but may contribute to both a continuing hypochondriasis and drug-dependency.

COMMENTARY: The author has found that several stressful environmental factors are usually present in recurrent psychogenic abdominal pain. Among the anxiety-provoking factors that the therapist should look for are the death of or separation from an important person in the child's life; physical illness, hypochondriasis, or chronic handicap in parents or siblings; severe marital discord; psychological illness in the parents; unsatisfying parent-child relationships; parental preoccupation with illness; the inability of the child to express aggressive or sexual impulses; inappropriate sleeping arrangements wherein the child may sleep with a parent or older sibling; and school problems, such as a specific learning difficulty. Moreover, some children develop this reaction because of a fear of their own death due to a current or past life-threatening disease.

SOURCE: Green, M. "Diagnosis and Treatment: Psychogenic Recurrent Abdominal Pain." *Pediatrics,* 1967, *40,* 84-89.

Operant Treatment of a Case Involving Recurrent Abdominal Pain

AUTHORS: Lawrence I. Sank and Anthony Biglan

PRECIS: Treating a ten-year-old boy with a two-and-a-half year history of recurring abdominal pain with operant methods (positive and negative reinforcement)

INTRODUCTION: The boy complained of severe pain attacks in the central abdominal area which usually lasted from five to twenty minutes but occasionally lasted several hours. Moreover, the boy reported the presence of low-level abdominal pain at all times. The attacks of intense pain occurred at least once daily. At the time of his admission to the hospital he had missed forty-five of seventy-two days of school. Extensive diagnostic work-ups at the hospital revealed no "organic" source.

TREATMENT: After a ten-day baseline period of recording the intensity and frequency of abdominal pain, the following contingencies were established. The boy received a point for every half day in which he had no severe attacks and had an average pain rating below his mean rating level during the baseline period. (During this period the boy had rated the intensity of pain every half hour on a ten-point scale from one, no pain, to ten, the most severe pain ever experienced.) As treatment progressed, the criterion for pain ratings was gradually reduced to 3.5, and the boy received a point for every half day of school he attended. He was not allowed to attend school unless he was below the pain criterion and had no severe attacks just before going to school. The points earned had an immediate cash value of five cents and, in addition, could be exchanged for various rewards, such as favorite meals, toys, books, and family outings (all of which were suggested by the boy). The parents gave attention and approval when the points were awarded. They also celebrated each milestone, such as a full week's school attendance.

When the boy was ill, in accord with one or more of the

above criteria, he was required to stay in bed for the rest of that half day. He could read schoolbooks but was not allowed to read other materials, listen to the radio, or watch TV. His mother was not to give him special attention while he was in bed.

During the course of treatment, longer periods of "well" behavior and school attendance were needed to obtain the rewards. First, the boy received two points for meeting the criteria for an entire weekend and no points if he showed any "pain" behavior on either day. Next, the criterion for earning points on each weekday included no overt pain behavior for the whole day and attending school all day. Subsequent steps required criterion performance for entire two- and three-day periods, and finally for four, five, and six days at a stretch.

Once treatment was instituted, there was immediate improvement in school attendance and a decrease in the intensity of pain and the frequency of attacks. All pain attacks ceased after seven weeks of treatment.

COMMENTARY: Since the parents were concerned that the boy's temperature was often elevated in conjunction with the pain attacks, the authors advised the parents to take the boy's temperature in the morning and again in the evening every day during treatment. These data indicated that there was no consistent relationship between the temperature and the frequency or intensity of the abdominal pain.

SOURCE: Sank, L. I., and Biglan, A. "Operant Treatment of a Case of Recurrent Abdominal Pain in a Ten-Year-Old Boy." *Behavior Therapy*, 1974, 5, 677-681.

Additional Readings

Apley, J. *The Child with Abdominal Pains.* 2nd ed. London: Blackwell, 1975.

A complete account of the diagnosis and treatment of children with recurrent abdominal pains.

Apley, J., and Naish, N. "Recurrent Abdominal Pains: A Field Survey of 1,000 School Children." *Archives of Disease in Childhood,* 1958, *33,* 165-170.

The authors note that this disorder is time-limited and that there are very few reported cases before age five or after age fourteen. Often the pain is attributed to excitement, worry, or "being worked up," feelings often associated with schooling. Pallor, headache, vomiting, and fever sometimes accompany the abdominal pain. The families of these children have an enhanced tendency to abdominal and "nervous" disorders. Appendectomy is rarely effective in relieving this disorder. Children with certain personality types seem commonly afflicted. They are timid, nervous, fussy, or overconscientious—just the types of children in whom emotional disturbances would be expected to develop. With these children, school or other difficulties often seem to have a "trigger effect" in evoking pains.

Heinild, S., Malver, E., Roelsgaard, G., and Worning, B. "A Psychosomatic Approach to Recurrent Abdominal Pain in Childhood." *Acta Paediatrica,* 1959, *48,* 361-370.

The authors studied a group of children with psychogenic abdominal pain. X-ray films of the stomach revealed increased peristalsis and alterations of the mucosal pattern. These changes were so pronounced that they were still present in three quarters of the cases when follow-up X-rays were taken three years later. Thus, even though the pain had subsided at this time, there were still signs of physical abnormality. Among the possible etiological factors noted were disharmonious homes, divorces, single mothers with outside jobs, poor housing, poor economic situation, authoritarianism, or poor childrearing. It would appear, then, that once the abdominal disorder has been triggered by external stress, aberrant physiological changes do occur and persist in the GI tract.

Liebman, W. M. "Recurrent Abdominal Pain in Children." *Clinical Pediatrics,* 1978, *17,* 149-153.

The clinical pattern of 119 children with recurrent abdominal pain, located most commonly in the periumbilical region, revealed no distinct features. The most frequent associated symptoms were pallor, tiredness, and anorexia. The most important psychosocial factors were marital turmoil in 44 percent, school difficulties in 32 percent, and perfectionism in 30 percent. Lab, X-ray, and fiberoptic endoscopic studies were uniformly unremarkable. Continuing counseling helped 105 of these children. Counseling often included advice about specific changes that should be made in the child's environment. Drugs ordinarily should not be given because they usually aggravate the family's concept of the pain, create an unnecessary dependency, and are almost always unrewarding.

Stone, R. T., and Barbero, C. J. "Recurrent Abdominal Pain in Childhood." *Pediatrics,* 1970, *45,* 732-738.

This report summarized the clinical features of a selected group of children hospitalized with abdominal pain, a group which can be considered as having the "irritable bowel syndrome of childhood." The pain in this group was variable, with no consistent pattern in time, duration, and intensity. Associated symptoms frequently included headache, pallor, nausea, vomiting, constipation, dizziness, and poor appetite. The main physical finding was tenderness on deep palpation of various sections of the abdomen. Some of the children were able to describe stressful events as precipitants of the pain episodes. A common clinical impression regarding the parents and child was that there was a contagious, circular anxiety about the disorder which seemed to heighten the child's pain and anxiety. An effective action by the therapist is to accept the pain as real and to develop a close, supportive relationship with the child and family. Hospitalization has proved effective when frequent outpatient visits have been unsuccessful.

Obesity

Obesity *is the accepted term for the presence of excessive bodily fat, and its prevalence is increasing. Obesity has been classified as a regulatory problem (improperly regulated food intake and exercise) or a metabolic (neurological, hormonal, or enzymatic) disorder. Eating behavior is influenced by physiological, social, and cognitive variables. At least 25 percent of all children and approximately 35 percent of adults are considered obese; that is, they weigh 20 percent more than they should, according to criteria established by the government. The incidence of obesity is higher at lower socioeconomic levels, in some ethnic groups, and with advancing age. More than 80 percent of fat children become fat adults, and family patterns of exercise, eating when anxious, and using food as a reward are enduring. The prognosis is poorest for obese adults who began to be fat as juveniles. Most obese children have enlarged (hypertrophic) fat cells, whereas massively overweight children who have more (hyperplastic) fat cells are very rare. The origins of diabetes, heart disease, and hypertension may be traced to childhood dietary habits. At least 80 percent of all diabetics are, or have been, obese. Cardiovascular-renal disease is almost twice as great in obese adults. Wide agreement exists for the need to teach good nutritional habits to all children. With obese children, weight loss combined with regulated food intake and exercise is necessary for the lifelong maintenance of appropriate weight. Efforts are being made to instill the basic concept of self-control in children, so that external control becomes unnecessary early in their development.*

113

Behavioral Treatment of a Child's Eating Problem

AUTHOR: Martha E. Bernal

PRECIS: Social attention and praise to reinforce gradual steps leading to self-feeding and the consumption of table food

INTRODUCTION: Bernal discusses "successive approximation" as a technique that sequentially reinforces the steps leading to desired behavior. Consequences are rearranged in order to produce or strengthen certain behaviors or weaken others. Bernal uses the example of giving social attention only for desirable behavior rather than for tantrums. This technique clearly requires parents to function as therapists for their own children. Bernal used closed-circuit television and telephone consultations in treating a four-year-old girl who refused to feed herself or eat table food. She only ate some types of strained foods. Feeding had presented difficulties since she was nine months old, and many food battles with her parents had reportedly been won by her. When her mother followed the pediatrician's advice and withdrew strained food, refusal to eat and vomiting led to her being fed by the mother (and refusal to feed herself).

TREATMENT: The strategy was to train the parents to gradually exert increased control over her eating habits, rather than to try to make an abrupt change. The therapist thought the parents would not be able to eliminate baby food and wait until she was hungry enough to eat table food. Therefore, breakfast was to consist of a limited amount of baby food so that her appetite would be great during the day. This limited breakfast also would allow her to maintain her weight even if she refused to eat for the rest of the day. Her mother would gain increasing control by using social rewards and food reinforcers for eating, rather than by coaxing, bargaining, threatening, or nagging. To prevent possible anemia or dehydration, for eight weeks before treatment she was required to drink four glasses of water and take two vitamin pills daily.

Videotapes were made at the clinic and at home. These revealed that social attention was given for playing with baby food, talking, and messiness and not for self-feeding. Usually she took a few swallows by herself, then refused, and was then fed by her parents, who made various comments, such as "You won't eat for me" and "Do you like to be sick and not feel well?" On the basis of these tapes, Bernal decided that all feeding was to be done by the mother, who was trained by the author. The mother was taught to withhold social attention (smiling, chatting, gazing) until her daughter put food in her mouth and swallowed. The child was not to be forced to eat and not cleaned until the meal was finished. Videotapes of subsequent feeding sessions were made, and the mother was provided feedback on how well she complied with instructions. For three sessions, the mother was told to give the child cottage cheese only after the girl had consumed nonpreferred strained vegetables and fruits. From week twelve through week twenty-one strained food was given only after the child ate new table foods. From weeks seven to ten, putting table food on her plate had not led her to sample it. Therefore, at week twelve all television viewing was terminated so that TV could be used as a reward: one program could be viewed following even a tiny bite of new table food. Various minor modifications in the program are described, with television viewing being allowed only after table food was eaten at mealtimes. Since television viewing was not a powerful reinforcer, this method was dropped. At one point, the mother gave in to pleading for chocolate milk, Koolaid, and chewing gum and was told to discontinue this and give her only four glasses of plain milk daily. The last step consisted of her eating very small portions of the family meal. This was rewarded by small amounts of preferred adult food and dessert. After thirty-two weeks, she was eating very well and had added fifty new and different foods to her diet.

Bernal sees the use of "shaping" (reinforcing gradual approximations of a goal) as successful in attaining both self-feeding and the eating of table foods. She cautions that strongly reinforcing one behavior (such as eating cottage cheese) can prevent the development of broader behaviors. Therefore, a class of

behaviors, such as eating many types of food, should be reinforced. Shaping was also used to train the mother to reinforce
self-feeding of strained foods through several steps to self-
feeding of table foods. Bernal points out how previously refused
foods were used as reinforcers once the child ate, and learned to
like, the new foods. Additionally, when the girl showed coercive
behaviors (tantrums, whining, milking, refusal to eat), the
mother was taught to ignore them. The mother was prone to
revert to her prior behavior of giving in and providing inappropriate food.

COMMENTARY: Bernal clearly cautions that health issues
must be considered when food refusal is being treated. Recordkeeping, frequent monitoring, and telephone contact are seen as
essential ingredients. Practically, the study offers useful guidelines in accomplishing a goal by the strategic planning and
attainment of subgoals. In this case, and in the case of other
disorders in this book, attempts to attain change in one step do
not succeed. In many therapeutic interventions, careful monitoring is often not planned. Parents' frequent tendency to revert
to maladaptive behavior should be anticipated and counter-
acted.

SOURCE: Bernal, M. E. "Behavioral Treatment of a Child's Eating Problem." *Journal of Behavior Therapy and Experimental
Psychiatry,* 1972, *3,* 43-50.

Behavioral Treatment of Obesity in Children

AUTHORS: Kelly D. Brownell and Albert J. Stunkard

PRECIS: Review of successful behavior therapy techniques, particularly useful for a pediatrician

INTRODUCTION: At least 25 percent of children are reportedly obese, and more than 80 percent of overweight children become overweight adults. Brownell and Stunkard review the problems of obese children as reported in the literature—being the target of peer abuse, having many personality difficulties and fewer friends, and so forth. Traditional approaches (caloric restriction, anorectic drugs, and exercise) have not been successful.

TREATMENT: Effective weight control requires major changes in eating behavior. By modifying children's habits, one can effect enduring changes. The behavioral approach requires a careful analysis of specific eating behaviors, including a study of the immediate antecedents and consequences of eating. Patients are asked to keep careful records of their behavior. Behavioral programs are designed to control the act of eating by altering the antecedent stimuli and then reinforcing the new behavior.

One study showed great success with ten children, ages eight to thirteen, from low socioeconomic backgrounds. The children and their mothers met weekly for ten weeks for two-hour meetings. The children kept a daily log of food consumed and their ability to do the prescribed behavior. Parents were taught how to give rewards, make contracts, and model appropriate behavior. Part of the weekly meeting was a group supper, where low-calorie, nutritional meals were served. Appropriate behaviors such as eating slowly, putting utensils down between bites, and self-monitoring were reinforced.

A similar study with forty children, ages two to eleven, is reviewed. Recordkeeping, stimulus control, and reinforcement were employed. Another study used two behavioral methods. Using the *deposit-refund* method, parents deposited the child's money with the therapist and refunded it for desired changes. Weekly refunds were given—25 percent for attendance of weekly meetings, 25 percent for completing charts, and 50 percent for losing a set amount of weight. Parents and children were taught stimulus control and nutrition and encouraged to exercise for thirty minutes a day. In the *deposit-refund plus reinforcement* method, nonmonetary rewards are also given for weight loss. Brownell and Stunkard discuss the slowing of the rate of eating as a central element in behavioral weight-control programs. Eating more slowly helps obese children control food intake. One study showed that the simple strategy of instruction and praise reduced the eating rate and decreased food consumption. Another study used self-monitoring, stimulus control, modification of eating, and reinforcement. In addition, cognitive restructuring was used to help adolescent girls become aware of their irrational thoughts concerning eating.

PRINCIPLES OF BEHAVIORAL TREATMENT:

Self-monitoring is a key element. A careful record must be kept of weight, food (calorie) intake, and physical activity. Self-monitoring plus social reinforcement has been effective. A promising technique is "premonitoring," or writing down what is about to be eaten. Monitoring effectively leads to awareness of previously unnoticed behavior, like snacking, and enables individuals to evaluate their behavior. At times, recording alone has led to positive change in eating behavior.

Stimulus control concerns events that precede the behavior to be controlled. High-calorie food is made scarce, and access to food is limited. Candy and nuts are not available, but celery and carrots are. Food requiring preparation is used, and spare change is eliminated to avoid impulse buying from machines. Eating often occurs at particular times or in association with specific activities, such as television viewing. In order to decrease stimuli that tend to elicit eating, all eating is to occur in one place (kitchen) at scheduled times. Even distinctive table settings with special silver or unusually colored placemats and napkins have been useful in controlling where the children eat.

Family intervention: Brownell and Stunkard believe that

families should be involved in any treatment program. Health and social problems associated with obesity have long-term negative consequences for the child; in contrast, eating provides immediate positive reinforcement. Therefore, the parents should be included in treatment in order to help them to encourage an adaptive eating pattern in their child. The parents can control the child's food intake and they can reinforce appropriate eating.

Slowing eating interrupts the chain of eating behaviors. Brownell and Stunkard see a positive effect in allowing time for the absorption of nutrients to produce signals of feeling satisfied. Some methods are putting utensils down between bits, counting each chew or swallow, and instituting one-minute delays. Patients are urged to make mealtimes a relaxed experience and to savor their food.

Reinforcement of behavior change and weight loss is a powerful method. Separate reward systems are most effective, with rewards for changing behavior having the greatest impact. Prompt reinforcement is necessary, and points are often used to earn toys, allowance money, television viewing, and attendance at special events. Considerable success is reported for contingency contracting. The patient agrees to do or omit certain behavior in return for rewards or avoidance of punishment. An explicit written, signed, and witnessed contract is used. Money or valuables (such as a record collection) are deposited and returned as goals are achieved.

Cognitive restructuring relates to the critical role that thoughts or private monologues often play in maintaining and controlling obesity. Negative self-statements are countered by positive and optimistic ones. One example given by Brownell and Stunkard is the patient's thinking "I keep finding myself thinking of how good chocolates taste." The more useful thought is "Stop that! It's just frustrating. Imagine lying on the beach in the sun" (or another pleasurable activity).

COMMENTARY: This very useful article points out several techniques that can be used specifically with obese children. Much of the prior literature concerns adults and adolescents.

The various strategies reviewed could be used with other psychosomatic disorders as well. Self-monitoring, stimulus control, and cognitive restructuring could be used to change any behavior that is physiologically maladaptive.

SOURCE: Brownell, K. D., and Stunkard, A. J. "Behavioral Treatment of Obesity in Children." *American Journal of Diseases of Children*, 1978, *132*, 403-412.

Emotional Aspects of Obesity

AUTHOR: Hilde Bruch

PRECIS: Establishing self-regulation of eating by having parents recognize a child's needs and offer food appropriately

INTRODUCTION: Bruch describes fat children as being bashful and ashamed of their bodies and looking awkward and slow. They are often teased, are rarely good fighters or self-assertive, and are often miserable and seclusive. Physical problems of complaints may lead to inactivity and more weight gain. Even adolescents who suffer socially find it very difficult to follow the rule of eating less and exercising more.

PSYCHOLOGICAL ASPECTS OF OBESITY: Bruch sees the family as wittingly or unwittingly encouraging overeating, inactivity, or other faulty habits. And, other sources of satisfaction may not have been developed. The parents, usually the mother, may find it difficult to follow advice and may act as if any restrictions constituted a starvation diet. Unfortunately, fatness often gives an insecure child a feeling of strength. One third of children seen in a pediatric clinic lost weight in what was viewed as a congenial family environment. The two thirds who did not lose weight came from families with an unrelenting preoccupation with weight or an unwillingness to face and correct the many conflicts and tensions. The children's personality development was inadequate, and they felt paralyzed by the family's rejecting attitudes. An unrealistic upbringing can lead to a feeling of being special or having to be "bigger and better than anybody else." Obese children often feel that they never achieve what they or their parents expect. Bruch thinks that dreams of glory cover a fear of being a nobody, and the children need continuous praise. The unrealistic goals lead to frustration and overeating as an attempt to cope with feelings of failure. Obesity acts as a protection, since being slim is seen as being necessary to fulfill their dreams and becoming slim would put them through a real test.

Bruch describes fat children as unable to resist the temptation of food because of an abnormal hunger awareness. They overeat because they do not recognize real hunger, and they misinterpret other states of discomfort (tension or dissatisfaction) as hunger. Most likely, the children were fed by well-meaning, insecure mothers whenever they expressed discomfort. In severe cases, such children may feel they do not "own" their own bodies and may seriously doubt their interpersonal effectiveness. Overprotective mothers prevent their children from trusting their impulses and activity, and they become passive, demanding, and easily frustrated. Additionally, they lack spontaneity, initiative, and self-reliance.

TREATMENT: Bruch believes success in treating obesity results from an accurate assessment of the underlying causes. Dietary instructions are usually successful with emotionally stable children whose families encourage individuality and independence. But these conditions are rarely present in long-standing cases of obesity. The pediatrician assesses the family stability, warmth, and mutual satisfaction. Psychiatric intervention may not be necessary, and the pediatrician's interest in the family may give the children encouragement to physiologically and psychologically outgrow obesity. In all cases, Bruch thinks that nutritional instruction alone is insufficient. The diet must help the child become aware of what she eats and lead to self-control of food intake. The child must take part in the planning or the child remains a dependent, passive receiver of parental instructions. In the case of older children it is even more important to involve them, to help them avoid conflicts with their parents, and to encourage their independence.

COMMENTARY: Bruch believes that unless the underlying causes are addressed, weight reduction in children with serious personality disorders may precipitate more serious problems. Pediatricians are seen as key figures in advising appropriate feeding based on a recognition of each child's needs. The goal is self-awareness and self-regulation of eating. This article outlines both the direction that psychological treatment should take and, more important, the necessity of preventing the development of obesity and the accompanying personality problems. The type of family analysis presented would be applicable to any psychosomatic disorder linked to a dysfunctional family system.

SOURCE: Bruch, H. "Emotional Aspects of Obesity in Children." *Pediatric Annals,* May 1975, pp. 91-99.

Regulation of Eating in Obese Children

AUTHORS: Leonard H. Epstein, Lynn Parker, James F. McCoy, and Gail McGee

PRECIS: Decreasing food consumption in seven-year-olds by putting utensils down between bites

INTRODUCTION: The authors reviewed studies suggesting that an early onset of obesity may lead to later resistance to treatment. Obese children in substantial numbers become obese adults, and early obesity causes an increase in adipose cells. The authors concluded that identifying high-risk children is important, and they sought a method for behavior change suited to obese children. Behavioral procedures are designed for problems in the regulation of food intake and exercise, not for metabolic disturbances. No studies had been done comparing the natural eating behaviors of obese and nonobese children. So for six months the authors examined children's lunchtime behavior. Their very careful, detailed observations of three male and three female seven-year-olds are described. Measured were their bite rate, sip rate, and concurrent activities.

TREATMENT: The researchers gave the children instructions in order to modify their eating rate. Each child was individually told that he or she was participating in an experiment to examine the ability of children to slow down their eating rate. They were told to place their utensils on the table or tray after every bite. Before each of approximately seven lunches, they were individually reminded to continue putting their utensils down after each bite. For another several lunches praise was added in order to assess whether it might cause increased compliance with the instructions. The observers made approving comments, such as, "You put your fork down more times than usual, that's good," when a child's compliance was above his or her own average during the instructions-only phase.

Detailed analyses are presented regarding the treatment's effect on and the food preferences of obese and nonobese children. Instructions combined with praise for compliance led to decreased eating rates for all children. The bite rate was reliably lowered but the sip rate was unaffected. In contrast to differences in bite rate between obese and nonobese adults found in past research, the two groups of children had similar bite rates. However, obese children drank more milk and nonobese children ate more bread.

COMMENTARY: The study highlights the efficacy of a simple procedure to slow down the eating rate of obese children and decrease their total food consumption. Parents may easily accomplish this by monitoring at home, giving praise for compliance, and suggesting that the procedure be followed at school or in other settings. The authors suggest that children who drink too much would not be affected by a program designed to change the intake of solid food. A quite promising approach would be to teach children to limit drinking to a set amount, and low-fat milk would be essential for obese children.

SOURCE: Epstein, L. H., Parker, L., McCoy, J. F., and McGee, G. "Descriptive Analysis of Eating Regulation in Obese and Nonobese Children." *Journal of Applied Behavior Analysis,* 1976, *9,* 407-415.

Controlling Obesity in Children

AUTHORS: Raymond G. Kingsley and Joan Shapiro

PRECIS: Behavioral weight-control groups for children alone, for children and their mothers, and for mothers alone

INTRODUCTION: Kingsley and Shapiro comment on the lack of obesity research with children, in view of findings that 80 percent of overweight children become overweight adults. They see drug treatment as being of little value and possibly harmful. Dieting and exercise have been successful with adolescents, but require a change in daily eating habits (behavioral self-control procedures have worked with adults). In this study, the involvement of parents was seen as possibly facilitating change in their children and in their own weight reduction.

TREATMENT: Twenty-four girls and sixteen boys, ages ten or eleven, were selected from people responding to a newspaper announcement of a weight-reduction program. All the children were above the ninetieth percentile in weight for their age group, and all mothers expressed a willingness to attend group sessions. Faithful participation led to the full refund of a thirty-dollar deposit, and one-hour weekly sessions were held for eight weeks. Children were assigned to one of four conditions: no treatment, waiting-list control; children only; mothers and children; mothers only. The treatment employed was an adaptation for ten- and eleven-year-olds of a published method by R. B. Stuart and B. Davis (*Slim Chance in a Fat World: Behavioral Control of Obesity*, Champaign, Ill.: Research Press, 1972). Factual information was given about obesity and nutrition. Weight loss was described as best attained by a negative energy balance resulting from reduced intake, increased expenditure of energy, or a combination of the two. Instructions were given in reducing caloric intake while maintaining good nutrition. Calorie-counting booklets were distributed and pocket-size diaries were used to record daily food intake. In each children's session, detailed procedures were given to them to be passed on to their parents. In one of these take-home instructions, the parents were requested to give tokens that could be exchanged for back-up reinforcers when the child followed all procedures. The same method was used with all three treatment groups, with the mothers in the mothers-only group teaching their children the procedures.

All three treatment groups lost weight (an average of three and a half pounds), while the control group gained an average of two pounds. Although the children were in a period of growth, 81 percent lost weight during treatment. The mothers in the mothers-only group lost significantly more weight than did mothers in the other three groups and maintained the loss. Analyses of weight gain after treatment showed all three treatment groups gaining weight at the normal rate expected for children their age. Kingsley and Shapiro suggest that improvement in eating habits, rather than dieting, was a key factor. All but one mother reported that her child's eating habits had improved or greatly improved. The children appeared to adopt a particular method suitable to them. Most children did record what they ate and exercised each day.

COMMENTARY: Kingsley and Shapiro adapted and assessed a method that has been successful with adults. The results are encouraging and point the way toward a more widespread use of instructional methods for weight reduction and maintenance with children. A striking finding is that, as in adult programs, continued weight loss did not occur after treatment (although weight gain was normal). The authors speculate that continued participation in a program or periodic monitoring may be necessary. A key ingredient is the change in eating habits that can result from the feeling of responsibility that is engendered by procedures that stress and teach "self-control."

SOURCE: Kingsley, R. G., and Shapiro, J. "A Comparison of Three Behavioral Programs for the Control of Obesity in Children." *Behavior Therapy*, 1977, *8*, 30-36.

A Diet Program for Emotionally Disturbed Children

AUTHOR: Mark A. Krueger

PRECIS: A positive self-image achieved by weight loss in three boys in residential treatment

INTRODUCTION: Krueger discusses behavior as being related to a child's feelings about himself. With this relation in mind, he designed a treatment plan to lead to improved physical appearance and therefore a positive self-image. This plan included dieting, since Krueger hypothesized that weight loss would lead not only to better self-images but to greater participation in activities and to getting more positive attention. The institutional staff had not tried a dieting approach before, fearing the possible negative consequences of food deprivation with deprived children. But achieving the goal of previous treatment—increased emotional growth—had not led to better diets, as had been hoped, and the heavy boys continued to fail at physical activities. Therefore they agreed to try Krueger's plan, in which the dieters were to be motivated by positive reinforcement (praise) from adults.

TREATMENT: Two of the boys treated were ten years old and one was nine. They had been at the institution for more than a year and were in the same group. All had been gaining too much weight. Their emotional problems were being treated according to an individualized plan. To treat their weight problem, the agency physician set a one-thousand-calorie diet, with the goal of attaining the average weight for their age and height. All ate three meals, and later they were allowed six ounces of diet soda at bedtime. A staff member recorded their weight each morning. All staff members were asked to avoid projecting negative feelings about overweight and to praise weight loss and other participation in activities. As a result of this plan, all three lost more than twenty-five pounds, in spite of staff reluctance and concern about the control of eating in an institution.

Since the boys were encouraged to look good, instruction in personal hygiene and grooming was provided. In addition, the institution bought them new clothes as they lost weight. Group participation was also encouraged, and activities were tailored to assure success. After doing simple projects or learning fundamentals, they took on more challenging activities. Before breakfast, the boys were required to exercise. The staff emphasized individual achievement, not achieving norms. As weight loss led to better running and athletic skills, they chose to play various ball games, rather than stay in their rooms. The staff focused on giving the boy responsibility for continuing the program while unsupervised, although they checked to see whether weight was gained on home visits.

The data presented show that the boys gained weight during the beginning of the program and near discharge. The reason for the gain, Krueger speculates, might be that the child was seeking parental attention by using earlier forms of behavior. Overall, though, the treatment succeeded: the boys' behavior improved and afterward they maintained a fairly constant weight. Krueger discusses one boy at length. He was very fearful and fantasized a great deal. His continuous talking kept adults at a distance. Several of his family members were overweight, and his father took a passive role in childrearing. During the program, the father became relatively more involved with the boy. After seven months, the son had lost forty-five pounds. His talk was still excessive but more positive in content. His new skills resulted in more positive feedback. In the community, he maintained a constant weight and his social involvement improved.

COMMENTARY: Krueger's report of adult negative expectations about children's dieting is a familiar one. It is true, as the negativists point out, that children can subvert the diet by obtaining food surreptitiously. However, whether at home or in an institution, positive expectations and praise by adults have worked very successfully. Weigh-ins are concrete examples of success that can be praised by meaningful adults. Striking are Krueger's attempts to ensure positive experiences in other areas, such as by designing appropriate athletic programs. As in other studies, weight loss occurs when dieting, exercising, positive experiences, and social praise are combined. Offering an individualized program within a positive social context is the most efficient way of changing any maladaptive behavior.

SOURCE: Krueger, M. A. "The Effect of a Dieting Program on Emotionally Disturbed Children." *Child Welfare*, 1973, *52*, 172-177.

Obesity in Childhood

AUTHOR: Charles U. Lowe

PRECIS: Review of causes and treatment procedures and the necessity for preventing obesity

INTRODUCTION: The long-term results of treating obesity are often disappointing, although Lowe cites evidence that death rates were reduced for overweight people who lost a significant amount of weight. Lowe reviews death rates of forty years ago and specific diseases in obese individuals.

INFLUENCES ON OBESITY:

Poor Regulation of Food Intake. In animals, lesions of the ventromedial nucleus of the hypothalamus result in increased food consumption and obesity, whereas lateral area lesions markedly diminish food intake. These centers receive impulses from various bodily organs via the autonomic nervous system, signaling the need for food or loss of appetite. Psychological stimuli such as arguments during mealtime also affect intake (loss of appetite). Lowe reviews this and other physiological theories about the role of food intake in obesity—theories having to do with metabolites, taste sensitivity, and so forth.

History of Obesity. The vast majority of obese children become overweight adults, and very obese children are even more likely to become obese adults.

Genetic Predisposition. The incidence of obesity in one or both parents of obese children has been reported to be from 60 to 88 percent. Further evidence of a genetic cause is the fact that identical twins, whether reared together or apart, have a very high weight correlation. And conversely, the weight of adopted children does not correlate at all with that of their adoptive parents. Lowe suggests that heredity may be more important in obesity than environmental influences.

Body Composition. Girls have slightly more subcutaneous fat than boys, and early in adolescence girls continue to gain body fat whereas boys begin to lose it. Lowe distinguishes between "lean body mass" and fat; the term *obesity* is used to describe children with a significant change in the ratio of lean body mass to body weight, a change due solely to an increase in fat.

Emotional Factors. Lowe cites reports of psychological disturbances being associated with obesity. When nonobese people are disturbed, they eat less, whereas obese people eat more when emotionally upset. According to Lowe, emotional overeating often results from having demanding, overprotective parents. Obese children of such parents feel helpless and inadequate. Another emotional factor, a result rather than a cause of obesity, is that some children develop psychological problems when forced to lose weight.

Endocrinous and Metabolic Problems. Lowe discusses the lack of studies of children and discusses metabolic disorders in obese adults. A diminished glomerular filtration rate, an elevated titer of antidiuretic hormone, and reduced renal clearance of water are present. Obese adults also have reduced rates of oxidation of glucose, palmitate, and beta-hydroxybutyrate. Various abnormalities of free fatty acids are listed, and some obese adults show adrenocortical hyperactivity. Higher insulin levels and other complications are discussed at length.

Insufficient Physical Activity. Obesity only occurs when the calories consumed are greater than the calories expended. In some children, decreased activity may perpetuate or actually induce obesity.

TREATMENT: Lowe warns that low-calorie diets must be used cautiously with children and adolescents because such diets have been shown to interfere with expected gains in height and with positive nitrogen balances in obese adolescents.

Use of Anorexigenic Agents. Sympathomimetic amenes, called central stimulating appetite distractors, have been used with children with only limited success. Even when initial weight loss is great, weight is often regained and undesirable side-effects may occur.

Formula Diets. While limiting calories, these diets can provide adequate daily protein, minerals, and vitamins. Some adults have successfully used this approach, but Lowe points out the lack of evaluation with children.

Fasting. Adults have successfully employed total fasting for periods of two to thirteen weeks. The ketonemia of starvation causes a loss of desire for food. Lowe questions whether fasting would be justified or effective with children.

Psychotherapy. Behavioral and developmental factors must be examined for clues to the emotional causation in a particular obese child. Lowe states that the effectiveness of this treatment cannot fairly be assessed, since hard-core failures are usually the ones referred to psychotherapists.

COMMENTARY: Lowe compiled this report as the chairman of a committee on nutrition. The article serves as a useful overview of the causes and treatments of obesity in children. This report was pessimistic about the long-term ability of children to maintain weight loss. Therefore he strongly advocates the prevention of obesity and sees the physician as playing a key role in high-risk families.

SOURCE: Lowe, C. U. "Obesity in Childhood." *Pediatrics,* 1967, *40,* 455-467.

Successive Approximation Control
of Eating in Juvenile Obesity

AUTHORS: Mary Ebel Wheeler and Karl W. Hess

PRECIS: Individualized treatment plans to gradually change eating behavior within the family context

INTRODUCTION: Wheeler and Hess review two types of weight-reduction programs—dietary programs with or without amphetamines and combinations of diet and exercise. In young children, modifying maternal behavior can lead to weight loss and more appropriate eating. Wheeler and Hess see the relation between analyses of the stimuli surrounding and maintaining excessive eating, rather than calorie reduction, as the essential ingredient in a permanent change in eating patterns. The authors help the family identify and manipulate the rewards supporting overeating, and the child and parent are active participants in the change process. In short, the authors focus on a gradual movement toward the final goal of changing the eating pattern, instead of on getting the child to follow a specific diet.

TREATMENT: Because analysis of the eating situation was crucial, a food intake record was used. The information recorded included where and when the food was eaten, how much was consumed, and what specific foods were eaten. The authors highlight certain patterns and suggest possible points of control. Different procedures are necessary for children who prepare their own food. A table is presented detailing eight of the most common problems encountered in forty obese children between two and eleven years of age (average 7.1 years). The eight problems were the consumption of large amounts of candy, cookies, and ice cream; eating on the run and getting snacks from kitchen; eating overly large meals; preparing their own food, which makes change difficult; consuming foods for which less-caloric substitutes are available; no exercise; parental sharing of their consumption of inappropriate foods; and much eating outside the home. The authors list guidelines for eliminating

and controlling each problem. How to provide appropriate situations and positive consequences is also outlined. For example,
if eating on the run is the problem, the kitchen can be out of
bounds and tempting foods locked up or eliminated. Set snack
times can be established, and outside activities assigned during
difficult eating times. Low-calorie snacks can be made easily
accessible, with a favored snack occasionally included. If a lack
of exercise is the issue, sedentary activities like television might
be curtailed and television viewed on a schedule. Revising
family activities and developing enjoyable new exercises are
other suggestions. Treats can be made contingent on the performance of certain activities, in which the parents participate.

In this study, parents met with the therapist to discuss
their views regarding the course of treatment. Changes in treatment occurred when weight loss did not occur or when the patient became dissatisfied. The therapists tried in each case to
develop a practical plan tailored to a given patient's environment. Careful analyses and recordkeeping were essential. At the
initial session the mother completed the forms concerning the
family situation and the child's food preferences. The child's
weight, height, skinfold thicknesses, blood pressure, and serum
cholesterol were recorded. And three semi-nude pictures were
obtained. Mother and child pairs were seen biweekly for half-
hour sessions, and then less frequently as progress occurred.
Children were considered to have achieved success if they came
closer to the mean weight for their age, sex, and height during
the study. The authors define and discuss the treatment and
control groups at length. Noteworthy is the discussion concerning the improvement of children who dropped out of the program. Wheeler and Hess believe that modest intervention works
with some children. The treatment results are reported as very
encouraging for those fourteen patients who remained in treatment.

COMMENTARY: Wheeler and Hess point out that since the
type of intervention described is possible as part of regular pediatric care, it can be long term. The contribution they make is
their emphasis on the gradual shifting of patterns rather than on

dramatic dietary changes. Additionally, because the adjustments are made within the family, temporary changes (alien to family patterns) that quickly lose their effectiveness can be avoided. And in keeping with the eclectic and practical theme of our book, they offer specific and realistic methods to families.

SOURCE: Wheeler, M. E., and Hess, K. W. "Treatment of Juvenile Obesity by Successive Approximation Control of Eating." *Behavior Therapy and Experimental Psychiatry*, 1976, 7, 235-241.

Additional Readings

Ferster, C. B., Nurnberger, J. I., and Levitt, E. B. "The Control of Eating." *Journal of Mathetics,* 1962, 87-109.

This is a detailed description of the application of reinforcement theory principles to eating behavior. Developing self-control is broken down into four steps: (1) what variables influence eating, (2) how these variables can be manipulated, (3) identifying the unwanted effects of eating, and (4) developing self-control. Eating habits were changed by a short-term small-group therapy program using stimulus and temporal control, chaining, prepotent repertoires, and the shaping and maintaining of self-control. Highlighted is the necessity to focus directly and specifically on future eating behavior, not on short-term weight loss.

Laron, Z. and Tikva, P. (Eds.) *The Adipose Child: Medical and Psychological Aspects.* Basel: S. Karger, 1976.

This book on childhood obesity was based on the proceedings of an International Symposium on the Adipose Child held in Tel Aviv. The authors discuss adipose tissue and fat metabolism in the infant, as well as the role of infant nutrition in the later development of obesity. The metabolic changes in and psychological problems of obese children are also described. The book covers a variety of therapeutic problems and practices, too.

LeBow, M. D. "Operant Conditioning-Based Behavior Modification: One Approach to Treating Somatic Disorders." *International Journal of Psychiatry in Medicine,* 1975, 6, 241-254.

Discussed are measuring, modifying, and evaluating the use of behavior modification in treating somatic disorders. Specifically, the treatment of obesity is discussed, including the use of behavioral contracts and modifying eating speed. Environmental Restructuring is used to teach the individual to reshape the environmental conditions that sustain obesity. Specific do's and don't's are developed for each person so he or she can alter the availability of irresistible food and engage in more exercise. A small electronic device is used to pace eating and increase intervals between bites.

Leon, G. R. "Current Directions in the Treatment of Obesity."
    Psychological Bulletin, 1976, *83,* 557-578.

This is an outstanding review of the effectiveness of a variety of methods to bring about and maintain weight loss, mainly
in adults. Behavior modification techniques are seen as the most
promising for weight-loss maintenance, especially those techniques that directly teach the modification of eating patterns. The
behavioral methods reviewed are the giving of rewards by the
therapist, contingency contracting, self-reward and self-monitoring, aversive procedures, covert sensitization, and coverant control. In addition, the author describes the group method, individual psychotherapy, and hypnosis. Also reviewed are various
dieting approaches, such as calorie reduction, less frequent
meals, and fasting or starvation. Medical approaches are drug
therapy and intestinal bypass surgery.

Loro, B. "Bibliography of Behavioral Approaches to Weight Re-
    duction and Obesity from 1962 Through 1976." *Professional
    Psychology,* 1978, *9,* 278-289.

This extensive bibliography contains 182 references about
weight loss in children and adults. It is a very helpful reference
source, since it describes behavioral approaches taken from a
large variety of journals. Especially helpful are the many articles
from the Dissertation Abstracts International. Many specific
and practical methods were employed in doctoral research,
which are conveniently listed here.

Marston, A. R., London, P., and Cooper, L. M. "A Note on the
    Eating Behavior of Children Varying in Weight." *Journal of
    Child Psychology and Psychiatry,* 1976, *17,* 1-4.

By unobtrusively observing eight pairs (one thin, one fat)
of six- to fourteen-year-old children, the researchers recorded
eating patterns. Like obese adults, mildly obese children bite
faster and chew less while eating than do children of normal
weight. Prevention and treatment lie in slowing down the eating. Appropriate behavior is eating slowly, putting the fork
down, chewing thoroughly, and not drinking while the mouth is
full.

Marston, A. R., London, P., Cooper, L. M., and Cohen, N. "In
    Vivo Observation of the Eating Behavior of Obese and Non-
    obese Subjects." Paper presented at the First International
    Congress on Obesity, London, 1974.

Obese and thin adult men and women were unobtrusively
observed while they were eating in a restaurant. The thin people
took smaller bites, had a slower biting rate, made more extraneous responses, left more food on the plate, and spent less time
at the table after the meal. The authors believe obese people can
be trained to employ this "thin eating pattern." To gain greater
satisfaction and eat fewer bites, the person should focus on tast-
ing the food. The authors make some interesting suggestions,
such as engaging in more extraneous activity (hesitating, toying
with food, putting utensils down, and so forth) and leaving food
on the plate rather than belonging to the "clean plate club."

Marston, A. R., London, P., Cooper, L. M., and Lammas, S. E.
    "Lifestyle: A Behavioral Program for Weight Reduction and
    Obesity Research." *Obesity and Bariatric Medicine,* 1976, 5,
    96-100.

A broad-based weight-reduction program for adults using
behavior modification is detailed. The program includes pre-
treatment assessment, keeping records of food intake and
energy output, self-control defined in terms of choice behavior,
skills training to control the starting and stopping of eating,
practice in slow eating, and detecting hunger cues. Exercise
tones and firms the body, leads to weight loss, counteracts dis-
couragement, and often improves the mood. Practical advice is
given for providing people with methods to avoid or overcome
fat habits. Very useful are relaxation and imagery training, finding nonfood rewards, and making contracts.

Mahoney, M. J. "Fat Fiction." *Behavior Therapy,* 1975, 6,
    416-418.

Mahoney examines unfounded general assumptions about
obesity and makes practical suggestions. An obese person may
not be an overeater. He may consume fewer calories than a
person of normal weight but lead a more sedentary life. Ma-

honey therefore suggests higher activity levels. Obese and non-obese people may not differ in eating styles either; although many approaches to weight reduction are based on slower eating and smaller bites, many obese people may in fact eat more slowly than thin people. Similarly, obese people may not be unduly influenced by food-related cues, even though many programs based on controlling these cues assume they are. Obesity is not just the result of learning maladaptive habits. Other causes must be taken into account—the genetic body type, the early onset of obesity (which causes an increase, rather than an enlargement, in adipose cells), differing metabolic rates, and the normal tendency for the relative percentage of body fat to increase with age.

Rau, J. H., and Green, R. S. "Compulsive Eating: A Neuro-psychologic Approach to Certain Eating Disorders." *Comprehensive Psychiatry,* 1975, *16,* 223-231.

    Rau and Green discuss the necessity of distinguishing between neurogenic compulsive eating and other medically or psychologically caused eating disorders. They define *compulsive eating* as the irregular, unpredictable consumption of large quantities of food "against the eater's will." *Overeating,* in contrast, involves a regular, psychologically predictable increase in food intake which the eater can control. The authors describe people of varying weights who have episodes of compulsive eating. They had abnormal electroencephalograms (resulting from cerebral dysrhythmias), and symptom remission occurred in nine out of ten patients following anticonvulsant medication (diphenyl-hydantoin). Illustrative case histories of two young adults are presented. One was a 79-pound female and the other was a 307-pound male.

Rodin, J. "Research on Eating Behavior and Obesity: Where Does It Fit in Personality and Social Psychology?" *Personality and Social Psychology Bulletin,* 1977, *3,* 333-355.

    Rodin exhaustively reviews the research literature concerning obesity. She sees eating as a system of motivated behaviors, involving the integration of physiological, sensory, cognitive, social, and cultural factors. To further understand eating behavior, she analyzes the internal and external stimuli and the social stigma attached to obesity. She also discusses stress-induced eating, pointing out that obese people eat more when they are unaware of the cause of their anxiety. The practitioner may find the review of various theoretical systems helpful in understanding the complexity of eating behavior. Listed are books and journals regarding recent developments in human feeding research.

Stunkard, A. J. "New Therapies for the Eating Disorders: Behavior Modification of Obesity and Anorexia Nervosa." *Archives of General Psychiatry,* 1972, *26,* 391-398.

Stunkard reviews published treatment programs for obesity (mainly in young adults) and finds that behavior modification procedures have been significantly more successful than alternative methods. Four principles are reviewed and detailed: the description of the behavior to be controlled, the modification and control of discriminatory stimuli governing eating, techniques to control eating, and prompt reinforcement of behaviors that delay or control eating. He also discusses the behavioral analysis of the environmental variables that control symptomatic behavior. Antecedent events may precipitate the inappropriate eating behavior and consequent events serve to reward and maintain it. Stunkard believes the therapist and patient can be more creative in modifying behavior as when they focus on discrete, clearly definable behaviors (not on motives, conflicts, and inner drives). The patient observes, records, and is shown how to use information in planning and performing tasks that help him or her achieve self-control.

Weiss, A. R. "A Behavioral Approach to the Treatment of Adolescent Obesity." *Behavior Therapy,* 1977, *8,* 720-726.

Obese adolescents were effectively treated by means of habit-change groups. A stimulus-control group was taught to only eat in one room of the house, do nothing else while eating (such as watching television), and chew each bite thoroughly. Each stimulus-control behavior resulted in earned points, which were exchanged for individually determined self-administered reinforcers. The other successful group used stimulus control plus a conventional diet, with earned points for dieting exchanged for reinforcers. Compared to the no-treatment, diet-no-reward, and diet-reward groups, only the stimulus-control and stimulus-control-diet-reward groups maintained their weight loss after one year. Weiss recommends the second of these for obese adolescents.

Winick, M. (Ed.). *Childhood Obesity.* New York: Wiley, 1975.
     The causes, prevention, and treatment of early-onset obesity are covered. Details are presented on cellular changes, obesity during critical growth periods, and lipid metabolism. The author discusses the basic concepts regarding the control of childhood obesity and devotes one section to the behavioral correlates of obesity. Hormone therapy and behavior modification are significant forms of treatment. Hormones, such as progesterone and thyroid hormones, are potentially quite useful, but extreme caution is advised. Winick describes a variety of behavior modification techniques intended to eliminate maladaptive behavior and promote appropriate, adaptive eating behavior.

Winikoff, B. "Changing Public Diet." *Human Nature,* Jan. 1978, pp. 60-65.
     Winikoff presents statistics concerning diseases and deaths caused by improper diet. The practical recommendations of the U.S. Senate Select Committee on Nutrition and Human Needs are discussed. Highlighted is the need for nutritionally valuable foods. Obesity in infants has been fostered by the production and consumption of fattening baby foods. Breast-feeding is advocated as a nutritionally superior way of preventing obesity in infants. Helpful comparisons are made among such food items as instant mashed potatoes, stuffing mix, and pared boiled potatoes. Stuffing has more carbohydrates, fat, and calories and less vitamin C than either of the potato dishes.

Wolff, J. M., and Lipe, D. *Help for the Overweight Child: A Parents' Guide to Helping Children Lose Weight.* New York: Stein and Day, 1978.
     This practical book written for parents· is also useful to professionals. Concrete information is given on the caloric con-

tent of a variety of foods, and recipes for healthful snacks are provided as well. Normative charts present weights according to size and age. Also discussed are the psychological and physical control of weight and how incentives may be used to change behavior. The well-known rationale is clearly spelled out: obesity is psychologically and physically harmful, and obese children often become obese adults. The concepts and specific instructions given are designed to help parents help their children lose weight. The prevention of overweight is stressed, and appropriate nutrition is clearly outlined.

Anorexia Nervosa

The chronic failure to eat is called anorexia (loss of appetite) nervosa (due to nerves). This distinct psychosomatic problem of self-starvation must be differentiated from other forms of food refusal or weight loss caused by depression, phobia, psychosis, or organic factors. This disorder is characterized by a distorted attitude toward food, a distorted body image, and a fanatic desire to be thin. It usually begins at puberty, or shortly thereafter. Females, especially in adolescence, far outnumber male anorectics. Approximately 20 percent of anorectic girls develop anorexia before having their first menstrual period. Other characteristic features are the pursuit of thinness as an indication of independence, delusional denial of thinness, hyperactivity, preoccupation with food, and a perfectionistic attitude. Anorectic girls frequently struggle for a sense of identity, self-respect, confidence, control, and effectiveness. Although no uniform agreement exists, there is a fairly wide consensus that a loss of at least 20 to 25 percent of the original body weight would classify a child as anorectic. There is also evidence of an increasing incidence of anorexia, and spontaneous remission is rare. The seriousness of this syndrome is indicated by the relatively high mortality rates reported of up to 23 percent.

Treating Anorexia Nervosa with Operant Conditioning and Environmental Manipulation

AUTHORS: Jacob Azerrad and Richard L. Stafford

PRECIS: The use of tokens, a reward system, and parent instruction to increase eating

INTRODUCTION: Azerrad and Stafford review two studies where reinforcement systems were used to restore eating. Both studies removed all potential reinforcers from the environment as part of their procedure. But in the present study, it was not possible to remove all potential reinforcers from the residential treatment center where the thirteen-year-old girl resided. She was very emaciated, extremely lethargic, and spoke very slowly and softly. She was quite manipulative at home, hoarded food in her room, and threw out food at mealtimes.

TREATMENT: The first approach was to help the family eliminate the manipulative behavior and increase eating. Socialization at mealtime was contingent on eating, and pleasurable activities could only occur if eating improved. Failing to eat was not discussed, and she was not to be allowed to control the activities of family members. All manipulative behavior ceased within a week, but her weight kept dropping and she was admitted to a residential treatment center. At the center, she hoarded food and various objects and was called a thief and thought to be psychotic by a psychologist. Daily supportive counseling occurred, but "depth therapy" was not employed. The counseling conversations related to her current problems.

The staff was instructed to weigh her every morning before breakfast. When she was observed taking food, the nurse was to ask her, with a minimum of social interaction, to return it. Staff members were told to not discuss eating problems with her, and parents were allowed only a one-hour visit per week. She could not make any telephone calls. Reward points were earned and used to purchase desirable items (such as hair curlers, writing paper, and stamps) that were not available at the center. Also purchased were special events such as movies, trips, and items from local department stores or catalogues. Reward points, in denominations of one, two, three, five, or ten, were printed on index cards. Points were earned each morning after the weigh-in: one point for maintaining the same weight as the morning before, one point for each .1 kg. weight gain, and no reward points until any weight loss was regained. After twelve days, points were made contingent on the amount of food eaten during the three previous meals. Careful observation was necessary to record food actually consumed. After thirty-five days, each food was assigned a point value, and cards were given after each meal. A nurse recorded all foods consumed. After fifty-eight days, extra days of home visits could also be purchased. Meanwhile, the parents were being seen weekly for one-hour sessions. They learned about the center's behavior modification program and how to be effective in the transition between the center and community living. A gradual program of longer home visits and meeting friends and relatives was followed.

The authors present detailed results regarding her continued weight gain. After discharge, she continued to gain approximately one pound a month. The initial failure to gain weight was seen as resulting from the points for weight gain being too far removed from the process of eating. When points were given for eating, both the food eaten and weight increased.

COMMENTARY: Azerrad and Stafford point out the powerful influence of the immediacy and amount of reinforcement following eating. Eating rates increased markedly when the reward system was changed to be more immediate or of greater value. Very significant is the use of this procedure while other reinforcers were present. Other studies had suggested that all other reinforcers had to be eliminated for weight gain to occur. This study is especially important because of the serious effects and possibly life-threatening consequences of anorexia. Finding the appropriate reinforcers and using them systematically are the challenges to be faced. The basic strategy of reinforcement should also be effective with other psychosomatic disorders, especially with obesity.

SOURCE: Azerrad, J., and Stafford, R. L. "Restoration of Eating Behavior in Anorexia Nervosa Through Operant Conditioning and Environmental Manipulation." *Behavior Research and Therapy*, 1969, 7, 165-171.

Observations of Hospitalized Children
with Anorexia Nervosa

AUTHOR: Richard Galdston

PRECIS: Anorexia seen as a phobic reaction to bodily desires; treatment focusing on the fear of eating food and getting fat

INTRODUCTION: Galdston sees anorexia as a result of a patient's efforts to establish the dominance of her mind over her matter. The need to seek self-control is caused by the patient's experience of disappointment as an intolerable personal fault. She seeks to remedy this by regressing and re-forming herself. Galdston treated forty-one girls and nine boys in a hospital over a period of twelve years. The average length of stay was three months, but stays ranged from one day to nine months. All children showed severe weight loss due to a failure to eat properly, and all girls who had passed menarche ceased menstruating.

TREATMENT: Most children claimed to be quite contented, denied any sadness, and upon hospitalization became very involved with various activities. Some sad children gave no explanation for their condition and said they were sad because they were not at home. Although attitudes toward food bordered on being delusional, clinical evaluation and psychological testing did not indicate psychoses. All the children were at least of average intelligence, most did very well academically, and all lacked pleasure in their lives. They were obsessively preoccupied with food and body image, and all felt that they were too fat and that eating was bad. Eating was seen as some form of personal sin. However, most children were intensely interested in food, often enjoying the preparation of meals and feeding others. Small or normal portions of food were often seen as being enormous. Their ideal often was to be light and airy sixty-pound girls who had no desires.

Many patients were very reluctant to discuss their feelings. However, all were able to recall and describe some emotionally significant disappointment. The loss of a friend or some other troubling situation was seen as a great letdown, and the discontent was attributed to fatness. Galdston reports many verbatim anecdotes illustrating various disappointments, such as losing favorite teachers, moving to a new community, and losing a friend or position of prominence with peers.

Galdston also reports the unusual fact that none of the fifty children was overtly defiant or rebellious. They were superficially compliant but quite manipulative, adhering to the letter of the law while violating the spirit and intent. They played with their food a great deal, and there were inordinately long mealtimes, with very little experienced satisfaction. Hoarding and hiding partially chewed food was a frequent occurrence. Much time was spent on caring for themselves, and many of them bit their nails, pulled cuticles, and picked their skin. Their work was laborious and painfully neat, and many compulsively exercised. All activities were done with minimal pleasure, and many children appeared prideful and disdainful of others. The staff often felt frustrated, exasperated, and hostile in response to the children's disdainful attitude and refusal of help. For the most part, the children were isolates, refusing to participate with others.

Treatment focused on the fear of getting fat, which led to a failure to eat. Therefore the staff was committed to the idea of protecting the patients from all harm, including excuses of any type. The therapists viewed meals as medicine for the physical illness of weight loss and for the inability of the patients to take care of themselves. The staff told the patients their daily weight and granted privileges according to weight gain. This behavior is seen by Galdston as a symptom of a phobia of bodily pleasure. Paying attention to pleasure was presented as an important aspect of learning to take care of oneself. The patients were to learn self-control of bodily pleasure and to not need others to protect them from their appetites. Under this program, significant weight gain was often achieved within two weeks of hospital admission, although at times it took one to three months for gain. Weight loss led to restrictions of activities. Frequently, staff members sat with patients and sometimes fed them. Galdston describes organic anorexics as immediately swallowing what they put in their mouths, whereas these patients ate with much protest and reluctance. The most effective staff attitude was expectant encouragement without intrusion. Monitoring and discussion were essential, since staff members tended to take over and do things for the patients rather than pressing them to do for themselves. Usually, the parents met with the clinical staff, provided essential information, and learned about appropriate treatment of their children.

Although psychotherapy was a significant part of everyone's treatment, the form, intensity, and frequency of interviews varied. Often, sessions were educational; the therapist discussed other children on the ward as examples of different ways of experiencing emotion. For verbal patients, the therapists used more traditional approaches, exploring present and past relationships and desires. Since weight gain was the focus, insight was seen as useful but not as an end goal. Release from the hospital was based on learning to enjoy activities and on gaining weight. All who achieved these two conditions were not readmitted for weight loss.

Psychodynamically, the children appeared slavishly devoted to the idea of perfection, often promoted by parental attitudes. Adolescence often led to their disappointment at their own imperfection. Their anger took the form of self-criticism and picking themselves apart, physically and psychologically. They concluded that being fat or large was sinful, and this became a dominating, fixed idea. Internal voices often told them to not eat. Galdston states that the fear of narcissistic supplies (proof of self-worth) is equivalent to the fear of death. A fear of this proportion led the children to the drastic reduction and revision of themselves.

COMMENTARY: Galdston's long experience led him to describe the dynamics of disappointment, perfection, and fear of bodily pleasure as underlying anorexia. He cites the necessity of hospitalization, a protective milieu, and appropriate psychotherapy. Like many authors referred to in this book, Galdston believes a combination of therapy, parental counseling, and specific approaches in the milieu is necessary. He makes a valuable contribution by stressing the need to understand and change the underlying fear and lack of enjoyment. While psychological treatment is occurring, the necessary health care and weight gain are achieved by controlling the environment and using rewarding and punishing consequences. The observational method used with many patients with the same problem would be applicable to other disorders, in that commonalities and successful approaches are revealed.

SOURCE: Galdston, R. "Mind over Matter: Observations on Fifty Patients Hospitalized with Anorexia Nervosa." *Journal of Child Psychiatry,* 1974, *13,* 246-263.

Family Involvement in Treating Anorexia Nervosa

AUTHORS: Ronald Liebman, Salvador Minuchin, and Lester Baker

PRECIS: Combining hospitalization, family therapy, lunch sessions, operant reinforcement, and weekly family therapy

INTRODUCTION: The authors see the family as a crucial factor in the development and perpetuation of psychosomatic symptoms. But before the family can be treated, the anorectic must first be hospitalized to have medical and neurological examinations so as to rule out the possibility that the disorder has organic causes. Next the therapist assesses the degree of negativism and anorexia by informally lunching with the patient. An operant reinforcement program is then used to initiate weight gain, and family lunch sessions aid this process. The maladaptive family patterns are modified by weekly outpatient family therapy. The patient is hospitalized from two to three weeks, and family therapy usually lasts five to twelve months.

TREATMENT: A fourteen-year-old girl who thought she was too heavy went from 112 to 85 pounds, even though she had been in psychotherapy for ten months and had made some progress in dealing with emotional immaturity, inhibition, and lack of self-confidence. No medical cause was found for her weight loss. By the time the authors saw her, she was down to 72 pounds and was extremely emaciated; she continuously wiped her mouth for fear that swallowing her own saliva would cause weight gain. A disturbed body image, misperception of internal stimuli, feelings of ineffectuality, and hyperactivity were also noted. The therapist used an informal lunch to gain information and briefly discuss the positive sensation of eating. The therapist offered his own food as a first step in the possible sharing of food. On the second day of hospitalization, the operant reinforcement program was begun. All physical activity was contingent on weight gain. In the morning, a weight gain (since the previous morning) of less than half a pound resulted in total bed rest. At least a half-pound gain resulted in being allowed to be out of bed to eat, watch television, have visitors, use the bathroom, and have four to six hours of unrestricted ward or hospital activity. Increased responsibility and autonomy were promoted by allowing her some selection of menu. She could have five or six small meals or three regular meals. She gained her first pound on the fourth day.

The team approach is illustrated by the first family-therapy lunch session on the sixteenth day. Included were the pediatrician, the psychiatrist, the patient, and her family (her father, stepmother, older stepsister, and younger stepbrother). The focus was on preventing power struggles and enabling the patient to eat in her parents' presence. Another issue was helping the family to see their conflicts rather than to only acknowledge having a medically sick child. The therapist told the girl that she could eat or not, but he immediately ate, saying how hungry he was. He even asked whether he might eat some of her food; this technique led to her eating her entire lunch. The family witnessed this and felt optimistic for a change. The pediatrician and therapist agreed that eating was no longer the problem in the family and that she could go home when she weighed 85 pounds.

After discharge, outpatient therapy focused on weight gain and changing dysfunctional family patterns. One change was to stop the family's scapegoating of the girl. The reinforcement program gave the parents a concrete method of handling her, which reduced their feelings of helplessness and anxiety. If she gained less than 2 pounds from Friday to Friday, they were not to allow her out of the house for the weekend and were to deny her any guests. If she did have to stay in, one other family member had to stay with her; this procedure caused the family to work together to ensure her eating. A 2- to 2½-pound gain resulted in either Saturday or Sunday activities, and more than 2½ pounds led to unrestricted weekend activity. In order to attend summer camp with her siblings she had to weigh 112 pounds, an objective she did accomplish.

Liebman, Minuchin, and Baker saw her problems as a result of dysfunctional family patterns, which were addressed during family therapy. The parents were ineffective, disorganized, rigid, and unable to deal with stress or resolve problems. Because of their weak marital relationship, she became inappropriately involved in parental affairs. Parental overconcern and preoccupation with the patient's problems were obstacles to resolving other problems. Her symptoms were reinforced by this family pattern, and the goal was to free her. The parents were instructed to privately discuss problems each evening and come up with some plan of action. After two months of outpatient therapy, the parents reported that eating was no longer a problem but that the patient had poor interpersonal relationships. Other interventions included sending the patient to parties with her sister and encouraging parental social evenings and vacations by themselves. A videotape was shown to the family illustrating the mother's overconcern for the patient and the father's peripheral role in the family. Specific plans were designed to promote the children's independence and responsibility. The latter part of the ten months of therapy dealt only with the parents' marital problems. An eighteen-month follow-up revealed no eating problems and continued progress by all family members.

COMMENTARY: The authors have used this approach with twenty cases and strongly advocate the therapeutic focus on the family to ensure the maintenance of weight gain and improved family functioning. Their approach is clearly different from family therapy, which is more nondirective and requires the family to develop specific childrearing practices. They freely suggest and teach courses of action to achieve the goals of reducing parental overprotection and promoting the patient's autonomy. This article is an outstanding example of the combination of behavioral and dynamic approaches. It demonstrates sensitivity to, and treatment of, the "whole" child and her family.

SOURCE: Liebman, R., Minuchin, S., and Baker, L. "The Role of the Family in the Treatment of Anorexia Nervosa." *Journal of Child Psychiatry*, 1974, *13*, 264-274.

Treating the Physiological and Psychological Needs. of Anorectic Patients in a Hospital

AUTHORS: Alexander R. Lucas, Jane W. Duncan, and Violet Piens

PRECIS: Separating patient from family, treating malnutrition, giving individually planned psychotherapy, and doing family counseling

INTRODÚCTION: The authors note the high mortality rate (up to 22 percent) of anorectics and the unsatisfactory results of coercive feeding or psychodynamic approaches alone. They conclude that the consensus of the literature is that treatment of anorexia is difficult and usually prolonged. Successful treatment efforts are seen as having common underlying principles: one therapist (or a cohesive team) using a consistent approach strongly influences the patient; the therapist has a genuine commitment to the patient, who is viewed as unique; contact occurs regularly over a long term; both the physiological and psychological problems are addressed; and treatment takes into account the family influences.

Characteristic of anorexia is the distorted attitude toward food and eating, with a strong desire to be thin. The central issues are the struggle for self-respect, identity, control, confidence, and effectiveness. Five boys and twenty-seven girls, between ten and twenty-one years of age, were treated in a hospital residential unit. Their weight loss had averaged 37 percent of body weight before treatment began, and none of the girls menstruated.

TREATMENT: The general treatment principles outlined above were followed. A carefully coordinated team worked on the physical and psychological problems of the patient. The child was separated from home in order to end the power struggles between child and parents. Malnutrition was treated by the staff's taking responsibility for eating behavior and gradually encouraging increased autonomy in the management of eating. The psychotherapist first took a supportive approach, later focusing on the expression of anger, ambivalence toward parents, and independence. Some amount of psychotherapy was continued after discharge. Counseling or intensive therapy also was provided to the family.

The anorectic patients ate in a separate dining room supervised by a nurse. A tray of food designed to maintain admission weight was served, with the expectation that it would be eaten. Gradually, small amounts of food were added. The nurse was firm, compassionate, patient, and alert to any deception. With progress the patients moved to the regular dining room, feeding themselves with gradually less supervision. A psychiatrist directed the medical treatment and provided psychotherapy. Essential was the acknowledgment that their form of dieting was destructive and out of control and that the patients had to stop losing weight and learn to eat according to their nutritional needs, not fears. The patients were asked to give up control and accept the staff's monitoring of food and fluid intake. Apathy, social distance, and inappropriate affect were not emphasized. Instead, discussions of the medical regime presented a specific, temporary dependence on the therapist which was thought to minimize the patients' anxiety regarding autonomy. As psychotherapy continued, the goal was psychic synthesis rather than analysis of defenses. Since the defense mechanisms of denial and projection interfere with awareness of reality, they were interpreted. The therapist pointed out the discrepancy between the patients' body image and their actual state. The patients' gradual acceptance of this discrepancy was aided by their relatively accurate perception of other anorectic patients. Another difficult task was helping the patient recognize the internal bodily sensations of hunger and satiety. All interactions with anorectic peers were discussed in therapy; in these sessions patients occasionally saw a repetition of their earlier relationships with their mothers. Spontaneity and a sense of humor were considered signs of recovery. When they left the hospital, therapy was usually dealing with peer and parental relations, expressions of anger, self-assertiveness, and independence.

The usual hospital stay was three to five months. The authors present a table detailing the results of weight gain for the thirty-two patients. Apathy, mental fatigue, and depression gradually lessened along with the gain in weight. Usually there was increased spontaneity and more freedom to express feelings. Most patients maintained their weight and generally showed improved adjustment for up to three years after discharge.

COMMENTARY: Lucas, Duncan, and Piens clearly indicate the need to carefully combine a medical and psychotherapeutic approach. Their approach appears to be quite inclusive in that they influence the patient in almost all aspects of functioning. Internal bodily sensations, distorted body image, the tendency to deny and project feelings, and many fears are all addressed. Clearly, the commitment of professional time and interest must be very great if effective and permanent change is to occur. In anorexia, and other psychosomatic disorders, short cuts are tempting but often more costly in the long run.

SOURCE: Lucas, A. R., Duncan, J. W., and Piens, V. "The Treatment of Anorexia Nervosa." *American Journal of Psychiatry*, 1976, *133*, 1034-1038.

Treating Anorexia Nervosa with Operant Reinforcement and Structural Family Therapy

AUTHORS: Lawrence M. Perlman and Sheila S. Bender

PRECIS: The use of directive, criterion-oriented approaches with the families of two young teen-age girls

INTRODUCTION: Perlman and Bender discuss the limitations of using only operant reinforcement. They combine reinforcement techniques with the restructuring of family interactions in order to formulate and achieve specific treatment goals. In action therapies, specific instructions and assignments are employed and interpretive statements are usually avoided. The two girls treated fit Bruch's description (H. Bruch, *Eating Disorders*. New York: Basic Books, 1973) of primary anorexia nervosa: the "pursuit of thinness in the struggle for an independent identity, delusional denial of thinness, preoccupation with food, hyperactivity, and striving for perfection" (p. 238). Both girls ate small amounts of food secretly, were overly dependent, and lacked a sense of autonomy. Typically, they responded to the demands of others rather than acted out of personal desires. They were unusually industrious, obedient, and perfectionistic. Both girls were shy, did not make direct eye contact, and had no relationships with boys. Both families were close-knit and somewhat inflexible, and in both the parents were overly involved with their children. Notable was the lack of channels for independent action.

Anorexia began shortly after puberty; both girls lost about thirty-five pounds, ceased to menstruate, and became depressed and irritable. One of the girls had been treated medically quite unsuccessfully with tube feeding and prescribed diet.

TREATMENT: The authors describe different aspects of treatment, during which the focus shifted from the patient to the entire family. The eating disorder was seen as affecting the whole family, and operant conditioning involved everyone. Weight gain, not the conflict-producing subject of eating, was the focus. Activity, typically treasured by anorectic girls, was made contingent on weight gain. For each pound gained, the girl was permitted a day of free and unlimited activity. No references to eating were permitted, and the mother was to confer with the girl regarding menus. The father was to monitor weight and enforce the activity allowance. Planning menus and activities gave the girls the opportunity to be more independent. But little or no weight gain occurred. Apparently the other family members were not complying with instructions, and the anorectic behavior was being maintained. The parents were protective, overly concerned, and doubtful about treatment. So the therapists had to firmly demand full family cooperation.

The therapist then became accepted into the family system and participated in family activities, such as meals and leisure activities. The parents followed instructions and the girls grudgingly gained weight. Perlman and Bender view the family as thereby being relieved of responsibility and the therapists as supporting the family structure, freeing the child from struggling against parental domination. The girl could become more autonomous and the parents could develop a more flexible position of authority. As the girl gained weight, the operant conditioning lost its effectiveness and became counterproductive. The girl had become more assertive, and weight regulation became her responsibility as a symbol of her maturity and independence. At this point, the focus of treatment shifted to family issues (especially parental interaction and conflicts), which the parents were now more willing to examine. Both girls achieved normal body weight on their own, made friends, participated in school, became more assertive and outspoken, and began menstruating again. Family tension diminished markedly. In discussion, it was clear that the parents were now functioning as a team and were able to discuss past and possible future problems. Ten months after treatment both girls were maintaining their normal weight and were much happier, friendlier, and more sociable.

COMMENTARY: Perlman and Bender stress the effectiveness of a male-female cotherapy team. They see the cotherapists as assisting each other and being more able to plan better therapeutic strategies; such a pair can more readily gain entry to the family system, too. Open-ended family sessions, from one to three hours, were used to promote intensive interventions. This article is in keeping with the growing trend to combine successful approaches in order to be more effective and efficient. The combined use of operant conditioning, a family-systems approach, cotherapists, open-ended sessions, and more active direct involvement with the family can serve as a possible model for interventions with other psychosomatic disorders.

SOURCE: Perlman, L. M., and Bender, S. S. "Operant Reinforcement with Structural Family Therapy in Treating Anorexia Nervosa." *Journal of Family Counseling,* 1975, *3,* 38-46.

Outpatient Treatment of Anorexia Nervosa Using Food as the Reinforcer

AUTHOR: C. B. Scrignar

PRECIS: Using a prescribed diet to increase appropriate eating and decrease vomiting

INTRODUCTION: Extreme dieting and voluntary vomiting are described as a typical start of anorexia by Scrignar. Weight loss, endocrine insufficiencies, amenorrhea, and metabolic changes soon occur. Scrignar reviews the psychoanalytic concepts of the disorder, including a fear of oral impregnation, ascetic reaction formation, and a fear of growing up or becoming sexually mature. He also cites the view that underlying causes are not relevant, that analyzing current eating behavior is sufficient. Successful results have been achieved by making privileges contingent on eating and weight gain and by the use of verbal praise. Systematic desensitization and the use of walking privileges have also been successful.

Scrignar treated an intelligent, conscientious, and energetic fourteen-year-old girl. A casual remark by her father that she was getting a bit big in the hips led to severe dieting. At first she induced vomiting with her finger after every meal; later she automatically vomited in the bathroom. Being very hungry, she often ate large quantities of food but always vomited.

TREATMENT: The girl was asked to keep a journal of all eating and to list foods she liked very much, liked, or disliked. Scrignar hypothesized that frequent vomiting had reduced stomach capacity to such a degree that normal eating made her feel stuffed. The habit sequence was eating, feeling stuffed, going to the bathroom, vomiting. Parental concern served to reinforce the process. Treatment began with her purchasing a scale and weighing all food. A well-rounded diet was designed that had fewer calories than average and included one multiple-vitamin pill. The most preferred foods were given at the end of each meal to serve as positive reinforcers. Scrignar presents tables listing her food preferences and a weekly diet. Bedtime snacks were used as delayed reinforcers, and foods "liked very much" were contingent on no vomiting during the day. If vomiting occurred, only "liked" food was to be eaten. The therapist dealt with her constant hunger by allowing her to eat celery, pickles, and popsicles at any time. These were "liked very much" foods that would not cause stuffiness. Weigh-ins were followed by a discussion with Scrignar. The diet was modified somewhat according to the patient's wishes. Meanwhile, the parents were told to ignore her eating patterns.

COMMENTARY: Scrignar reports successful weight gain and maintenance. The striking aspect of this report is the relative economy and efficacy of the program in view of the limited amount of professional time involved. Using the most preferred foods late in a meal as reinforcers appears to be a simple expedient to increase food intake. This technique is in stark contrast to the frequently reported prolonged inpatient stays of anorectic patients. It may be employed in situations where extensive treatment is not available or not feasible. Possibly this approach might be tried first, and only if it were unsuccessful would the more extensive and expensive procedures be instituted.

SOURCE: Scrignar, C. B. "Food as the Reinforcer in the Outpatient Treatment of Anorexia Nervosa." *Journal of Behavior Therapy and Experimental Psychiatry*, 1971, *2*, 31-36.

Additional Readings

Ayllon, T., Haughton, E., and Osmond, H. O. "Chronic Anorexia: A Behaviour Problem." *Canadian Psychiatric Association Journal,* 1964, *9,* 147-154.

Although concerned with adult schizophrenics, this article contains useful theoretical discussions in addition to practical methods for treating a chronic refusal to eat. Rejecting food is considered a learned behavior that must not be followed by social reinforcement. Without adequate control, maladaptive behavior continues to be produced and maintained. In treatment, the therapists must have complete control over food. Patients must have access to food only under prescribed conditions, and food should be available for a limited time only (twenty to thirty minutes) and then removed. Patients are not coaxed, talked to, or offered special foods. The authors stress the importance of not talking to the patient about his or her failure to eat. Social reinforcement (smiles, pleasant looks, conversation) is paired with the intrinsically rewarding properties of eating. If the person hesitates or rejects food, social reinforcement is immediately withdrawn.

Blum, S. "Children Who Starve Themselves." *New York Times Magazine,* November 10, 1974, p. 63.

This article is a good review of different approaches to anorexia, particularly the Philadelphia Child Guidance Clinic's family therapy methods. Consistent diagnostic patterns are discussed. Families are described as overaccommodating and not knowing how to resolve conflicts. The parents blame each other, and rather than fight them, the child refuses to eat. Therapy is focused on the family system and on restoring the rights of both parents and child. The parents are assisted to exercise power, and food fantasies are never discussed with the child.

Bruch, H. *The Golden Cage: The Enigma of Anorexia Nervosa.* Cambridge, Mass.: Harvard University Press, 1977. *Eating Disorders: Obesity, Anorexia Nervosa, and the Person Within.* New York: Basic Books, 1973.

Two books by a pioneer in the field of eating disorders. Early diagnosis and treatment are stressed, and narrative case histories are used to illustrate Bruch's psychodynamic treatment approaches. Middle-class families with professional, hard-driving, perfectionistic parents are prone to have bright, attractive, anorectic children.

Casper, R. C., and Davis, J. M. "On the Course of Anorexia Nervosa." *American Journal of Psychiatry*, 1977, *134*, 974-978.

Useful comparisons are made between anorexia and starvation. The physical symptoms are similar, but anorectics show high initiative, the ability to suppress hunger, hyperactivity, and distorted body images. Anorexia follows a three-phase course. Phase one usually includes precipitating events resulting in a loss of self-esteem and increasing self-consciousness about physical appearance. Pride in the ability to lose weight and an unreasonable fear of eating are characteristic of phase two. Because of the severity of their symptoms, patients admit they are ill by the third phase.

Crisp, A. H., Palmer, R. L., and Kalucy, R. S. "How Common Is Anorexia Nervosa? A Prevalence Study." *British Journal of Psychiatry*, 1976, *128*, 549-554.

This study demonstrates that anorexia is more common in England than had been assumed, and the incidence is increasing. Girls were diagnosed only if they had lost at least 30 percent of their body weight, had prolonged amenorrhea, and bizarre dietary attitudes. In boarding schools, there was one severe case out of every two hundred girls, a ratio that probably reflects the greater number of cases among middle-class girls. Families are often (mistakenly) advised to send a girl to boarding schools as a form of treatment. Crisp, Palmer, and Kalucy see the rapid biological growth in girls during puberty and self-consciousness regarding fatness as causal factors in anorexia. In addition, they report almost universal dieting attempts by female adolescents and increasing existential problems among adolescents.

Debow, S. L. "Identical Twins Concordant of Anorexia Nervosa: A Preliminary Case Report." *Canadian Psychiatric Association Journal*, 1975, *20*, 215-217.

Identical fourteen-year-old twin sisters were both treated for anorexia. They joined their moderately overweight father in dieting and engaged in many emotional outbursts concerning food. After they lost more than 20 percent of their body weight, they were hospitalized. The subsequent therapy focused on the competition between the twins and their frequent use of denial (especially denying their anger). During and after hospitalization, the family therapist concentrated on the communication of caring and hostile feelings. The twins maintained their body weight but were not gaining weight after discharge.

Goetz, P. L., Succop, R. A., Reinhart, J. B., and Miller, A. "Anorexia Nervosa in Children: A Follow-Up Study." *American Journal of Orthopsychiatry*, 1977, *47*, 597-603.

The authors consider anorexia a serious problem, with an increasing incidence. In their study, they did not use hospitalization, feeding techniques, drugs, or behavior modification. Psychotherapy is their treatment of choice, although they view the techniques of the therapist as less important than the therapist's being comfortable with a personal style. They discourage symptom management alone, and once-a-week outpatient collaborative psychotherapy for the child and parents is suggested. They also discuss in detail the different possible prognoses and conclude that the outcome is largely determined by the patient's personality structure. Anorectics with schizoid personalities did worst and hysterical-manipulative types did best in their study.

Hauserman, N., and Lavin, P. "Posthospitalization Continuation Treatment of Anorexia Nervosa." *Journal of Behavior Therapy and Experimental Psychiatry*, 1977, *8*, 309-313.

Hauserman and Lavin, after citing the inadequacy of providing only in-hospital treatment, describe the posthospital behavior therapy they provided to a female college student. The treatment included behavioral contracts, cognitive restructuring, systematic desensitization, and group assertiveness training. The student gained weight in the hospital but quickly lost eight pounds at home. Consequently, the therapists decided she would be returned to the hospital if she lost weight on any of the next ten days or if she did not gain four pounds in those ten days. After being monitored by her aunt, she gradually assumed self-monitoring and was not rehospitalized. She also was trained to recognize and modify her emotional reactions. Her inappropriate and magical beliefs were identified and discussed: she did not have to be nurtured by others, she could tolerate rejection and not have to love and care for everyone, she could assert herself without being ungrateful, and she did not have to be perfect.

Heron, G. B., and Johnston, D. A. "Hypothalamic Tumor Presenting as Anorexia Nervosa." *American Journal of Psychiatry*, 1976, *133*, 580-582.

Heron and Johnston provide the very helpful warning that repeated neurological and endocrine evaluations are essential when anorectic patients are unresponsive or only partially responsive to psychiatric treatment. Negative initial medical evaluations, obvious psychopathology, and some response to treatment do not rule out organic disease. These warnings were emphasized by the case of a young adult male who was found to have a pinealoma affecting the hypothalamus. He had behavior abnormalities without endocrine or neurological deficits. The authors state that anorexia caused by infections or extracranial malignancies may be ruled out by the usual medical examination. They advise giving special attention to tumors affecting the pituitary-hypothalamic axis (symptomized by headaches, visual field changes, and endocrine abnormalities). Ectopic pinealomas, they point out, usually affect adolescent and young adult males and cause diabetes insipidus, pituitary dysfunction, and neurological deficits. Although a behavior modification regimen increased the weight of their patient, he was readmitted after five months in a serious condition (semicomatose, dehydrated, and almost totally blind). Hormonal replacement and radiation therapy were successfully instituted. Skull films are most helpful, because they may reveal a calcified pincal. Additionally, abnormal urine specific gravities and decreased levels of serum cortisol and gonadal and thyroid hormones are diagnostic indicators. Pneumoencephalography indicating a hypothalamic mass is usually definitive.

Hogan, W. M., Huerta, E., and Lucas, A. R. "Diagnosing Anorexia Nervosa in Males." *Psychosomatics,* 1974, *15,* 122-126.

Extensively reviewed are the criteria and methods for diagnosing anorexia. Clinical and laboratory features are detailed for eighteen typical cases of anorexia in males (ages eleven to twenty). In descending frequency, bradycardia, overactivity, lanugo, self-induced vomiting, and bulimia were found. These features are remarkably similar to those found in girls (who show a much greater incidence of anorexia). Treatment occurred on an adolescent inpatient unit and included separation from home, firm encouragement of eating and a restriction of activity, individual psychotherapy, and parent counseling.

Kellerman, J. "Anorexia Nervosa: The Efficacy of Behavior Therapy." *Journal of Behavior Therapy and Experimental Psychiatry,* 1977, *8,* 387-390.

The author considers behavior therapy the treatment of choice for anorexia. He reviews the literature and refutes two criticisms of behavioral approaches, asserting that weight gain was not temporary and other positive psychological changes did accompany weight gain. Kellerman also states that the therapeutic focus should be determined by a behavioral analysis. The patient is asked to describe all the stimulus antecedents, and his or her anxiety-mediated responses must be considered and modified. The techniques employed include operant conditioning and systematic desensitization. Freeing individuals from unadaptive learned behavior creates greater autonomy and satisfaction.

La Pook, E. "They Choose to Starve." *Of Westchester,* February 1977, p. 56.

Written for the general public, this article provides helpful diagnostic indicators and a profile by Dr. Jack Katz of a typical anorectic girl. Yes answers to twelve of the fifteen questions posed by Katz serve as an alert to families. The questions are clear and conform to the existing literature on anorectic family patterns. This article informs the public of the need to recognize anorectic patterns and treat the situation early.

Leitenberg, H., Agras, W. S., and Thomson, L. E. "A Sequential Analysis of the Effect of Selective Positive Reinforcement in Modifying Anorexia Nervosa." *Behavior Research and Therapy*, 1968, *6*, 211-218.

The authors successfully treated two girls, fourteen and seventeen, for anorexia by reinforcing progressive gains in the amount of food eaten and in weight. Ignoring their physical complaints had eliminated those but had not worked in restoring normal eating. Verbal praise for increased eating and tangible privileges for weight gain were effective. A daily four-thousand-calorie diet was given in four meals; no snacks were allowed. They ate in a private room for thirty minutes. Pleasurable activities were not allowed until they began to gain weight. A graphic record was kept by the girls of mouthfuls eaten and daily weight. Examples of response-contingent positive reinforcement are "You gained nicely today; would you like to watch TV for an hour tonight?" and "Your weight has been progressing at a good pace this week; would you like to go look at the snow sculptures on campus tomorrow afternoon?"

Lesser, L. I., Ashenden, B. J., Debuskey, M., and Eisenberg, L. "Anorexia Nervosa in Children." *American Journal of Orthopsychiatry*, 1960, *30*, 572-580.

Treatment is described in detail for fifteen anorectic girls from ten through sixteen years of age. Coordinated efforts and communication were necessary among all hospital staff members. Tube feeding was used in only two cases, but the girls were informed that it would be used if necessary. The authors believe hospital care is essential for a majority of anorectic cases, because they see a united and sincere medical effort as a corrective emotional experience for the child caught up in parental conflicts. They show how both pediatrician and psychiatrist can intervene in family interaction patterns. Anorectic girls are described as frequently involved in seductive, conflictual relationships with their fathers and very dependent relationships with their mothers.

Liebman, R., Minuchin, S., and Baker, L. "An Integrated Treatment Program for Anorexia Nervosa." *American Journal of Psychiatry*, 1974, *131*, 432-436.

The authors state that early family involvement promotes significant and rapid weight gain in inpatients, and outpatient treatment leads to a restructuring of family patterns to prevent relapses. In the hospital, physical activity is permitted only when weight gain occurs. At home, weekend social activities are dependent on weight gain. Family therapy lunch sessions are held to enable eating without any power struggle and to redefine anorexia as a family problem. Weight gain is considered only a first step in restructuring the family system. The parents must work together and support each other in carrying out the operant reinforcement food program. The assignment of family tasks leads to changes in the structure, organization, and functioning of the family. The aim is to improve family relationships.

Minuchin, S., Rosman, B. L., and Baker, L. "Psychosomatic Families: Anorexia Nervosa in Context." Cambridge, Mass.: Harvard University Press, 1978.

Family therapy techniques are applied to cases of anorexia. A new theory of psychosomatic disease is proposed and supported by data and clinical studies. The therapist stimulates crises that shake up the system and lead to forming new and healthier patterns. The course of therapy with four families is carefully described. Specific initial and continuing strategies are employed and suggestions for modifications are made. New possibilities are described for traditionally untreatable psychosomatic disorders.

Pillay, M. "Some Psychological Characteristics of Patients with Anorexia Nervosa Whose Weight Has Been Newly Restored." *British Journal of Medical Psychology*, 1977, *50*, 375-380.

Patients and sometimes families need intensive psychological help in dealing with panic, shame, and low self-esteem. Anorexia serves to inactivate the usual problems of puberty and maturation that weight gain rekindles. The therapist can learn more about the patient's general sensitivity and social anxiety by administering the Edwards Personal Preference Schedule, the Hysteroid Obsessional Questionnaire, the Fear Survey Schedule, and the Social Questionnaire. Implications for treatment can be found in Pillay's findings of timidity (not a lack in social adeptness), obsessive traits of conscientiousness, precision, and perfectionism, and a need for maximum predictability.

Rollins, N., and Piazza, E. "Diagnosis of Anorexia Nervosa: A Critical Reappraisal." *Journal of Child Psychiatry,* 1978, *17,* 126-137.

Rollins and Piazza found varying criteria and definitions in the literature regarding the diagnosis of anorexia. They believe that a 25-percent weight loss is too restrictive for diagnosing anorexia, stating that a 20 percent loss would be more appropriate. Amenorrhea was present in 100 percent of their twenty-seven cases of anorexia, and they agree that amenorrhea should be retained as an essential diagnostic criterion. In contrast to the reviewed literature, they believe that body-image distortion is the one psychopathological indicator that is basic in anorexia.

Taipale, V., Larkio-Miettinen, K., Valanne, E. H., Moren, R., and Aukee, M. "Anorexia Nervosa in Boys." *Psychosomatics,* 1972, *13,* 236-240.

Five anorectic boys were treated. They had a definite feminine identification and weak identification with their fathers. The authors believe adolescence was frightening to the boys because their parents were not helpful in their growing into manhood. Fasting is viewed as their wanting to remain children and to be appealing to their mothers. All the mothers had frustrating and nonsatisfying relationships with their husbands. Four to ten weeks of hospitalization resulted in maintained weight gain, but social and emotional adjustment remained marginal.

Van Buskirk, S. S. "A Two-Phase Perspective on the Treatment of Anorexia Nervosa." *Psychological Bulletin,* 1977, *84,* 529-538.

Research concerning the treatment of anorexia is reviewed in great detail. Operant conditioning is discussed, particularly room restriction and making activities and privileges contingent on weight gain. Several studies combined operant techniques, drug therapy, supportive psychotherapy, or systematic desensitization. A variety of psychodynamic approaches are discussed and summarized. Useful tables are presented concerning the short- and long-term outcomes of various types of therapy. Van Buskirk points out the need for better controlled and more conclusive research. She also highlights a variety of weaknesses in the literature, including the inappropriate combining of patients who do not fit any agreed upon definition of anorexia and the lack of comparisons of patients' actual weight with their ideal weight. Continuing care after hospitalization is stressed.

White, J. H., Kelly, P., and Dorman, K. "Clinical Picture of Atypical Anorexia Nervosa Associated with Hypothalamic Tumor." *American Journal of Psychiatry*, 1977, *134*, 323-325.

In atypical (or secondary) anorexia, the patient realizes that his or her emaciated state and bizarre eating pattern are abnormal. Hyperactivity is absent, but depression and hysteria are frequent. Though primary anorexia occurs almost exclusively in females, the secondary type is found in both sexes. The authors describe their medical and psychological findings on a fifteen-year-old boy who was treated for anorexia in a residential center. A large tumor was found in the midline displacing the anterior aspect and the floor of the third ventricle superiorly and posteriorly. After the boy was metabolically stabilized, a right frontal craniotomy revealed a cystic tumor between the anterior cerebral arteries and above the optic chiasm. All signs of anorexia disappeared after successful surgery and radiation therapy on the hypothalamic area. Strikingly, the history was typical of anorexia and the original tumor evaluation was completely normal. Periodic reevaluations for tumor are suggested as long as anorectic behavior continues.

Young, J. K. "A Possible Neuroendocrine Basis of Two Clinical Syndromes: Anorexia Nervosa and the Klein-Levin Syndrome." *Physiological Psychology*, 1975, *3*, 322-330.

Incomplete maturation of the hypothalamus leading to hypersensitivity to sex steroids is seen as a primary cause of both anorexia and the Klein-Levin syndrome. Whereas anorexia is almost exclusively a female syndrome, Klein-Levin occurs almost entirely in males and is quite rare. In Klein-Levin, attacks of sleepiness or drowsiness and sudden, ravenous cravings for sweets occur. The symptoms of the two syndromes are seen as mirror images of each other. Both disorders are viewed by Young as resulting from defects in the hormonal regulation of energy balance (feeding, activity, and body temperature). Administration of sex hormones is discussed as an appropriate treatment.

3

Neuromuscular
Disorders

In this section we will be dealing with two disorders involving the voluntary muscles: tics and tension headaches. We have limited the discussion to these two because the available literature concerning psychosomatic disorders of the neuromuscular system contains few reports on other disabilities.

There are two important characteristics of the voluntary muscle system—the fact that constant or extreme muscle contractions are painful and that gross striated muscle activity results in visible movement—that draw attention to disorders in which it is involved. The first characteristic is evident in tension headaches and the second in tics. Although both disorders are related by their underlying stimulus and by the system they belong to, the actual mechanisms involved, the resulting manifestations, and their impacts are quite different. The tic is generally more evident to the observer than to the person suffering with it. This tends to lead to problems in socialization. The headache, in contrast, is usually more evident to the sufferer than to the observer. In some instances, however, secondary gains from headache behavior (moaning, grimacing, and so on) become of such paramount importance in the process that the reverse may be true.

Tics are irregular and spasmodic movements of isolated groups of muscles, movements that are not associated with any organic disorder. The disorder, which most commonly involves the facial muscles, is far more prevalent in children than adults. It has long been noted that the frequency of tics increases when the child is under stress or excited. An important pediatric textbook states that "on occasion the origin of a tic may be traced to interference with normal motility during early childhood due to illness or artificial restraint such as that imposed by casts or elbow splints" (W. Nelson (Ed.), *Textbook of Pediatrics,* Philadelphia: W. B. Saunders, 1975, p. 100).

There is some disagreement about the psychologic mechanisms that result in the manifestation of a tic, and predictably this disagreement is based on differing schools of thought. Psychoanalysts see tics as instinctual impulses of an erotic or aggressive nature that are continually escaping through pathologic discharge. Others consider them simply a manifestation of tension, while a third view is held by learning theorists, who believe tics are a learned response maintained by operant reinforcement. Obviously the way a therapist looks at the problem will have a decisive impact on his or her choice of a therapeutic plan. The section that follows includes representations of different types of treatment approaches which have shown some efficacy in handling what is generally a difficult disorder to eradicate.

Tension headaches have long been considered to be due to excessive muscular contractions in the scalp, neck, and shoulders that result from an increase in emotional stress. The first true evidence to support this view was found in the early 1950s, when two British researchers used a rather new device, the electromyograph (EMG), in an experiment. The EMG measures the electrical activity within a muscle. This activity is directly correlated with the amount of contraction being generated by the muscle. The researchers found that the resting EMG levels measured in the frontalis (scalp) muscle of headache patients were significantly higher than those measured in nonheadache controls (P. Sainsbury and J. F. Gibson, "Symptoms of Anxiety and Tension and Accompanying Physiological Changes in the Muscular System," *Journal of Neurology, Neurosurgery, and Psychiatry*, 1954, *17*, 216-224).

Since then a great deal of work has been reported on using the EMG not only as a measure but as a feedback tool. Although EMG biofeedback has been used therapeutically with frequent success, the underlying assumption that the headache is caused by increased muscle contraction has been called into question. A recent study concluded that there was greater reactivity in the frontalis muscle in tension headache patients in response to stressful images than was noted in nonheadache control subjects (C. Phillips, "Tension Headache: Theoretical Problems," *Behavior Research and Therapy*, 1978, *16*, 249-261), but this finding was in no manner consistent for all headache subjects. Other reports questioning the true role of muscular contraction in the development of tension headache pain have appeared in the literature, leaving some doubt about whether or not tension headache can continue to be considered synonymous with muscular contraction headache.

This issue aside, EMG feedback has been repeatedly shown to be beneficial for tension headache patients. Some might question the accuracy of labeling a program that involves a voluntary function true biofeedback in the classical sense, but the label has appeared a sufficient number of times to be accepted by investigators. The reports that muscle contraction may not be a universal constant in tension headaches have led some to reexamine the rationale of using EMG feedback as a therapeutic technique. Hauri speculates that the relief that tension headache patients obtain with EMG feedback programs may be due more

to the "subtle change in lifestyle" that accompanies the programs than to the feedback itself. (P. P. Hauri, "Biofeedback
and Self-Control of Physiological Functions: Clinical Applications," *International Journal of Psychiatry in Medicine*, 1975, 6
(1/2), 255-265). He points out that the EMG feedback programs with the greatest success involve periods of home study
and practice during which the subject must sit quietly for at
least a half hour concentrating on relaxing the muscles in the
scalp, neck, and shoulders. This quiet time may itself be the
most important factor in headache relief because of its effect on
reducing overall stress. In addition patients are conceivably
aided by the development of a feeling of mastery over their condition.

The following section includes treatments that incorporate
general relaxation training as well as feedback training using
alpha wave production (EEG). The promising results produced
by both kinds of training may be another indication that the
precise cause of the pain in tension headaches is not the increased contraction of a discrete muscle group, but something
else less directly measureable. There is no question in most investigators' minds at this juncture, however, about the importance of internal stress in triggering whatever mechanism is
involved in causing the pain.

Tension Headaches

Tension headache is generally felt to be due to excessive muscle contraction in the scalp, neck, and shoulders. It is one of the most frequent physical complaints encountered in medicine and is responsible for a great deal of discomfort and disrupted school and work time. Increased emotional stress and anxiety are important triggers of the reaction leading to pain.

Treatment of Tension Headaches
with EMG Biofeedback

AUTHORS: Thomas H. Budzynski, Johann M. Stoyva, Charles S. Adler, and Daniel J. Mullaney

PRECIS: Using EMG biofeedback to decrease headache pain

INTRODUCTION: The authors noted in a previous study that the level of EMG activity in the frontalis (scalp) muscle was higher in tension headache patients than in nonheadache sufferers. A subsequent study revealed that the frequency and severity of tension headaches seemed to be diminished when patients were taught to reduce frontalis muscle tension using EMG biofeedback training. The present study was designed to determine whether the results were due to the training or were, in fact, due to a placebo or suggestion effect.

METHOD: Three groups of tension headache patients were chosen for the purposes of the study. The first group (A) received EMG biofeedback training. Group B received "pseudo-biofeedback" training—the feedback signal was not in any way connected with actual EMG measurement. The third group (C) served as a control and received no training.

During an initial two-week baseline period no training was conducted and all subjects recorded hourly their subjective assessment of headache intensity. Once these data were accumulated, training began for groups A and B.

The "BIFS" EMG feedback system (Bio-Feedback Systems, Inc., Boulder, Colorado) was utilized. Electrodes (half an inch in diameter) were placed four inches apart, each one inch above the eyebrows. A reference electrode was placed in the center of the patient's forehead. The electrodes were connected to a preamplifier that was in turn connected to the "BIFS" unit. A clicking sound whose rate was directly related to the level of muscle activity was supplied over headphones. Subjects undergoing the training were kept in a dimly lit room. They reclined on a couch and were instructed to keep their eyes closed during the sessions, which generally lasted thirty minutes and were conducted twice weekly for two months (sixteen sessions).

Specific instructions were given to each group undergoing training. Group A subjects were told the following:

> Tension headaches are primarily due to sustained contraction or tightness in the muscles of the scalp and neck.
>
> The goal of this study is to learn to relax your muscles so that the tension level never gets too high, and you no longer get headaches. This will involve a great deal of work on your part, both here in the lab and also at home.
>
> In order to help you learn, we are going to provide you with information on the level of muscle tension in your forehead region. You will hear a series of clicks in the headphones. The click rate will be proportional to your forehead tension; that is, the higher the tension, the faster the click rate. Your job will be to find out what makes the click rate slow down, because this means lower muscle tension. Try to eliminate those things that make the click rate go faster. Do not try too hard, or this will defeat your goal of deep relaxation. Remember to keep your attention focused on the clicks—do not let your mind wander.
>
> This session will last about thirty minutes.
>
> Remember—do not go to sleep.
>
> Any questions?

Group B subjects were given similar instructions, except they were not told the click rate was associated with muscle tension. Both groups were instructed to practice relaxing at home for two twenty-minute sessions each day. No specific instructions on how to relax were given.

During the course of the training the trainers noted that both groups that received training significantly reduced the level of EMG frontalis muscle activity. However, the drop was significantly greater in group A subjects than in group B subjects. Three months after the termination of training additional readings revealed that these changes persisted. Of more importance was the finding that actual headache activity was markedly reduced in four of the six group A subjects as compared to only one in six of group B subjects. Group C subjects showed no improvement. A follow-up eighteen months after training ended (obtained on four group A subjects) revealed that the three subjects who had initially reported improvement continued to do well, whereas the fourth, who had not benefited greatly from the training, reported a mild reduction in headache severity and frequency.

COMMENTARY: The authors utilized other measurements of benefit from EMG biofeedback training, and their results were also impressive. The use of analgesics in the A group was markedly reduced after the training. But only half of those in the B group were able to significantly reduce their use of analgesic medications. Many of the medications used regularly by these headache sufferers have the potential for abuse. Certainly a method as simple and safe as the training described is a far better treatment than the use of abusable substances. This consideration is of particular concern when dealing with an adolescent population.

SOURCE: Budzynski, T. H., Stoyva, J. M., Adler, C. S., and Mullaney, D. J. "EMG Biofeedback and Tension Headache: A Controlled Outcome Study." *Psychosomatic Medicine,* 1973, *35,* 484-496.

Treating Tension Headaches with Relaxation

AUTHORS: Daniel J. Cox, Andrew Freundlich, and Robert G. Meyer

PRECIS: A comparison of electromyograph (EMG) feedback training, verbal progressive relaxation, and placebo medication in the management of tension headaches

INTRODUCTION: Muscle contraction in the neck and scalp appears to play an important role in the etiology of tension headaches. As a result, a number of investigators have attempted to use various relaxation techniques to treat this very common condition. The authors cite the results of several such studies which incorporated, alone and in various combinations, such methods as electromyograph feedback, verbal relaxation instructions, and Jacobson's progressive relaxation training. The outcomes have varied and have been further confused by applying methods simultaneously. The present study was designed to determine the specific contributions that EMG feedback, verbal relaxation instructions, and placebo medication can make to the therapy of tension headaches.

PROCEDURE: The group of twenty-seven subjects ranged in age from sixteen to sixty-four years. All fulfilled the criterion of suffering three or more times a week from tension headaches with no organic etiology, according to their family physicians. They were divided into three study groups after two initial pre-treatment assessments during which baseline studies were made and a personal history was taken. The two groups that received training attended eight one-hour sessions over a four-week period. Each subject was seen individually.

During the first half hour the biofeedback subjects received biofeedback training using an auditory signal triggered by the amount of electrical activity measured in the scalp muscle over the forehead. This activity parallels the degree of contraction of the muscle. Signals were picked up by three electrodes placed on the forehead and were fed into a biofeedback unit that emitted an auditory signal (details available from the Electronics Systems Development Corporation, P.O. Box 18223, Louisville, Kentucky). Immediately following the training the subject was instructed to maintain a relaxed condition and focus on his or her natural breathing rhythm while simultaneously thinking "relax" (cue-controlled breathing). As training progressed the machine was gradually altered so that progressively lower levels of EMG activity were necessary to lower the auditory signal. As the subject improved, intervals of no signal were introduced in order to fade out feedback dependency. At home each subject practiced the relaxation technique twice daily and the cue-controlled breathing before each meal in order to generalize the biofeedback effect to other environments. Following the third session the subjects began to apply the techniques at the first sign of a headache.

The verbal relaxation instruction group spent the first half of each of the first three sessions tightening and relaxing sixteen muscle groups in sequence. The second half was spent practicing the cue-controlled breathing technique. During the final five sessions the number of muscle groups used to attain relaxation was progressively reduced until each subject could relax without the need for any exercises. At home they practiced twice daily and employed their cue-controlled breathing before meals, just as the biofeedback group did.

The placebo medication subjects attended weekly hourly sessions during which they received a glucose capsule they were told contained an effective peripheral-acting time-release muscle relaxant.

All subjects attended two weekly posttreatment assessment sessions immediately following and again four months after the training sessions. Follow-up data were gathered, and the results revealed that the biofeedback and relaxation groups benefited significantly from their training to a statistically similar extent while the placebo group did not improve significantly. The criteria used for measuring improvement were a headache score incorporating total hours of pain and its intensity, scalp-muscle EMG activity, medication requirements, and the number of additional psychosomatic complaints offered.

The four-month follow-up revealed a trend to increasing improvement for the trained groups.

COMMENTARY: The authors point out that the successful treatment of tension headaches using a relaxation approach requires four steps: learning to lower EMG activity, increasing periods of daily relaxation, recognizing the onset of a headache early, and appropriately applying relaxation techniques. It should be kept in mind that such an approach can only work if the underlying cause of the headache is increased neuro-muscular activity. Although those involved in this study were mostly adults, some adolescents were included. The techniques taught were not difficult to master and could be applied to older children who are properly motivated.

SOURCE: Cox, D. J., Freundlich, A., and Meyer, R. G. "Differential Effectiveness of Electromyograph Feedback, Verbal Relaxation Instructions, and Medication Placebo with Tension Headaches." *Journal of Consulting and Clinical Psychology*, 1975, *43*, 892-898.

Treatment of Headache with Electroencephalographic Biofeedback

AUTHORS: Richard E. McKenzie, Wayne J. Ehrisman, Penelope S. Montgomery, and Robert H. Barnes

PRECIS: Teaching relaxation with the aid of alpha wave feedback

INTRODUCTION: During the course of exploring the usefulness of an electronic device to induce sleep, one of the authors noted that although subjects did not sleep, they did achieve a state of relaxation. This state coincided with increased alpha (slow) wave production as measured by electroencephalographic (EEG) recording of electrical activity within the brain. Further study revealed that there was a definite relationship between muscular relaxation and alpha wave production.

Tension headaches have been reported to be due to increased tension in the muscles of the head, neck, and shoulders. With this in mind the authors decided to find out whether or not people suffering from tension headaches would improve if given a feedback program that stimulated alpha wave production.

METHOD: The feedback device is described as follows:

We typically monitor at least four channels of EEG or brain wave information. The two electrodes give us a single channel of information which is fed into an amplification system to increase the signal, to shape it, and to eliminate unwanted signals or noise. We then feed this signal into a filtering network which acts to divide the raw brain wave signal into four frequency bands: beta—twenty-five to thirteen cycles; alpha—twelve to eight cycles; theta—seven to four cycles; and delta—four to one cycle. These four channels are then fed into another "black box" which converts the signal into one suitable to drive a display. In this case the display is a series of four colored lights, each one representing one of the frequency bands.

Experimental subjects were chosen after thorough history takings and physical examinations verified the diagnosis of tension headache. Baseline data covering the location, duration, frequency, and severity of headaches were obtained for a one-week period before training, during the entire training period, and for two follow-up study periods one and two months post-training. Sessions were held twice weekly for five weeks.

Electrodes were attached to the subjects, who sat viewing a screen similar to a television set on which colors corresponding to the production of wave types were displayed. Alpha waves caused a diffuse blue light to appear, whereas beta waves were associated with a diffuse red color. Patients were told that their brain waves were being fed back to them over the screen and were instructed to keep the blue light on as much as possible while eliminating the red light.

It was found that the number of sessions necessary to achieve a significant alleviation of symptoms ranged from four to twelve. The authors present EEG tracings that demonstrate increased alpha wave activity in seven of the subjects studied. Coincidental headache charts revealed substantial reductions in the hours of headache each week for these same subjects. The two follow-ups after terminating training showed continued benefit. The members of a simultaneously studied control group who did not receive the feedback but were given relaxation instructions also were improved, but not as much as those who received the feedback training. It was noted that their alpha wave production increased as they achieved the relaxation state.

COMMENTARY: Though the number of subjects studied is not specified, the implication is that most were benefited by the feedback training. The authors feel that better results could be obtained if auditory rather than visual feedback were used because visual stimulation tends to arouse the subject, thereby reducing alpha wave production.

The beneficial responses found in this study occurred earlier than did those in studies utilizing other forms of feedback (such as EMG). The equipment is more complex when EEG feedback is used, but a more rapid response may be an important factor, especially when using the technique to treat subjects who are easily frustrated by delays in improvement.

SOURCE: McKenzie, R. E., Ehrisman, W. J., Montgomery, P. S., and Barnes, R. H. "The Treatment of Headache by Means of Electroencephalographic Biofeedback." *Headache,* 1974, *13,* 164-172.

A Simple Relaxation Approach
to Tension Headaches

AUTHORS: Donald L. Tasto and John E. Hinkle

PRECIS: A progressive muscle relaxation technique to relieve the symptoms of college students suffering with tension headaches

INTRODUCTION: The authors felt that some of the behavioral therapies for tension headaches being reported by researchers required an excessive amount of time and expense to implement. The study they conducted was designed to determine whether a nonprofessional, a nurse, or a paraprofessional could teach tension headache sufferers a simple muscle relaxation technique that could be effective in reducing symptoms. In addition, they hoped to show that this skill could be taught with a minimum of therapist-patient contact.

METHOD: Six college students, all diagnosed by the health service as suffering with tension headaches, were used as subjects. Each was seen initially to record baseline data and then was given a notebook in which to record the frequency and duration of headaches over a one-week period before training. Subjects were seen individually in four weekly sessions during which they were taught a muscle relaxation method by an undergraduate psychology student previously trained in the procedure. When training began, each subject received a second notebook in which to keep a record of relaxation practice sessions conducted daily.

The participants were informed that it was very important to practice the relaxation technique every day in order to improve their abilities to become more deeply relaxed and to decrease the time necessary to achieve the relaxed state. Only with such practice would the treatment method become effective in actually controlling their headaches. In addition each subject was told to institute relaxation where possible whenever they felt the slightest indication that a headache was starting.

During the training sessions the technique was practiced and the entire process was reviewed. Though details of the exact method of training are not included by the authors, it apparently involved a progressive relaxation technique similar to that initially described by Jacobson. This involves sequentially tensing and relaxing a number of muscle groups. With practice the number of muscle groups required to achieve the relaxation state is reduced until, ultimately, the relaxation state can be reached without the need for any exercises.

Follow-up results were obtained two and a half months after training was terminated and revealed that all subjects experienced marked decreases in the number and duration of their headaches.

COMMENTARY: Despite the small size of the study, the results obtained were impressive. As described, this is an easy and inexpensive approach to conducting a behavioral therapy program for a very common malady. The authors point out the importance of the participants' maintaining daily records of their practice sessions. In this way they are more likely to maintain a daily practice schedule, and frequent practice diminishes the need for numerous therapist-patient contacts.

SOURCE: Tasto, D. L., and Hinkle, J. E. "Muscle Relaxation Treatment for Tension Headaches." *Behavior Research and Therapy*, 1973, *11*, 347-349.

Additional Readings

Norton, G. R., and Nielson, W. R. "Headaches: The Importance of Consequent Events." *Behavior Therapy,* 1977, *8,* 504-506.

   The authors distinguish between headache due to a stress situation that triggers tension and headache being maintained by external reinforcement of the headache-related behavior. The person treating the headache patient should perform a functional analysis of pain-related behavior in order to determine whether the headache is being controlled by consequent events. If this is found to be the case, then behavior therapy (feedback, relaxation, meditation, and so on) may have to be supplemented with other forms of therapy designed to extinguish the pain-related activities along with the pain.

Blanchard, E. B., and Young, L. D. "Clinical Applications of Biofeedback Training: A Review of Evidence." *Archives of General Psychiatry,* 1974, *30,* 573-589.

   This is an excellent review article that objectively evaluates many of the studies that have been performed in which biofeedback is used. The treatment of tension headaches with EMG feedback is noted to be one of the more successful applications of the technique. An extensive bibliography is included.

Tics

Tics (or twitches) are habitual and spasmodic movements of specific muscle groups, often of the face. Some theorists consider tics to be a compulsion or a form of conversion reaction. Others, including us, consider tics as a separate entity, since they may be caused by tension, maladaptive learning, or possibly by a dysfunction of the central nervous (Tourette's syndrome). The onset is usually between the ages of four and ten. Tics are much more frequent in boys, and spontaneous remission can occur, particularly at puberty. Examples of tics are shoulder hunching, head bobbing, eye blinking, grimacing, throat clearing, making various sounds, and grunting. For years, tics have been treated by traditional psychotherapy, since many theorists believe that unacceptable erotic and aggressive impulses are expressed through this symptom. Head shaking, for instance, has been viewed as a symbolic no to various perceived stresses. Eye blinking has been discussed as a refusal to see and accept painful situations and feelings. Hunching and arm

twitches are thought to be symbolic expressions of anger. Another belief is that tics are caused by tension, and a variety of tension-reducing methods have been used (behavior therapy or tranquilizing drugs). Today there is a growing tendency to view tics as a learned response that can be counter-conditioned. Antagonistic muscles can be trained to counteract the often strengthened muscles causing the tic.

Tourette's syndrome is included here because tics are its outstanding symptom, and inarticulate noises and words often develop. Rhythmic and purposeless tics occur anywhere from once to thousands of times per hour. Without treatment, the frequency of tics periodically diminishes or increases. Onset usually occurs between the ages of two and fourteen years. Some evidence suggests that Tourette's syndrome is organically caused by an impairment in the central nervous system. Others believe that evidence points to psychological causation, and they use only psychological forms of treatment, such as reinforcement of incompatible behavior, self-monitoring, and massed practice. Haloperidol is the drug most often reported as successful in treating Tourette's syndrome.

Eliminating Tics with Habit-Reversal

AUTHORS: Nathan H. Azrin and Robert G. Nunn

PRECIS: Practicing movements the opposite of the tic, increased awareness of the habit, and social approval for inhibition

INTRODUCTION: Azrin and Nunn discuss nervous habits and tics as being highly resistant to general types of treatment. Psychoanalytic treatment is based on the person's learning that repressed impulses cause the problem and expressing the impulses in some manner. Two kinds of treatment follow from the view that nervous habits are caused by tension. Negative practice requires the person to perform the tic rapidly, thereby preventing the tic from reducing tension. Tranquilizing relaxant drugs are used to directly reduce tension. Another view is that nervous habits are learned and maintained by operant reinforcement. Aversive stimuli are used to counteract the effect of the reinforcers. The authors' approach is based on the belief that the habit starts as a normal reaction, possibly to an extreme event such as physical injury or psychological trauma, or as an increased frequency in, or alteration of, normal behavior. The behavior is called a nervous habit when it persists after the trauma and has an unusual form and high frequency. If the movement blends into normal movement, it becomes automatic and escapes personal awareness (which ordinarily would inhibit the movement). For some tics, repeated movement strengthens some muscles and opposing muscles become weakened. The social reinforcement of sympathy strengthens the movements.

TREATMENT: Twelve clients, ages five to sixty-four years, were treated. All had been unsuccessfully treated by various professionals. The authors discuss a variety of habits, but we will focus here on the clients with tics. Two clients had a shoulder-jerking tic. One of them had an upward right-shoulder jerk, and the other's right shoulder jerked up and his elbow simultaneously jerked against his ribs. One client had a violent, jerky upward head movement.

Awareness training was accomplished by several methods. The client described the details of the movement, using a mirror if necessary, while reenacting the movement (Response Description Procedure). The client was alerted by the counselor when a tic occurred (Response Detection Procedure). The earliest sign of the habit movement was taught (Early Warning Procedure). Incompatible muscles were tensed (Competing Response Practice), and the client described the usual situations when the habit occurred (Situation Awareness Training).

The Competing Response Practice was used to strengthen behavior opposite the problem behavior. The responses were maintained for several minutes, tic muscles were tensed isometrically to heighten awareness, the responses were socially inconspicuous, and the antagonistic tic muscles were strengthened. The clients did the competing responses for about three minutes following tic temptation or occurrence. Competing responses followed each type of tic: shoulder jerking—shoulders depressed downward; shoulder jerking and elbow flapping—shoulders depressed down and hands pressed to sides; head jerking—neck tensed; head shaking—neck tensed.

Several procedures were used to increase a client's Habit Control Motivation. The counselor and the client reviewed the inconveniences, embarrassment, and suffering caused by the habit (Habit Inconvenience Review). To enhance the client motivation, family and close friends were asked to use Social Support Procedures. They praised his efforts and improved appearance and reminded him to practice his exercises. Also, the counselor telephoned periodically to praise the client's efforts to inhibit the habit. In the case of young, often uncooperative, children, parents and teachers guided them through exercises whenever they failed to exercise volitionally. Family and friends often saw tics as being neurologically caused and not subject to voluntary control. A Public Display Procedure was used where the family observed a demonstration of self-control during a counseling session. Afterward, the client and counselor informed friends, teachers, and so forth of the incidents of self-control.

Generalization Training was accomplished by showing the client (with instructions and practice) how to control the habit in everyday situations. A Symbolic Rehearsal Procedure was used to teach the client to be aware of the habit in many situations. He imagined common and habit-eliciting situations and pretended to detect the habit and perform the exercise. The list of situations was obtained from the previously described Situation Awareness Procedure. For a half hour the counselor had a casual conversation with the client in which the client was to detect the habit and do the competing exercise for three minutes while the conversation continued. If the client did not detect the habit, the counselor would stare at the limb or make a low sound to indicate habit occurrence.

For every client, the habit was reduced at least 90 percent, and for ten clients the habit was gone by the third week of treatment. Usually, only one counseling session occurred, and a five- to seven-month follow-up revealed that the average of 99 percent reduction achieved after three weeks was persisting. Clients and observers all reported that no new habit developed.

COMMENTARY: The habit reversal procedure appears to be a strikingly effective way to treat a variety of "nervous habits." It is quicker and more effective than negative practice, psychotherapy, or drugs. The analyses of the problem and the multiple methods used can serve as a model for any type of intervention. Using family and friends to reinforce progress and the generalization training are both powerful methods for enhancing progress and the performance of habit elimination. Training a competing response by exercise is an outstanding idea that may be employed with any type of inappropriate habitual movement.

SOURCE: Azrin, N. H., and Nunn, R. G. "Habit-Reversal: A Method of Eliminating Nervous Habits and Tics." *Behavior Research and Therapy*, 1973, *11*, 619-628.

Behavioral Treatment of Tourette's Syndrome

AUTHORS: Daniel M. Doleys and Paul S. Kurtz

PRECIS: Reducing jerking, guttural sounds, and compulsive swearing by reinforcing incompatible behaviors and enlisting the help of people in the community

INTRODUCTION: Doleys and Kurtz report that the literature contains no definitive treatment for behavioral tics or Tourette's syndrome. Success with drugs has led to theorizing an interaction of functional and organic factors. Recently, tics have been seen as learned responses or as operant responses (modified by changing the response consequences). Massed practice techniques and aversive stimuli have been used, but the improved behavior that resulted was seldom sustained in the natural environment. In this study, Doleys and Kurtz used tokens and social reinforcers to strengthen incompatible behavior. A fourteen-year-old boy had a five-year history of behavioral tics, including compulsive swearing (coprolalia) frequently accompanied by guttural sounds, arm jerking, and sticking his tongue out. He had a low rate of eye contact with people and generally poor social skills. Because of his behavior he was removed from school and lived on a farm with his family. The results of a neurological examination were normal. As had been found in similar cases, his tics occurred less frequently during manual or other competing activities. Reading or conversation increased tic frequency.

TREATMENT: The initial intervention focused on increasing eye contact and reducing jerking, guttural sounds, and coprolalia in the office setting. A special education teacher saw him in a small room. He had to place a block in a box when he heard music and remove a block when he heard noise. When all twenty blocks were in the box, he was given a choice of rewards. Music was played when eye contact, conversation, and fifteen seconds of no tics occurred. When he pressed a switch, the teacher would look at him for ten seconds. If he looked at the teacher, he heard music. Jerking, guttural sounds, or coprolalia resulted in the playing of white noise. After four weeks, he was taken to a restaurant for a soda reward for obtaining twenty blocks. Play dimes were used to reinforce appropriate behavior. A finger snap indicated the loss of a dime for inappropriate behavior. Other appropriate social interaction was rewarded, and play money was exchanged for material rewards. When he was speaking with the waitress, his disruptive behaviors increased, and as agreed beforehand, she politely left when tics occurred. He also received verbal reinforcement (and tokens) from parents and the waitress for appropriate behavior and neat appearance. After fourteen weeks, he was taken to a university student union, where he encountered a small group of students who had agreed to ignore disruptive behavior and pay attention to him for appropriate behavior. Treatment was terminated after five months.

The authors present detailed results. Reinforcing incompatible behaviors (conversation, reading, and so forth) and reinforcing the nonoccurrence of tics significantly reduced inappropriate behaviors at the clinic. Initially, public places caused an increase in vocal and body tics. But using reinforcement contingencies and people in a more natural environment led to the transfer of the behavioral changes.

COMMENTARY: Doleys and Kurtz do not see their success as either supporting or negating an organic basis for the tic syndrome. What is more important, they believe, is that behavioral procedures can reduce tics without the usual drug administration. The usefulness of their study lies in the detailed description of a reinforcement method and the enlisting of people in the community. Other procedures fail to promote the transfer of improved social behavior and reduced tics to the natural environment. Using community members to reinforce appropriate behavior (and ignore inappropriate behavior) is a significant contribution to the treatment of tics and should be employed to ensure generalization.

SOURCE: Doleys, D. M., and Kurtz, P. S. "A Behavioral Treatment Program for the Gilles de la Tourette Syndrome." *Psychological Reports,* 1974, *35,* 43-48.

Self-Monitoring for Tourette's Syndrome

AUTHORS: Robert R. Hutzell, Denna Platzek, and Patrick E. Logue

PRECIS: Self-observation, recording, role playing, and the reduction of head jerking and barking

INTRODUCTION: Gilles de la Tourette's syndrome consists of multiple motor tics and unprovoked loud utterances (barks) appearing during latency. During adolescence the barks become compulsive swearing (coprolalia). Hutzell, Platzek, and Logue report that the literature reveals only limited success in using psychological and pharmacological treatment. They describe a successful case using self-monitoring procedures, which they employed with an eleven-year-old boy, and include a follow-up (since short-term improvement can follow almost any type of treatment).

TREATMENT: The boy had developed a skipping motion while walking, a severe head jerk, and a barking noise. Haloperidol had been administered by previous therapists with some short-term effect, but the symptoms had continued. Positive reinforcement had also been used with no success. The authors' work with him focused on the head jerking and barking, both of which occurred frequently and very intensely. The boy was highly motivated for treatment, since he was very sensitive to the social embarrassment that resulted. Two therapists saw the boy twice a week for half-hour sessions. He was given a hand-held cumulative counter to record each head jerk. One therapist demonstrated his head-jerking behavior, and the boy was instructed to model the therapist. He then role played for two minutes by purposely jerking his head and recording each jerk. Following this, he played a simple game with the other therapist and was told to make as few head jerks as possible but to accurately record each jerk. After each five minutes (there were six five-minute intervals), the boy and the observer compared the number of head jerks each had counted. If the scores were equal, the boy was praised for his accuracy. Eight sessions were concentrated on the head jerking, and then ten sessions were devoted to the barking noises, using the same procedure.

In order to maximize generalization, the mother was taught the observing and recording techniques when therapy terminated. During therapy, the barking increased as the head jerking decreased. Then the barking decreased when he monitored it himself. Follow-up sessions held after one and a half, two and a half, and twelve months disclosed that the frequency of both behaviors had vastly diminished and remained very low both at the clinic and in the natural environment.

COMMENTARY: Self-monitoring is an efficient and useful procedure for greatly reducing tics and barking noises. One might speculate on the possibly increased efficiency and lower costs of training parents to use the methods described. Hutzell, Platzek, and Logue suggest that if motivation is not high, some form of external control may be necessary (such as "time out" punishment for habitual behavior). The sequence of instruction-demonstration-modeling-role playing is quite similar to effective methods used by learning theorists to reduce all types of habitual behaviors (see C. E. Schaefer and H. L. Millman, *Therapies for Children,* San Francisco: Jossey-Bass, 1977).

SOURCE: Hutzell, R. R., Platzek, D., and Logue, P. E. "Control of Symptoms of Gilles de la Tourette's Syndrome by Self-Monitoring." *Journal of Behavior Therapy and Experimental Psychiatry,* 1974, *5,* 71-76.

Controlling Tics by Maternal Reinforcement

AUTHOR: Michael Schulman

PRECIS: Nonreinforcement of tics by maternal ignoring, and a discussion of the role of family interaction

INTRODUCTION: Schulman discusses the behavioral treatment of tics in the therapist's office. Negative practice and using music as a reinforcer are described. Social contingencies were manipulated at home for a fourteen-year-old boy with a nine-year history of multiple tics. He had facial, arm, leg, and torso spasms along with grunts or shouts at times. Three tics a minute were observed when he was with his mother at calm periods. During a conflict with her, tics would occur at least fifteen times a minute, often in bursts of three or four tics. No medical abnormalities were discovered. The tics occurred almost exclusively in the mother's presence. The boy and his father related well, but he frequently fought with his mother. His younger brother's artistic talent had been recognized shortly before his tics had become more pronounced.

TREATMENT: The mother was told to totally ignore the tics (extinction procedure). She was warned that any attention would maintain or intensify the tics (partial reinforcement). Ignoring was difficult, since the mother's attention to the tics was part of the pattern of interaction with her husband. The author initiated family therapy, using contingency contracting, positive and differential reinforcement, and behavioral rehearsal. The parents kept records of the antecedents and consequences of tic occurrence. The boy, who was not told about the extinction procedure, continued to believe that the tics were caused physiologically.

The frequency, duration, and intensity of the tics progressively diminished. During the fifth week there were two tic-free days. Family relations were improving, with a much lower frequency of major arguments, but the parents terminated therapy against Schulman's advice. A two-month follow-up revealed more family conflicts, maternal attention to tics, and tics occurring at the midtreatment rate.

COMMENTARY: Schulman's article highlights two significant points. One is the efficacy and efficiency of reducing parental reinforcement by instructions to totally ignore all tics. Second, the role of the family interaction in tic maintenance is clearly seen. With only a brief intervention, a nine-year habit was virtually eliminated. But family conflicts and maternal reinforcement led to symptom recurrence. By altering the causes and consequences of tics and reducing family conflicts, the therapist probably can reduce or eliminate the symptoms. Even brief, focused family therapy may lead to more satisfying, less destructive, family interactions.

SOURCE: Schulman, M. "Control of Tics by Maternal Reinforcement." *Journal of Behavior Therapy and Experimental Psychiatry*, 1974, *5*, 95-96.

Additional Readings

Bruun, R. D., Shapiro, A. K., Shapiro, E., Sweet, R., Wayne, H., and Solomon, G. E. "A Follow-Up of Seventy-Eight Patients with Gilles de la Tourette's Syndrome." *American Journal of Psychiatry,* 1976, *133,* 944-947.

Seventy-eight patients with Tourette's syndrome, for whom psychotherapy alone had not resulted in any substantial improvement, received chemotherapy. The authors describe the clinical course of the syndrome afterward. At the initial evaluation, they rated severity ratings, from one (mild) to four (severe), of the patient. The authors found that the type of tic, the severity of symptoms, and the patient's history were not meaningful bases for prognosis. Having administered many other drugs with little positive effect, they consider haloperidol the most effective treatment, but many patients cannot tolerate the adverse side-effects.

Golden, G. S. "Tourette Syndrome: The Pediatric Perspective." *American Journal of Diseases of Children,* 1977, *131,* 531-534.

The clinical findings and the course of treatment are reported for fifteen children with Tourette's syndrome. Eye blinking was the most usual first sign, followed soon by tics and abnormal vocalizations. In all these cases the syndrome was not correctly diagnosed for several years because, as often happens, Tourette's was confused with childhood transient tics. Another reason for the delay was that physicians are reluctant to give a Tourette's diagnosis in the absence of echolalia or coprolalia—tics and a noise are seen as the minimum diagnostic criteria for Tourette's. Many of these children had school problems and "soft" neurological signs. Doses as low as one and a half milligrams a day of haloperidol were effective, with some increase necessary when symptoms recurred. Good or excellent results were achieved with three quarters of the children.

Rafi, A. A. "Learning Theory and the Treatment of Tics." *Journal of Psychosomatic Research,* 1962, *6,* 71-76.

Two adults were treated for tics (foot tapping and a spasmodic head movement, respectively). The tics were seen as conditioned avoidance responses that became reinforced. "Massed practice" was used twice a day; that is, the patients accurately produced the tic and repeated it without pause while being very attentive to the tic. Massed practice and strengthening an incompatible response were very successful in dramatically reducing foot tapping. The other patient achieved good results with the additional use of systematic muscle relaxation. He practiced fifteen to thirty minutes a day and used general muscle relaxation during the day.

Shapiro, A. K., Shapiro, E., Wayne, H. L., Clarkin, J., and Bruun, R. D. "Tourette's Syndrome: Summary of Data on Thirty-Four Patients." *Psychosomatic Medicine,* 1973, *35,* 419-435.

The authors present an extensive summary of characteristics and treatment. They view Tourette's syndrome as an organic impairment of the central nervous system. Detailed histories, interviews, and psychological testing results are described. There were four times as many males as females in the sample, a ratio consistent with that found in other studies. The age of onset was below twelve years for 91 percent of the patients. Useful tables give the first symptoms, the number of movements, and the ratings of central nervous system abnormalities (psychological, electroencephalogram, neurologic, and psychiatric indexes). The psychiatric ratings were based on organic indicators, such as hyperactivity, concrete thinking, perseveration, perception impairment, and clumsiness. Problems in differential diagnosis are reviewed. For patients taking haloperidol faithfully, the improvement rate was 85 percent after one month and more than 90 percent after one year. The dosage depends on the clinical response and must be individualized.

Thomas, E. J., Abrams, K. S., and Johnson, J. B. "Self-Monitoring and Reciprocal Inhibition in the Modification of Multiple Tics of Gilles de la Tourette's Syndrome." *Journal of Behavior Therapy and Experimental Psychiatry,* 1971, *2,* 159-171.

An eighteen-year-old male was treated for multiple tics, including barking and jerky neck and hand movements. His behavior was assessed and modified in a natural, rather than a laboratory, environment. A key technique was self-monitoring of the vocal tic by use of a quiet-lever counter. Later the patient also counted his neck movements. After a training period with an observer he was able to count his tics accurately. He learned to relax, too, and the therapist systematically desensitized him to tension-producing imagined scenes. With this treatment vocal tics decreased rapidly and significantly and then disappeared. The frequency of the neck tic also declined quickly, and although movements still occurred, they were almost unnoticeable. The patient was taking haloperidol, which probably contributed to tic reduction.

Tophoff, M. "Massed Practice, Relaxation, and Assertion Training in the Treatment of Gilles de la Tourette's Syndrome." *Journal of Behavior and Experimental Psychiatry*, 1973, *4*, 71-73.

A bright thirteen-year-old boy in three years had developed a complete Tourette's syndrome. He had motor tics (head jerking, finger in mouth), echolabia, a verbal tic ("eh"), and coprolalia. Haloperidol had no effect on the tic and resulted in drowsiness and parkinsonism. Similarly, supportive psychotherapy and progressive relaxation were not effective. What did work—it reportedly led to a complete recovery—was a combination of three things: massed practice twice weekly, thirty minutes per tic, for fourteen sessions; instructions to the parents to ignore the tic and thereby avoid inadvertent reinforcement; and the learning of assertive behavioral alternatives. Tophoff stresses the need to pay attention to social factors while massed practice is employed.

Yaryura-Tobias, J. A., and Neziroglu, F. A. "Gilles de la Tourette Syndrome: A New Clinico-Therapeutic Approach." *Progress in Neuro-Psychopharmacology*, 1977, *1*, 335-338.

Extensive medical, psychiatric, and psychological evaluations were made of twenty patients (ages five through fifty-two) with Tourette's syndrome. In all cases the onset had occurred in childhood; 89 percent had obsessive-compulsive symptoms, 75 percent showed aggressive behavior, 54 percent had abnormal oral glucose tolerance tests, and 36 percent had EEG abnormalities. Ten patients did not benefit from taking haloperidol. The tricyclic antidepressant chlorimipramine (25 to 350 mg.) was administered because of its efficacy with obsessive-compulsive symptoms. Within two to three weeks, chlorimipramine controlled 80 to 90 percent of Tourette's symptoms. In addition, this drug's low toxicity and relatively mild side-effects lead the authors to recommend it as an alternative to haloperidol. They conclude that this study supports previous work suggesting that Tourette's syndrome has organic causes along with a psychological component.

4

Central Nervous System Disorders

The brain and the spinal cord compose the central nervous system (CNS). The other part of the nervous system is the peripheral nervous system (PNS). Various nerves connect to the CNS through spinal and cranial nerves. All nerve impulses go to the CNS, which acts as an integrating and coordinating mechanism. The PNS has two divisions—the somatic nervous system, where the nerves go directly from the spinal cord to organs, and the autonomic nervous system, where ganglia are an intermediate between the spinal cord and the organs. The sympathetic (mobilizing) and parasympathetic (energy-conserving) systems make up the autonomic nervous system.

In this chapter, we are considering the functioning of the CNS. Hysterical somatic symptoms (paralysis, blindness, and so forth) can mimic symptoms of CNS damage. Of crucial importance is understanding the effect of any type of brain damage when one is trying to differentiate psychologically caused from organically caused symptoms. Subtle brain damage can cause impairments in intellectual, visual, auditory, motor, reading, writing, and calculating functions. Expressive and receptive language are often affected by chemical imbalances or lesions in the brain. The emerging field of neuropsychology is concerned with the most sophisticated assessment of the relationship between brain functioning and behavior. A detailed examination pinpoints performance deficits, which often indicate the probable area of brain dysfunction. Recent evidence points to two different (but integrated) systems in the brain: one regulating internal functions and the other receiving external information. Recognizing the various structures within the brain is essential, since the modern consensus is that these structures are dynamically interrelated and hence a focal lesion often affects total brain functioning.

In this book, we are concerned with the psychological problems that cause, or exaggerate, somatic disorders. Because of the interrelatedness of brain structures, tension and conflicts affecting any brain structure can lead to a variety of difficulties. For instance, prolonged stress can cause hypertension, which can lead to a stroke in a blood vessel supplying a specific area of the brain. Stress may also bring about some type of subtle chemical imbalance or electrical discharges within the brain, causing behavioral symptoms. In children with a constitutional predisposition to seizures, a relatively stable environment may preclude the appearance of seizures, whereas relatively stressful experiences may lead to their appearance and to the exaggeration of both their severity and frequency. Abnormal electrical discharges in the brain, called seizures, are covered in this chapter. In cases of severe epilepsy, electrodes implanted in the brain have been used to induce electrical excitation in a competing area. The discharge does not spread, and a seizure can thereby be prevented.

Seizures

We use the words seizures *and* epilepsy *synonomously.* Epilepsy *denotes disturbed electrical rhythms in the central nervous system typically manifested by convulsive attacks (often with clouding of consciousness). Sudden (paroxysmal) bursts of neuronal activity result from lesions or improper chemistry in the brain. These discharges may affect motor, sensory, or cognitive functions. Since* epilepsy *refers to a symptom complex and not a specific disease, one must find the cause whenever possible. An electroencephalogram is used to pinpoint the type of discharge and the affected area of the brain. Emotional stress has long been known to precipitate seizures, especially in cases of temporal lobe epilepsy. In hysterical convulsions (as opposed to epileptic seizures), the patient usually does not bite his tongue or injure himself; neither is there incontinence or an abnormal pupillary reaction to light. Seizures have been treated successfully with medication, traditional psychotherapy, psychophysiological desensitization, reward management (including operant conditioning), and cortical biofeedback. Approximately 25 percent of patients are refractory to medication. Recently, seizures have been conceptualized as the final link in a behavioral chain of events. By identifying and modifying preseizure behavior, the therapist can eliminate or reduce seizures. Roughly one out of every two hundred people has recurrent seizures.*

Behavior Therapy for Psychogenic Seizures

AUTHOR: James E. Gardner

PRECIS: Altering family reinforcement contingencies so that parental attention is given to appropriate behavior and not to inappropriate behavior such as seizures

INTRODUCTION: Gardner briefly reviews two views of psychopathology—that underlying disease causes a symptom or that neurotic or maladaptive learning is the cause. The former model uses insight or catharsis, and the latter focuses on relearning. Behavior therapy accomplishes relearning through manipulating environmental reinforcement contingencies, counterconditioning or extinction, or providing appropriate social role models. Gardner describes the direct manipulation of the environment of a ten-year-old girl with nonorganic seizures.

CASE STUDY: The girl, the oldest of three children, had an intense rivalry with her next youngest sister for parental attention. A few months before the onset of seizures, her mother may have provided a model of psychosomatic behavior by having a severe headache, rocking and banging in pain, and being taken to a hospital. The girl recently had many somatic complaints and several temper tantrums, one of which looked like a convulsion. One episode began with a stomach ache and became a headache accompanied by rhythmic head rolling and hair pulling. Her parents took her to a hospital, where physical tests, including an electroencephalogram, were negative or ambiguous. Psychological tests indicated a hysteric-type personality, with no severe emotional disturbance or neurological impairment. Seizure-inhibiting medication was not employed, and no counseling was used with the child. Instead, the parents were seen for three weekly one-hour sessions. The focus was on analyzing reinforcement contingencies and altering them so as to change the girl's deviant behavior. Instead of giving direct suggestions, the therapist encouraged the parents to develop or elaborate appropriate responses to their daughter. In effect, the psychologist shaped their behavior after presenting the behavioral principles involved. During the first session it was agreed that the parents would be deaf and dumb to any seizures or deviant behavior such as tantrums. Appropriate behavior, such as playing with siblings, helping her mother, and drawing, would be rewarded with parental attention. Any increased somatic complaints would receive the parental deaf-and-dumb response. During the next two sessions, the plan was refined and clarified.

Every other week for thirty weeks, telephone interviews took place. The frequency of the somatic complaints, tantrums, and seizures was recorded. The parents had estimated that before hospitalization, she had somatic complaints six to eight times a week and tantrums five to six times a week. Within two weeks of hospital discharge, the seizures disappeared and tantrums occurred about three times a week, stopping altogether after one month. Somatic complaints continued at a rate of about three per week. To demonstrate a functional relationship between seizures and parental attention and to distinguish between psychogenic and organic seizures, the psychologist asked the parents to again attend to the deviant behaviors. Within twenty-four hours, the child's problem behaviors occurred hourly. As agreed, the parents returned to the plan; the seizures disappeared, two tantrums occurred, and somatic complaints rose to seven a week (gradually returning to about three a week).

COMMENTARY: Gardner suggests that when the girl's somatic complaints increased, the parents may have become desensitized and did not pay attention to her. Dramatic behavior (such as hair pulling or convulsive behavior) did elicit serious parental attention. This case study illustrates the power of using parental attention in a strategic manner. Psychogenic seizures would be very responsive to this quick and economical method. Because of the link between feelings and the triggering of physiologically based seizures, this approach should diminish the frequency of such behavior. The parent can handle the child matter-of-factly, not paying undue attention after a seizure has occurred. This article illustrates a practical and useful approach to the gamut of psychosomatic disorders.

SOURCE: Gardner, J. E. "Behavior Therapy Treatment Approach to a Psychogenic Seizure Case." *Journal of Consulting Psychology,* 1967, *31,* 209-212.

Intensive Psychotherapy with Epileptic Children

AUTHOR: Louis A. Gottschalk

PRECIS: Eliminating, diminishing, and modifying the form of seizures through psychoanalytic psychotherapy

INTRODUCTION: Gottschalk first reviews the literature on the role of psychological factors in the elaboration or exacerbation of epilepsy. He then describes the psychotherapy of three children with "idiopathic epilepsy" as diagnosed neurologically. Studied was the possible modification by psychotherapy of the form and frequency of convulsions, since psychological factors were hypothesized. Also, the neurotic conflict of family members was hypothesized to affect convulsive frequency and form. (We discuss below two of the three cases.)

CASE STUDY I: A five-year-old boy was seen four times a week for 60 sessions and then three times a week, for a total of 140 sessions. The diagnosis was idiopathic epilepsy, with atypical and possible *petit mal* seizures and inhibited, infantile character disorder. When he was almost three, sudden explosive twitching and jerking of hands, arms, and face occurred daily (usually at nighttime), with or without loss of consciousness. Also occurring were frequent transient trancelike states, with brief disturbances of consciousness. Other problems included enuresis, night terrors, temper tantrums, and negativism. The administration of Dilantin (.03 gm. four times a day) and phenobarbital (.03 gm. three times a day) resulted in milder seizures but unchanged or worse behavior.

At the beginning of psychotherapy, movements such as speaking, eating, or excreting appeared to be associated with hurting or being hurt. He feared retaliation and loss of security. In his play, he showed a wish to be strong and powerful, and his play gradually became bolder. While shooting a dart gun he would become gleeful and then suddenly tense and anxious. Rhythmic hip movements and a need to urinate were seen by Gottschalk as his associating genital-urinary activities with injuring himself or someone else. During a three-month period, he displayed muscular jerks and, facial grimaces and then hand washing. Gottschalk reports that twitching and grimacing appeared immediately after paint smearing or cutting with scissors. Stuttering was diminished when his unexpressed emotion was openly dealt with. Acted out were such themes as wanting to marry his mother. He asked questions about childbirth and procreation, and these themes were worked through. A series of temper tantrums and a prolonged nocturnal *grand mal* seizure occurred at a time when his mother was discussing with a social worker her fear of injuring him. After five months of therapy and withdrawal of all anticonvulsive medication, the epileptic seizures stopped permanently. Enuresis, night terrors, feeding difficulties, and stuttering all reportedly stopped as well. Play and social relations with children improved.

CASE STUDY II: A ten-year-old boy was seen once a week for 100 sessions; therapy was ended when the therapist had to leave the city. The diagnosis was idiopathic epilepsy with frequent daily psychic or atypical seizures, occasional psychomotor fits, and very rare *grand mal* seizures in a hysterical character disorder. The various electroencephalograms reported disclosed paroxysmal discharges in the right parietal area and *petit mal* discharges. While looking through a screen (window screen or striped patterns on cloth), he stared and had uncoordinated, usually symmetrical, shaking of his arms like bird flapping. He usually stood and would rarely fall or bite his tongue. During these episodes, he could not be communicated with or recall what happened. The onset was at age five. At age ten, psychomotor seizures began in which for fifteen to thirty minutes he was very destructive—tearing clothing or breaking furniture. The few tonic and clonic *grand mal* seizures occurred during a "screen" spell. Gottschalk reports that at age five, the boy's mother turned to him for security because her husband had left for the army. She was inconsistently seductive and compulsively perfectionistic toward the boy. Anticonvulsive medication (bromides, phenobarbital, diphenylhydantoin, or trimethadione) had no effect on the frequency or form of the seizures.

After three months of therapy, the screen spells diminished and then stopped while psychomotor seizures increased. When he described to the therapist what he thought, felt, and did throughout the psychomotor seizures, the seizures soon disappeared. The therapist provided information to the boy about his behavior during these seizures. During therapy, he began to be more communicative and admitted to being terrified by his crazy and destructive thoughts. His usual submissiveness gave way to more assertive and spontaneous behavior. Screen spells could be averted if the therapist helped him formulate a question or reason for having unacceptable impulses. When therapy was discontinued, psychomotor seizures had stopped and screen spells occurred infrequently at home. His relationships with friends and his father had improved, but he had distressful feelings about his mother. One year later he had a few *grand mal* seizures while working during the summer.

Gottschalk hypothesizes that wishing to see or witnessing sexual intercourse between his parents was the origin of looking as the trigger for the screen spells. When he was between three and six years of age, his bedroom was separated from his parents' room by an open doorway partially blocked by a checkered screen. Gottschalk reports that the boy wanted to see women tortured and attributed magical and omnipotent powers to looking or being looked at.

COMMENTARY: Gottschalk reports a raising of the seizure threshold and a decrease in seizure frequency as a result of psychotherapy. A successfully treated adolescent is also described. This article is a good example of a psychoanalytic approach to seizure disorders. The material and the psychological pretesting and posttesting are quite detailed. Theoretically, the approach described (and therapy with the parents) would be applicable to all psychosomatic disorders.

SOURCE: Gottschalk, L. A. "Effects of Intensive Psychotherapy on Epileptic Children." *A.M.A. Archives of Neurology and Psychiatry,* 1953, *70,* 361-384.

Eliminating Epileptic Seizures by the Use of Relaxation and Conditioning

AUTHOR: Laurence P. Ince

PRECIS: Behavior modification as treatment for seizures when drug therapy has failed

INTRODUCTION: This case study illustrates how a behavioral technique may be employed for a problem that usually is treated in other ways. Ince describes a twelve-year-old boy who had had recurrent seizures of the *petit mal* and, to a lesser degree, the *grand mal* type over a four-year period. The child developed secondary psychological problems that further incapacitated him. He was fearful, overly sensitive, reluctant to attend school, and subject to psychosomatic complaints. Except for his epileptic disorder he behaved normally, did well academically, and was a good athlete. When first seen, he was receiving Dilantin and Mysoline, and later, Tegretol and Celontin were administered, none of which controlled his seizures.

TREATMENT: Therapy consisted of two phases: (1) the removal of anxiety, and (2) treatment for seizures. After talking with the boy, the therapist selected certain anxiety-producing situations to concentrate on. These included seizures in school, seizures on a baseball field, being ridiculed by other children, and receiving a new experimental medication. The therapist divided each situation into four or five scenes that aroused increasing anxiety in the child. During each treatment session, the boy imagined each scene in sequence until he could visualize the "final scene" without experiencing any anxiety. He was also trained in relaxation using a "pseudo-hypnotic suggestion tape recording." He listened to the tape at home twice a day in order to practice relaxing. It took two therapy sessions for complete relaxation and another five sessions over four and a half weeks to eliminate his anxiety. At this point the reduction of seizure activity was undertaken. He was given the word *relax* and told to associate this cue word with his relaxed body state. He practiced in the office and at home, saying "Relax" slowly to himself once he was deeply relaxed. He was also instructed to tell himself "Relax" repeatedly when he felt the approach of a seizure. He saw the therapist one hour a week for three months.

COMMENTARY: During the first four weeks of the treatment for anxiety there was no significant change in the seizure activity. But the seizures definitely decreased when therapy to reduce them began in the tenth week. The boy needed one visit to reinforce the treatment during weeks twenty-two to twenty-five while he was at a camp, and he needed to be reminded to practice relaxing at camp. There were no seizures from then on, and a nine-month follow-up after the termination of therapy showed no seizure activity. This article illustrates an alternative to drug treatment for seizures. Behavioral techniques may not work in all cases, but certainly they can be used as an adjunct to or replacement for drug therapy. Because seizures are rarely eliminated completely, these results are most encouraging. Striking is the *combination* of anxiety desensitization and deconditioning the seizure response.

SOURCE: Ince, L. P. "The Use of Relaxation Training and a Conditioned Stimulus in the Elimination of Epileptic Seizures in a Child: A Case Study." *Journal of Behavior Therapy and Experimental Psychiatry,* 1976, 7, 39-42.

Contributions of Psychology
in Treating Epilepsy

AUTHOR: David I. Mostofsky

PRECIS: The role of psychology in diagnosing, treating, and developing theories about epilepsy

INTRODUCTION: Mostofsky reviews some erroneous views of epilepsy—that it is genetically caused or accompanied by retardation, that patients swallow their tongues, and that treatment consists only of drugs or surgery. Scars, lesions, or improper chemistry cause a predisposition to sudden bursts of neuronal activity. However, lights, sounds, the time of day, stresses, and fears trigger seizures. Mostofsky sees a need to translate psychosomatic factors into intervention strategies.

INTERVENTION: When conventional medical treatment has resulted in limited success, behavior therapies and biofeedback training have proven effective. In diagnosis, Mostofsky states that it is imperative to assess the person's capacity for self-control and tolerance of stress. Four successful treatment modalities are reviewed: psychotherapy, reward management, psychophysiological procedures such as desensitization to trigger stimuli, and cortical biofeedback. Mostofsky provides an overview of basic treatment procedures, such as attaining an hour-by-hour, ten-week baseline and questioning the patient extensively. The patient can reveal the possible precursors of seizures and subjective reactions that would be helpful in designing an effective intervention. Eliminating mental health problems can often reduce seizure frequency as well as the need for medication. Mostofsky points out the need for people (siblings, parents, teachers, and so forth) to monitor, cue, and reward appropriate behaviors. By carefully describing successful treatment tactics, he believes, we can evolve a concept of epilepsy and discover which particular approach would be successful.

COMMENTARY: Mostofsky's article serves as a good overview for the practitioner. He stresses the need to appreciate the complexity of epileptic disorders, using the suitably complex term *psychoneuropharmacobiosociophysiological syndrome* to describe them.

SOURCE: Mostofsky, D. I. "Epilepsy: Returning the Ghost to Psychology." *Professional Psychology*, 1978, *9*, 87-92.

Psychobiological Control of Seizures

AUTHORS: David I. Mostofsky and Barbara A. Balaschak

PRECIS: An exhaustive review of specific behavioral intervention methods for seizures

INTRODUCTION: Mostofsky and Balaschak see the emergence of behavioral medicine in the context of the increasing success of classical psychotherapy and behavior therapies in remediating many central and autonomic nervous system dysfunctions. They review all the known published reports on behavioral treatment programs for reducing the frequency or severity of epileptic seizures. Although researchers and clinicians use a variety of often overlapping techniques, Mostofsky and Balaschak use their own classification system to describe therapeutic procedures. They present many cases, involving both children and adults, in great detail.

TREATMENT:
    A. Reward Management
        1. Denial of reward—the seizure is ignored and therefore extinguished; care, concern, or attention does not follow seizure occurrence. The authors also discuss covert extinction—patients imagine having seizures to which no one pays any attention.
        2. Penalty—the patient enters a time-out room or closed ward where there is no access to reinforcement immediately after having a seizure. Other penalties are the denial of visits or off-ground privileges, eating meals with others, recesses, favorite games or activities, and so forth. Therefore, rewards become contingent on the reduction of seizures.
        3. Relief—negative stimuli (shocks, putrid medicines) are administered and continued until seizures are reduced. This method has been used for reducing clinical seizures and electrical spike-and-wave paroxysms of the brain.
        4. Punishment—seizures are immediately followed by a noxious stimulus, such as shouting at the patient, using over-

correction, administering an electric shock, or presenting an uncomfortable noise or flash of light. In one case the authors describe, an unpleasant odor was used to eliminate long-standing seizures in a woman who, after pairing two stimuli, learned to control all seizures by thinking alone. Electric shock successfully eliminated hundreds of seizures per day in a five-year-old retarded boy. Overcorrection helped a three-year-old whose head rolling preceded *petit mal* episodes. For two minutes his head was moved in various positions by an adult. Mostofsky and Balaschak consider punishment and overcorrection very useful in cases of self-stimulated seizures.

5. Overt reward—rewards, praise, or tokens are given for seizure-free periods or for significantly fewer seizures during a specific time interval. The criterion time is gradually extended to several hours or days. On seizure-free days, time to talk with a therapist has been used as a reward. The authors describe a nine-year-old girl who was told to talk to the teacher when anxious; this talking thus provided an alternative to seizures. Verbal praise and candy have also been used successfully as rewards. In another case a reward (root beer) was given, but time-outs (being put to bed after a seizure) was also used. For a fourteen-year-old girl, reinforcers were used for nonepileptic falling. Her rewards were going home for a weekend, playing cards, using a tape recorder, and having soft drinks and candy.

6. Covert reward—the patient imagines scenes while relaxed and then is told to imagine rewards or no rewards for non-seizure behavior or seizure-provoking behavior, respectively. In one case, a female adult imagined scenes of having a seizure to which no one paid attention. Additionally, she was taught to stop her worrisome thoughts by saying a sharp "Stop" to herself. Very important was having all the people in her life completely ignore her seizure episodes so that reinforcement did not occur and so extinction would take place.

B. Self-Control

7. Relaxation—progressive muscle relaxation is taught, and the patient induces relaxation when stress or preseizure behavior occurs.

8. Desensitization/Hypnosis—while relaxed, the pa-

tient visualizes or thinks of seizure-provoking scenes. Deep muscle relaxation led to an improved mood, attention span, and physical appearance in an adult male. Traditional anxiety hierarchies were constructed for him and presented twice a week for fifteen weeks; this procedure completely eliminated multiple daily seizures.

9. Traditional (Dynamic) Psychotherapy—in group or individual therapy the patient learns to understand and resolve underlying anxieties and conflicts. The authors describe in detail three children who were successfully treated by psychoanalytically oriented psychotherapy. Another case concerns the use of video-replay with five adults. These patients viewed their seizures and had therapeutic interviews in which they developed a "conscious awareness of the association between the specific emotional stimulus and the seizure."

10. Self-Control—techniques are often developed by the patients to help them prevent, diminish, or stop seizures. For instance, patients shake their head vigorously, talk themselves out of having a seizure, tell the seizure to go away, make arm movements, and remain motionless.

11. Habituation or Extinction—when seizures are triggered by a sensory stimulus, the stimulus is presented below threshold and the frequency or intensity is gradually increased until the stimulus no longer provokes a seizure. The authors review many cases in which seizures induced by various visual and auditory stimuli (including music-induced seizures) were treated successfully.

12. Biofeedback—when patients create a particular electric pattern or wave form, they are either punished or rewarded (a light or sound appears or concrete rewards are given). For example, an eighteen-year-old female was successfully taught to relax and given both EMG and EGG (alpha) training, resulting in significantly fewer seizures and less apprehension. A nine-year-old girl responded very well to photic stimulation (a five-second burst of light at a flash rate of 3.5 c./sec.), which she described as mildly unpleasant. When her EEG indicated paroxysmal activity, photic stimulation was immediately administered. The authors discuss many other cases as well.

OTHER PROMISING TECHNIQUES:

A. Overcorrection—for seizures self-induced by hand waving, a child stands with eyes closed and tenses and relaxes his fist sixty times.

B. Palliative strategies—patients control their seizures by learning to have them at particular times (such as during sleep) or in particular places (such as in bed).

C. Flooding—extinction is achieved by repeatedly evoking the seizure response in the presence of nonreward. Mostofsky and Balaschak recommend this for *petit mal* but not for *grand mal* seizures.

COMMENTARY: Mostofsky and Balaschak provide an invaluable service in this article by exhaustively reviewing the literature concerning seizure control. In addition, they call for more consistent methods and a reporting system that would lead to uniformity and clarity in the field. They suggest that future studies include a description of the patient, the symptoms and diagnosis, the etiology and form (time of onset and duration), EEG data, the medication given, the location of treatment, all baseline data, all trigger stimuli, the aura (the subjective sensation of the patient that often precedes the seizure) the treatment procedure and schedule, a description of the therapist, the results and follow-up data, and comments and conclusions. This overview, in recognizing that multiple approaches to seizure disorders can be taken, strongly supports the purpose of our handbook.

SOURCE: Mostofsky, D. I., and Balaschak, B. A. "Psychobiological Control of Seizures." *Psychological Bulletin,* 1977, *84,* 723-750.

EEG Feedback Training to Reduce Seizures

AUTHORS: A. R. Seifert and J. F. Lubar

PRECIS: Visual feedback of appropriate sensorimotor rhythm and epileptiform brain activity

INTRODUCTION: Seifert and Lubar review the successful operant conditioning of various electroencephalogram frequencies. They point out the efficacy in seizure control of reinforcing the 12-14 Hz. frequency range (the range characteristic of what is called the sensorimotor rhythm). Details are presented concerning research using different types of equipment. They used an analog and digital processing system capable of precisely indicating 12-14 Hz. activity and of not responding when this activity is accompanied by slow waves, epileptiform spikes, or gross movements.

TREATMENT: Six epileptic adolescents were treated. They had varying degrees of mental retardation, and their seizures were not well controlled by high levels of anticonvulsant medication. Baselines were established for the emission of 12-14 Hz., and each adolescent received three forty-minute training sessions a week. They were told to keep the green light on—which indicated slow wave amplitude. A digital display showed a running count of criteria met per minute. The history and problems of the three boys and three girls are described in detail. They ranged in age from twelve to nineteen and had from thirty-two to fifty-four training sessions. Five showed significant reductions of seizures during the first three months. The youngest, age twelve, did not show a reduction in seizures. He was afraid of being alone in the experimental room and had great difficulty paying attention to the task.

COMMENTARY: Seifert and Lubar suggest that 25 percent of epileptics have seizures that are not well controlled by drugs. This training offers a method that could lead to their ability to control their seizures. Most promising would be a combination of biofeedback training, interrupting behavioral chains, and reinforcement methods.

SOURCE: Seifert, A. R., and Lubar, J. F. "Reduction of Epileptic Seizures Through EEG Biofeedback Training." *Biological Psychology,* 1975, *3,* 157-184.

Interrupting Preseizure Behavior

AUTHORS: Steven Zlutnick, William J. Mayville, and Scott Moffat

PRECIS: Reducing the frequency of epileptic seizures by identifying and modifying preceding seizure behavior

INTRODUCTION: The authors review research in which seizures were eliminated or reduced by conditioning procedures, such as presenting eliciting stimuli until extinction occurred. They discuss how to apply consequences to behaviors (headaches, spasms, and so forth) that reliably precede seizures. Seizures are viewed by them as the terminal link in a chain of behaviors. In their own study they employed two operant procedures—contingent interruption and reinforcement of behavior incompatible with seizures. The interruption method consisted of shouting "No!" loudly and shaking the child vigorously.

TREATMENT: The authors discuss the cases of five children, providing the baseline data and measurable outcomes of their research, including information on a reversal phase in which the experimental contingencies were removed. In the following digest, only treatment strategies are presented.

A seven-year-old boy received eight one-quarter-grain tablets of Dilantin daily and still averaged twelve seizures a day. Two preseizure behaviors were identified—a fixed gaze at a flat surface and subsequent bodily rigidity. Violent shaking (myoclonic spasms) followed, and he fell to the floor. The fixed stare was observed to precede every seizure. School staff members used the interruption procedure whenever visual fixation occurred. No consequences were applied once the seizure occurred. When this procedure was used, seizures only occurred when staff members were unable to interrupt the staring within ten to fifteen seconds. The method immediately diminished the frequency of seizures, and seizures stopped after seven weeks. During this period the medication was reduced until none was being given at the end of seven weeks of treatment. Spontaneous generalization occurred at home and in the community: the staring and seizures diminished and finally stopped.

Various anticonvulsive medications were unsuccessfully used with a four-year-old moderately retarded boy with epilepsy of the minor motor type. Two types of seizures occurred: decreased activity, followed by sudden flexion of arms and head; and twenty to thirty seconds of vacant staring, terminated by brief vomiting. The boy's mother used the interruption method when she observed the lowered activity level. In school, interruption was used at the onset of vacant staring. As a result, flexion episodes and vomiting were reduced. However, vacant staring was unaffected, and the authors speculate that this is a seizure in itself and not preseizure behavior.

In spite of anticonvulsive medication, a four-year-old brain-damaged boy with reduced dexterity on the left side averaged twelve seizures a day. A difficult-to-define, subtle behavior change was followed by sudden flexion of the arms and head. His mother used the interruption method when she perceived the subtle behavior change, quickly reducing the number of seizures to six or seven per day. Follow-up data were not available.

A fourteen-year-old girl had had seizures since eighteen months of age. She raised her right arm parallel to her head, a movement that was always followed by myoclonic jerking and vacant staring. The diagnosis was epilepsy of the minor motor and focal types. With medication, seizures still occurred usually twice daily, much more often during menstrual periods. The severity and regularity of the seizures had led to home tutoring instead of school attendance. As treatment, her mother employed the interruption procedure. After six months, the seizure frequency was far below the baseline level. Reportedly, the method was later used sporadically, and consequently the frequency returned to the baseline rate.

Despite large doses of Dilantin and phenobarbital, a seventeen-year-old mentally retarded female with major motor epilepsy had multiple daily seizures. Her body became tense and rigid, she clenched her fists and raised her arms at a ninety-degree angle, her head snapped back and she grimaced, and a major motor seizure followed. She was treated at a training center. Instead of an interruption procedure, differential reinforcement was used. As soon as she raised her arms, they were placed back down, and after five seconds she was praised and given candy for having her arms lowered. This resulted in an almost total elimination of seizures. A nine-month follow-up revealed a near zero level of seizures, even though the procedure had not been used during that period.

COMMENTARY: Recently there has been a great deal of interest in the application of methods derived from the behavioral sciences to medical problems. This article highlights how environmental manipulation can affect organically caused seizures. The authors point out how parents and nonprofessionals can easily carry out the procedures. Indeed, the concept of behavioral chains may be as useful in analyzing and treating other psychosomatic disorders. One inference drawn by the authors is that a procedure more intense than saying "Stop!" and shaking the child might produce even more dramatic results.

SOURCE: Zlutnick, S., Mayville, W. J., and Moffat, S. "Modification of Seizure Disorders: The Interruption of Behavioral Chains." *Journal of Applied Behavior Analysis*, 1975, *8*, 1-12.

Additional Readings

Adams, K. M., Klinge, V., and Keiser, T. W. "The Extinction of a Self-Injurious Behavior in an Epileptic Child." *Behavior Research and Therapy*, 1973, *11*, 351-356.

A case history is presented of a fourteen-year-old girl with *grand mal* and *petit mal* epilepsy. She was admitted to the hospital neurology service because of increased seizure frequency, a choreoathetotic gait, and severe bruises due to frequent falling episodes. Detailed are the behavioral diagnosis and the treatment designed to eliminate nonepileptic falling. Rewards and punishments were planned, carried out, and always explained to the girl. Extinction occurred, and after six weeks of treatment, no further falls occurred. Appropriate alternative behaviors were positively reinforced.

Anthony, J., and Edelstein, B. A. "Thought-Stopping Treatment of Anxiety Attacks Due to Seizure-Related Obsessive Ruminations." *Journal of Behavior Therapy and Experimental Psychiatry*, 1975, *6*, 343-344.

A twenty-four-year-old woman had obsessive fears of having a seizure even though medication had eliminated all seizures for two years. She had had a seizure following an anxiety attack, and her ruminations resulted in palpitations, nausea, and vomiting. The therapist told her to record all information regarding any anxiety attack for two weeks and then taught her thought stopping. The therapist interrupted overt, and then covert, thoughts of having a seizure in a public place. The patient overtly, and then covertly, interrupted covert thoughts. Pleasant imagery followed each thought stopping. She practiced twice a day and initiated the procedure at the onset of any obsessive ruminations. By the fifth week she could successfully eliminate any obsessive worries.

Balaschak, B. A. "Teacher-Implemented Behavior Modification in a Case of Organically Based Epilepsy." *Journal of Consulting and Clinical Psychology*, 1976, *44*, 218-223.

A teacher used a contingency-management program to significantly reduce seizures in a very dependent eleven-year-old girl. In spite of receiving Dilantin and phenobarbital, she had been having an average of three seizures a week in school. New or anxiety provoking situations (especially rejection and criticism) often triggered seizures. The treatment goals were to reduce seizure frequency and increase self-initiated, independent behavior. Rewards of candy and praise were given for a seizure-free week at school. Balaschak states that the behavioral program led to dramatic improvement, although later the seizure rate returned to that of the baseline period. The author cites environmental reasons (wearing a helmet and taking medication, which may have led her to doubt the effectiveness of her self-control procedures) for this return.

Balaschak, B. A. "Behavior Modification with Epileptic Children: Preliminary Case Reports." Paper presented at the meeting of the American Psychological Association, Washington, D.C., August 1976.

Two eleven-year-old boys and a ten-year-old girl were successfully treated for seizures. A diagnostic method (Child's Pre-Treatment Questionnaire) was developed in order to ascertain the child's perceptions and feelings concerning his or her seizures. Additionally, a Seizure Disorder Survey Schedule was administered to parents in order to have a standardized record of seizure history. The behavior modification techniques of rewards and time-outs were successful, whereas medication had not reduced seizures. The rewards used included praise for non-seizure periods and weekly rewards (candy, movie attendance). Either seizures were ignored or time-outs were used. (A time-out for blinking consisted of having to stand up, close the eyes, and count to sixty.) Parents, teachers, and hospital staff members were able to reduce the seizure frequency, and medication was reduced.

Cabral, R. J., and Scott, D. F. "Effects of Two Desensitization Techniques, Biofeedback and Relaxation, on Intractible Epilepsy: Follow-up Study." *Journal of Neurology, Neurosurgery, and Psychiatry,* 1976, *39,* 504-507.

Three young female adults were treated for intractible epilepsy and associated anxiety and phobic symptoms. One had *petit mal* and *grand mal* seizures; the second, *petit mal* seizures only; and the third, psychomotor seizures. During three months of biofeedback training, the patients learned to produce the alpha rhythm with their eyes closed. For another three-month period, Jacobsonian muscle relaxation was taught. The patients were then systematically desensitized to anxiety-provoking images (related to their anxiety and phobias). Relaxation lowered the heart rate by 15 percent, while biofeedback increased alpha activity from approximately twenty-two to sixty-four alpha waves in a two-minute interval. Both forms of desensitization led to behavioral and EEG improvement, which was maintained during the subsequent fifteen-month follow-up period.

Daniels, L. K. "Treatment of *Grand Mal* Epilepsy by Covert and Operant Conditioning Techniques." *Psychosomatics,* 1975, *16,* 65-67.

Thought stopping, covert reinforcement, and operant conditioning were used to successfully eliminate *grand mal* seizures in a twenty-two-year-old female. Deep muscle relaxation was used to countercondition the anxiety responses that preceded a convulsion. Thought stopping was used to inhibit the nausea present as an aura. After saying "Stop," she was taught to imagine relaxing and safe scenes. She earned points and a backup reward for not having a seizure, for taking medication, and for other socially appropriate behaviors. Her seizures were eliminated and vast social improvement resulted, but later the seizures resumed when stressful life situations occurred. Using successful strategies and improving her environment reduced these renewed seizures to rare occurrences.

Feldman, R. G., and Paul, N. L. "Identity of Emotional Triggers in Epilepsy." *Journal of Nervous and Mental Disease,* 1976, *162,* 345-353.

Some adults who had long suffered from a partial epilepsy with complex psychomotor symptoms managed to decrease their seizures significantly when the emotional triggers of the seizures were identified and controlled. In exploratory interviews the therapist first determined the seizure patterns and stressful stimuli. Then he selected and played "stimulated recall" audiotape recordings of stressful conversations to elicit clinical seizures. In the self-confrontation portion of the treatment, the patient watched videotapes of his listening to the audiotape and then having a seizure. This procedure made him aware of responses ordinarily forgotten because of ictal amnesia. Thereafter periodic reminders and viewing of the videotapes alerted the patient and led to his ability to avoid the emotional response that brought on a seizure.

Finley, W. W. "Operant Conditioning of the EEG in Two Patients with Epilepsy: Methodological and Clinical Considerations." *Pavlovian Journal*, 1977, *12*, 93-111.

Seizure reduction in a thirteen-year-old boy and a twenty-four-year-old man was achieved with sensorimotor rhythm biofeedback. The boy experienced eighty to one hundred akinetic seizures a day, lasting from twenty seconds to thirty minutes. An ultra-sharp band-pass filter and the use of epileptiform inhibit and feedback circuitry were developed. Monetary rewards and noncontingent feedback and reinforcement were used as control techniques. The man, a psychomotor epileptic, also benefited from sensorimotor training (operant conditioning of 11-14 Hz. electroencephalogram activity). The detailed tables and technical advances presented illustrate the anticonvulsant potential of long-term sensorimotor training.

Green, S. A. "A Case of Functional Sleep Seizures." *Journal of Nervous and Mental Disease*, 1977, *164*, 223-227.

Green describes functional nocturnal seizures in an eighteen-year-old male and views conversion reactions as communications about unacceptable feelings or wishes. In spite of hospitalization and totally normal medical findings, the boy continued to have nightly seizurelike episodes. Phenobarbital was not effective, and he was completely unresponsive to psychotherapy. He blamed others and accepted no personal responsibility for his problems. He frightened and controlled people by being aloof during the day and by having temper tantrums while asleep. The conversion symptom served to communicate rage.

Lewis, D. O. "Delinquency, Psychomotor Epileptic Symptoms, and Paranoid Ideation: A Triad." *American Journal of Psychiatry*, 1976, *133*, 1395-1398.

Lewis stresses the need to examine delinquent children for the possible presence of psychomotor epilepsy. In two years, eighteen children referred to a juvenile court were found to have psychomotor epileptic symptoms (the loss of fully conscious reality contact—characterized by blackouts, staring episodes, falling—and auras: funny sensations, visual distortions, dizziness). Paranoid thoughts were found in sixteen of the eighteen children. They had such delusions as being persecuted, whispered about, attacked, and stalked by a murderer. Because of their aggressiveness, they often responded to these imagined threats. Serious head trauma had been experienced by fifteen of the children. Lewis discusses the auditory and visual misperceptions, the fluctuating accuracy of perceptions, and the anxiety that precedes psychomotor seizures. This perception of an unpredictable, threatening, and anxiety-provoking world may lead to paranoid thinking and behavior.

Parrino, J. J. "Reduction of Seizures by Desensitization." *Journal of Behavior Therapy and Experimental Psychiatry,* 1971, 2, 215-218.

Grand mal seizures in a thirty-six-year-old man progressively decreased and then ceased after he was desensitized to several anxiety hierarchies. Before this treatment he had poor recent memory, several *grand mal* seizures, right-sided twitches and loss of balance, and a diffusely abnormal electroencephalogram with questionable temperoparietal spikes. Anticonvulsive medication had had no effect on seizure activity or other symptoms. In general, his daily rate of seizures was directly related to his level of anxiety. The anxiety-provoking situations that triggered seizures included socializing, interacting with authority figures, initiating conversation, and mention of family-related material. Deep muscle relaxation and the anxiety-hierarchy technique were employed twice a week. Seizures were gradually eliminated, and the form of the seizures changed from gross motor movements to ticlike mannerisms. On follow-up he was seizure-free without any medication.

Roussounis, S. H., and Rudolf, N. de M. "Clonazepam in the Treatment of Children with Intractable Seizures." *Developmental Medicine and Child Neurology,* 1977, 19, 326-334.

A new benzodiazepine derivative, clonazepam, was administered to twenty-two children (ages five months to fourteen years) with seizures, mainly of the minor motor type. The dosage was .025-1 mg./kg. daily. A 90 percent reduction in seizures was seen in seven patients and a 50 percent reduction occurred for fourteen patients.

Roy, A. "Hysterical Fits Previously Diagnosed as Epilepsy." *Psychological Medicine,* 1977, *7,* 271-273.

Roy distinguished seventeen adults with "hysterical fits" from a matched group of seventeen epileptic patients. Five factors are suggested as aiding this discrimination. Hysterical patients showed a family and personal history of psychiatric disorder, attempted suicide, and sexual maladjustment and currently demonstrated an affective syndrome. Staff members observed the attacks, slowly removed anticonvulsant drugs, and serially recorded EEGs. Several patients had attacks while the EEG was recording, and there was an absence of any epileptic abnormality on the EEG.

Russman, B. S. "Convulsive Seizures in Infancy and Childhood." *Pediatric Annals,* 1976, *5,* 39-54.

Russman presents a very useful, practical guide for pediatricians in diagnosis and treating seizures. Information is presented in tabular form, with such headings as "Acute Management of Seizures" and "Etiology of Seizures." Laboratory procedures are described and definitions are given for *grand mal,* focal, psychomotor, *petit mal,* and minor motor (akinetic and myoclonic) seizures. The diagnosis of paroxysmal behavior must differentiate it from hysterical seizures, syncopal attacks (fainting), breath holding, sleep disturbances (night terrors, sleep walking and talking), and migraine headaches. The need for follow-up care is discussed, especially in view of the high percentage of epileptic children who have learning problems.

Sterman, M. B., and Macdonald, L. R. "Effects of Central Cortical EEG Feedback Training on Incidence of Poorly Controlled Seizures." *Epilepsia,* 1978, *19,* 207-222.

Eight adult patients with mixed seizure patterns were given EEG feedback training with reward contingencies. Significant and sustained seizure reductions occurred in six patients using 12-15 or 18-23 Hz. in the absence of 6-9 Hz. In five patients the maximum seizure reductions occurred after at least six months of training. Protection against abnormal discharge may be achieved through enhancing normal EEG patterns by rewarding 12-15 Hz. Rewarding 18-23 Hz. activity may increase normal discharge along reticulocortical pathways, which desynchronizes abnormal cellular recruitment. Sterman sees EEG normalization as explaining the therapeutic effects of various feedback studies.

Wells, K. C., Turner, S. M., Bellack, A. S., and Hersen, M. "Effects of Cue-Controlled Relaxation on Psychomotor Seizures: An Experimental Analysis." *Behavior Research and Therapy,* 1978, *16,* 51-53.

Cue-controlled relaxation has been successfully used for treating test anxiety, public-speaking anxiety, snake phobia, and epileptic seizures in a thirteen-year-old boy. A twenty-two-year-old woman was having two to eight psychomotor seizures a day, in spite of her daily ingestion of one thousand milligrams of Tegretol, two milligrams of Clonapin, and two and a half milligrams of Prolixin three times a day. Cue-controlled relaxation involved teaching her muscle relaxation and saying "Relax" twenty-five times during exhalation. While she clearly imagined situations involving preseizure auras, the therapist said "Relax" until a deep state of relaxation was again achieved. Whenever auras occurred, she was instructed to use the cue word "Relax." The frequency of seizures fell gradually, and follow-up revealed no seizure activity for three months.

Whitehouse, D. "Behavior and Learning Problems in Epileptic Children." *Behavioral Neuropsychiatry,* 1976, *7,* 23-29.

Objective neurological and psychological evaluations of two hundred children were performed to clarify the nature of behavioral and learning problems in children with seizure disorders (*grand mal,* psychomotor, *petit mal,* minor motor, akinetic, myoclonic, and convulsive equivalents). Detailed neurological and psychological test data are reported, including electroencephalogram recordings. Significant learning defects were found in 70 percent of the children, requiring special educational placement, and 30 percent had minor learning problems causing difficulties in regular classes. Tables are presented describing the IQ distribution by the type of seizure disorder. Like children with learning disabilities without seizures, many of these children showed the dyscontrol syndromes of hyperactivity, attentional difficulties, and emotional lability. Learning problems require corrective educational procedures, not just medication. Whitehouse states that medication combining stimulant drugs with anticonvulsants is effective for minimal brain dysfunction. Phenobarbital may aggravate behavioral syndromes and mephobarbital or primidone can be substituted. Counseling for parents and teachers should be similar to that successfully used with children with central nervous system dysfunctions without seizures.

Wright, L. "Aversive Conditioning of Self-Induced Seizures." *Behavior Therapy*, 1973, *4*, 712-713.

A significant decrease in self-induced seizures (trancelike states) was achieved with a five-year-old retarded boy. He induced several hundred seizures a day by waving his hand before his eyes or blinking while looking at a light. Every time he waved his hand, an electroshock was administered to his thigh by a ninety-volt battery connected to a potentiometer for adjusting voltage. Conditioning was given for five one-hour sessions over three days. After the third session, he never again waved his hand to induce a seizure. The same method was used to condition blinking, which was inducing 407 seizures an hour. The seizures gradually decreased from 175 on the first day to 36 on the fourth day. Conditioning resulted in greater alertness, better cognitive functioning, and improved interpersonal relations. Follow-up revealed no hand-waving seizures, and the blinking seizures had decreased to 10 percent of the base-rate frequency. Later he received medication, which produced drowsiness, poorer interpersonal behavior, and more seizures.

5

Respiratory System Disorders

A discussion of those psychosomatic disorders in children centered in the respiratory system is essentially a discussion of asthma. Not only is asthma the most prevalent disorder that may be considered psychosomatic in this system, it is the leading cause of chronic physical illness during childhood and consequently has received a great deal of attention from researchers over the years.

Asthma is a *reversible* respiratory disorder found in 5 to 10 percent of children and is characterized by hyperactivity of the airways in response to a variety of stimuli. The three essential aspects of the reaction include constriction of the smooth-muscle lining of the large and small airways, edema of the mucosal lining of the bronchial tree, and the excessive accumulation of thickened secretions in the airways. The resulting symptom is increasing respiratory distress due principally to difficulty in exhaling air trapped in the hyperinflated lungs by the obstructive process.

The variety of stimuli that can trigger these changes is extensive and includes specific allergens, irritant fumes, smoke, strong odors, cold air, and strenuous exercise. B. B. Wolman, J. Egan, and A. O. Ross, the editors of a *Handbook of Treatment of Mental Disorders in Childhood and Adolescence* (Englewood Cliffs, N.J.: Prentice-Hall, 1978, p. 180), state that skin testing and history can only account for specific allergens triggering asthma attacks in 60 percent of the cases. A. U. Khan, after reviewing much of the literature on the subject, concluded that "there is a subgroup of asthmatics, as high as 50 percent, which is quite suggestible, essentially nonallergic, and in which emotions rank high among the precipitants of asthmatic attacks" ("Present Status of Psychosomatic Aspects of Asthma," *Psychosomatics,* 1973, *14,* 195-200).

The usual management of asthma involves therapy specifically aimed at counteracting the abnormal reaction of the respiratory tract. Medications such as epinephrine and theophylline are injected to produce bronchodilation. Metaproterenol, isoproterenol, and other potential bronchodilators are introduced into the respiratory tract to work directly on the lining cells. Steroids are occasionally used in more severe cases to help control the allergic reaction and to reduce the amount of edema in the mucosal lining. Expectorants and copious amounts of water are employed to help loosen and mobilize secretions. More recently medications like cromolyn sodium have been added and used to attempt to prevent the initial reactions.

Despite the numbers and variety of medications available to the physician for treating asthma, it still continues to be a major health problem, responsible for significant morbidity and mortality and the cause of one quarter of all school absences due to chronic conditions (E. F. Ellis, "Asthma," in M. Green and R. J. Haggerty (Eds.), *Ambulatory Pediatrics II,* Philadelphia: W. B. Saunders, 1977, p. 325). This situation has no doubt been responsible for stimulating the large amount of research being conducted into alternative treatments for childhood asthma. Much of this work has come out of residential treatment facilities such as the one in Denver, for it is in these centers that the most intractable cases are found—those who have not been adequately controlled with any of the drug measures currently available.

Investigations into the psychological characteristics of the asthmatic have resulted in confusing information. Many people still question whether the abnormalities noted are the primary causes of asthma or are, in fact, secondary results of the condition. A recurrent theme is that childhood asthmatics suffer from a fear of separation from the mother. In effect the child learns early in life that an asthma attack brings him or her closer to his or her mother and helps to relieve the fear. This theory led to the practice of removing the child from the parent ("parentectomy") as a therapeutic technique. The reasoning is that once the child is away from the parent, the fear and anxiety will no longer be operating. This action was further encouraged by the common observation that many children improve markedly as soon as their parents leave them in the hospital and deteriorate once they return home.

As is evident from the digests that follow, many different types of behavior therapies have been applied to asthmatic children over the past few decades. T. J. Knapp and L. A. Wells, in a review article, noted that those therapies most frequently employed involved some variant of relaxation training or operant conditioning ("Behavior Therapy for Asthma: A Review," *Behavior Research and Therapy,* 1978, *16,* 103-115). Present evidence indicates that most asthmatics will gain substantial benefits from the various medications available for asthma, but a significant portion will require further treatment with other means. In addition, many of those currently doing reasonably well with medication alone might indeed do better if behavior therapies were added to their overall treatment plans. Morbidity and mortality statistics indicate that there continues to be great room for improvement.

Also included in this section is a small selection of digested articles that discuss the treatment of chronic coughs of a non-organic nature. In general the feeling among investigators is that chronic coughing of this type is a learned operant behavior, reinforced by the responses of others in the patient's environment. Most therapies employed have sought to alter the operant behavior by reducing secondary gains or by shaping and re-directing the patient's original inappropriate behavior toward more appropriate action. The small number of digests cited is a reflection of the amount of literature currently available concerning this topic. However, the articles included offer much insight and can be of great help in the treatment of this difficult disorder.

Asthma

Asthma is a reversible obstructive lung disorder that, at times, presents great difficulties in management. A number of different stimuli have been identified that are capable of causing the obstructive reaction. Included among them are emotional factors of a chronic underlying or acute nature.

Relaxation Training for Asthmatic Children

AUTHORS: A. Barney Alexander, Donald R. Miklich, and Helen Hershkoff

PRECIS: Using a modified form of Jacobson's systemic relaxation technique with asthmatic children, whose peak expiratory flow rates showed significant increases

INTRODUCTION: A large number of asthmatic children can have an attack precipitated by exercise. This fact has led to speculation that the reverse—relaxation—may well be beneficial to asthmatics in distress. The authors cite the work of a number of investigators who have studied different procedures designed to promote a more relaxed state in the asthmatic in order to find whether or not an improvement in symptoms results. Such techniques have included psychotherapy, hypnosis, and systematic relaxation training. Though the results had not been conclusive, the authors felt that the theory and accumulated information warranted further investigation. Thus their study was designed to determine the effects of purposeful systematic relaxation on the clinical condition of asthmatic children.

METHOD: The authors selected two groups of asthmatic children, matched according to age, sex, and degree of disability, and ranging in age from ten to fifteen years. One group served as the control; the other received the training. Each subject attended at least three sessions, and the entire experiment covered an eight-day period.

To determine the effects of the training the investigators employed two measurements. The first was a subjective rating by the participants of their feelings of relaxation on a scale from one to ten, the lower being "not relaxed at all" and the higher being "very relaxed." Relaxation ratings were given before and after each session. The second measurement was more objective, an assessment of the Peak Expiratory Flow Rate (PEFR) using the Wright Peak Flow Meter (Air-Med Ltd., England). The PEFR is a measure of the maximum rate of air flow from the lungs during a forced expiration and is adversely affected by airway obstruction (as occurs with asthma). The subject must voluntarily exert the maximum expiratory effort or the reading will be lowered in a false manner. Since no error can make the PEFR higher than it should be, each subject was measured three times before and after each session and the highest value of the three was used.

The sessions lasted for twenty minutes each. Subjects in the control group were informed that "we want to find out if inactivity affects your peak flows," and they were told to sit quietly for fifteen minutes. Quiet activities such as talking, reading, and sewing were allowed. Those in the training group were told "we want to find out if relaxation effects your peak flows." For the next fifteen minutes they were taught a modified form of Jacobson's systematic relaxation technique, which consisted of tensing and then relaxing muscles in the following order: hands and forearms, biceps, upper face, calves, and feet. During the session the trainer encouraged feelings of warmth and relaxation. Subjects in both groups sat in comfortable chairs during their sessions.

The results of the study revealed that, as a group, the controls had no real increase in their subjective feelings of relaxation after the session as compared to before, and the measurements of their PEFRs were not significantly altered. In contrast, the trained group did increase their subjective feelings of relaxation after the session, and the overall improvement in their PEFRs was statistically quite significant. Furthermore, the improvement increased after each succeeding training session. Though the mean improvement in PEFR was 11 percent and not impressive enough to represent a reduction in actual symptoms, the elimination of the six out of sixteen training group subjects who showed the least improvement left a mean improvement in PEFR of 32 percent, which is compatible with symptomatic improvement.

COMMENTARY: The results obtained with the purposeful relaxation approach are impressive, especially when one considers that the improvements shown were greater as the subjects received more training in the technique. Since no plateau effect was reached in any of the subjects, one can only speculate on the maximum effectiveness of this therapeutic mode.

The investigators mention that the variability in individual responsiveness to the training is similar to the varying responsiveness of asthmatics in general to most treatment approaches. Certainly such training holds promise. Although the authors needed to formalize and standardize their sessions for the sake of uniformity and documentation, the training itself could be performed at the bedside with essentially no equipment.

SOURCE: Alexander, A. B., Miklich, D. R., and Hershkoff, H. "The Immediate Effects of Systemic Relaxation Training on Peak Expiratory Flow Rates in Asthmatic Children." *Psychosomatic Medicine*, 1972, *34*, 388-394.

"Time-Out" from Positive Reinforcement in the Treatment of Hospitalized Asthmatics

AUTHOR: Thomas L. Creer

PRECIS: Reducing the number and duration of hospital admissions by withdrawing the secondary gains provided to two male asthmatics in a residential treatment center.

INTRODUCTION: Recently the use of the time-out procedure to treat inappropriate behavior has increased. In essence, the procedure involves removing the child exhibiting such behavior from the environment where reinforcement occurs until the behavior ceases. Much of this work has been done in relation to temper tantrums in children. The child is placed in a room alone when a tantrum occurs until he or she stops. The physical removal prevents the child from receiving positive reinforcement in the form of the secondary gain available in the original setting. The author (therapist) felt that such an approach might be beneficial in the cases of asthmatic children who seemed to spend an inordinate amount of time in the hospital and who presented symptoms in such profusion and of such a nature that a diagnosis of malingering was strongly considered.

CASE STUDIES: The subjects were two ten-year-old males who were patients in a residential treatment center for intractable asthmatics. In between attacks they lived in as normal an environment as possible, attending public school and participating in a variety of social and recreational activities. Don had been living at the center for sixteen months, during which time he had had eighty-eight admissions to the hospital for a total of 248 days. Jack had lived there for eighteen months, had forty-nine admissions, and had been hospitalized a total of 137 days. Both seemed able to deliberately increase their symptoms in various voluntary ways, and each complained of other symptoms unrelated to asthma once their attacks cleared. These new complaints required continued hospitalization while their doctors pursued additional tests to determine whether or not their complaints were genuine. A great many times their complaints did not appear to be medically justified. The therapist decided to attempt to decrease the frequency and duration of their hospitalizations by reducing the secondary gains present in the hospital setting.

An initial six-week period, during which each boy followed the normal hospital routine whenever he required hospitalization, was used to collect baseline data. After this a six-week time-out period was put into effect. Strict instructions were followed whenever either boy had to be admitted: (1) Each boy was placed in a room alone. (2) No visitors other than medical or nursing personnel were allowed. (3) No visiting was permitted with other patients. (4) No comic books or television was allowed, only school books. (5) The boy could only leave the room to go to the bathroom—with a nurse escort. And (6) all meals were eaten alone in the boy's room. This phase was followed by a three-week "reversal" period during which all restrictions were removed. Finally another eight-week time-out period occurred.

At the conclusion of the study the accumulated data revealed that the frequency and duration of hospitalizations were drastically reduced during the time-out periods as compared to the prestudy and baseline periods. There was some slippage during the reversal period, but neither boy required anywhere near the number of admissions he had needed before the time-out.

COMMENTARY: This is not an uncommon problem, and it extends to children suffering with other types of chronic illnesses as well. In the case of these boys, both had mothers who were themselves asthmatics. Being aware from first-hand experience how a child can use his asthma to manipulate others, they were rather firm in their approach to their sons. The nurses at the hospitals where the boys had gone before coming to the center described them as the "darlings of the nursing staff." So it is not too hard to understand why the boys may have preferred the hospital setting to home on occasion. One may speculate about the positive value of family therapy in the long-term management of such children.

SOURCE: Creer, T. L. "The Use of a Time-Out from Positive Reinforcement Procedure With Asthmatic Children." *Journal of Psychosomatic Research,* 1970, *14,* 117-120.

Biofeedback Training Applied to Asthmatic Children

AUTHOR: Gary M. Feldman

PRECIS: Training severe asthmatics to lower their respiratory resistance utilizing biofeedback training techniques

INTRODUCTION: Feldman points out that biofeedback training has led to subjects' being able to exert control over such activities as heart rate, blood pressure, vasomotor response, and brain-wave activity on EEG. Other researchers have used a combination of biofeedback and reinforcement techniques to train children to reduce experimentally induced bronchial muscle spasms, a combination that resulted in improved breathing. The many factors that lead to difficulty in breathing during an asthmatic attack include edema of the bronchial mucosal lining, blockage due to accumulated secretions, and increased tone of the bronchial musculature, leading to narrowed airway passages. There are neural and hormonal effects on these factors. In fact it has often been observed that asthmatics' respiratory condition can be greatly affected by their emotional state. Techniques that have been used with differing degrees of success to improve this emotional state include relaxation training, hypnosis, psychotherapy, and separating the child from his parents (parentectomy). The author feels that biofeedback training involves a more direct link between the asthmatic's mental state and the degree of respiratory difficulty.

TECHNIQUE: For this pilot study four severe asthmatics and one nonasthmatic were selected. Case One was a sixteen-year-old female who had had serious asthma since the age of two and who was not responding well to daily medication. One indication that the asthma was psychosomatic in nature was the fact that her condition worsened predictably after her parents' visits. Case Two was a ten-year-old male whose asthma had become severe after age six. His family life was very disrupted, and he had become quite withdrawn and depressed. Case Three was a

ten-year-old male who had developed severe asthma at age three
when he was placed in foster care after his father's hospitalization for psychosis. He was returned to his mother at age eight,
and his attacks and their severity soon increased. It was noted
during his hospitalization that his condition deteriorated after
emotional upsets or home visits. Case Four was an eleven-year-
old male whose asthma began at age six months. His frequent
attacks worsened after his mother remarried a strict disciplinar-
ian who was described as rejecting.

Feldman describes in detail the equipment used. The subject was instructed to synchronize his or her breathing with the
sound of breathing heard over earphones, which were attached
to the Somanetic Model 950 breathing trainer. The subject also
was requested to breathe into an apparatus that was set up to
measure the total respiratory resistance (TRR) in the patient.
The TRR is a sum total of the various resistances encountered
in the respiratory system and includes the lower airway resistance (smooth muscle tone), upper airway resistance, and the
viscous tissue resistance of the lung and chest wall. The TRR
was measured by a forced oscillation technique. The signal
developed was passed through a voltage-controlled oscillator,
which generated an audio output to a speaker. The subject
heard a continuous tone whose pitch varied with the
TRR.

Each subject was given a series of thirty-minute sessions
with either biofeedback training or inhaled isoproterenol (via
intermittent positive pressure breathing). During the session the
subject was told to relax and match his or her breathing to that
of the trainer and was told that "a lower tone means you are
breathing better. Try to lower the pitch of the tone." Immediately before and after each session pulmonary function
studies were performed to document any changes (specifically
the peak flow rate and the mean midexpiratory flow rate).
Using the biofeedback technique each of the subjects was able
to lower the TRR to a degree consistent with the use of the
inhaled isoproterenol. However, although all the subjects demonstrated improvement, all also failed to reach expected normal
values on their pulmonary function studies.

COMMENTARY: The author is careful to point out how attempts were made in the course of designing the study to correct for the possibility that other factors might be influencing the outcome. The resulting technique as illustrated seems to be effective in leading immediately to reducing bronchial smooth muscle tone in severe asthmatics whose illness has significant psychosomatic components. As pointed out, this was a pilot study and was not designed to demonstrate whether or not the training had any lasting effects.

SOURCE: Feldman, G. M. "The Effect of Biofeedback Training on Respiratory Resistance of Asthmatic Children." *Psychosomatic Medicine,* 1976, *38,* 27-34.

Behavior Therapy Techniques Applied to an Emotionally Disturbed Asthmatic Child

AUTHOR: James E. Gardner

PRECIS: Applying several behavior therapy techniques, including reinforcement, extinction, and conditioned placebo, to the asthma and acting-out behavior of a six-year-old

INTRODUCTION: Gardner describes a young child with life-threatening asthma and severe emotional disturbance. The child acted out in a number of ways and successfully manipulated others around him by threatening to have an asthma attack. The author explains how the problem was organized into a conceptual model that reduced it to the individual activities involved and enabled the therapists to formulate a treatment plan that employed several different behavior therapy techniques so that all inappropriate behaviors could be intervened with simultaneously. The therapists felt that the child's life-threatening condition warranted a treatment plan that would result in a rapid response.

CASE STUDY: The patient (P) was a six-year-old male who had suffered with severe asthma since the age of one. His asthma was considered to be dangerous enough to justify a standing order for admission to the hospital whenever he developed asthmatic symptoms. P also exhibited severe behavioral problems characterized by hyperactivity, unpredictability, and antisocial behavior, including excessive swearing at visiting time. He had a number of tics and twitches and often attempted to manipulate others with the threat of an asthma attack. On admission he was described as having tenuous reality ties, a great deal of emotional lability, and separation anxiety.

P's life had been frequently disrupted and was marked by a series of moves from one caretaker to another. His natural parents had not been seen since his infancy, and he had lived with a succession of different relatives. After several admissions he was removed from an aunt's home and sent to a sanitarium, where

his asthma did not improve and his overall behavior deteriorated. At that point he was admitted for treatment.

The boy's therapists, in formulating a treatment plan, first
constructed a conceptual model of his inappropriate behaviors.
They felt that much of his behavior was based on learned responses that had been reinforced by the reactions of the adults
around him. His tics and hyperactivity were seen as tension reduction behaviors. The tensions arose from the negative feelings
directed toward him by others because of his manipulative and
inappropriate behaviors, from his separation anxiety based on
his unstable life history, and from his fears for his life, which
was indeed put in jeopardy during his asthma attacks. The
asthma was felt to be based on the child's psychologic responses
and also on his pursuit of secondary gain in the form of increased adult attention.

The planners considered the model and various limitations
present in a hospital setting and settled on four different procedures. First they asked the hospital staff to stop responding to
inappropriate manipulative behaviors as much as possible and to
increase their attention in response to appropriate behaviors.
The second procedure was a rather elaborate means of rewarding appropriate behaviors and encouraging P to reduce his level
of activity. It employed a system of dispensing various colored
poker chips that could be traded for desirable toys located in
the therapist's office. The therapist set toys of differing interest
to P on shelves above different colors that corresponded to the
colors of the chips. P was told he could earn any of the toys by
accumulating chips. Red chips (the lowest denomination) could
be traded for red toys or five could be saved and traded for a
white chip (medium denomination). White chips could be used
for white toys or two could be traded for a blue chip (highest
denomination). Blue chips were good for any toy in the office.
To earn chips, P was instructed to simply "settle down and relax." The time period for reduced behavior was initially set at
three minutes for each red chip, but gradually that was increased to five and then ten minutes. The author felt that the
human contact in delivering the chips to P was an important
part of the process because of the attention P gained for appro-

priate behavior. Despite some setbacks due to P's carelessness in losing chips and to his acting out when frustrated by not following the rules of the program, his behavior was noted to improve markedly in all settings where the token system was maintained, including his aunt's home.

The third procedure used fantasy stories involving space adventures to teach alternative responses to stress. The therapist incorporated P in the stories in the role of a space hero who acted in very positive and assertive ways when faced with adventures on the moon, and contrasted him with another character who was weak and developed asthma attacks whenever faced with difficulties and dangers in outer space. Two weeks after the start of the stories P announced that he was no longer going to have asthma attacks, since he did not want to act like the asthmatic boy in the stories. And in fact the number and severity of his attacks declined. The final procedure was the use of a placebo in the child's drug regimen. His physician noted that his demands for adrenaline shots to control his asthma were excessive and possibly indicated an acquired or psychological dependence. When the subsequent injection of saline eliminated the need for adrenaline about half the time, the therapist felt that introducing a conditioned placebo in pill form might be beneficial in reducing P's medication needs. On discharge from the hospital P was given a supply of placebo pills and told to take one at the first sign of any asthma symptoms. As a precaution, however, his aunt and his teachers were told about the nature of the pills and advised to seek medical aid if his condition was not promptly relieved.

In response to this multidimensional approach P was reportedly doing well in the follow-up period. His asthma attacks were markedly reduced, he was attending school regularly, and he no longer was exhibiting hyperactivity or tics. In addition he was no longer resorting to manipulative behaviors.

COMMENTARY: This article is a good example of how a child with a physical problem that has a tremendous amount of emotional overlay can be effectively managed. The use of a conceptual model in the preparation of a treatment plan can allow for rapid progress by employing a number of modalities simultaneously in an organized fashion. The author clearly shows how therapies were applied to each facet of the problem. The total treatment regimen required a great deal of team effort by all the caregivers involved, both inside and outside the hospital. All members of the management team must be informed of the plan and its purpose so that problem behaviors can be handled consistently.

SOURCE: Gardner, J. E. "A Blending of Behavior Therapy Techniques in an Approach to an Asthmatic Child." *Psychotherapy: Theory, Research, and Practice,* 1968, *5,* 46-49.

Relaxation and Assertive Training
for Asthmatics

AUTHORS: R. A. Hock, C. H. Rodgers, C. Reddi, and D. W. Kennard

PRECIS: A comparison of training in relaxation alone, assertiveness training alone, and a combination of the two

INTRODUCTION: The authors note that previous studies have demonstrated an association between stress and the severity of bronchial asthma. In addition, other reports have appeared in the literature stating that asthmatics are deficient in assertive skills—unable to express anger or aggression. The study they undertook examined the effectiveness of relaxation and assertiveness training alone, and in combination, in improving pulmonary functioning or reducing the frequency of attacks or both.

METHODS: Several groups of adolescent male asthmatics were selected. The study groups received relaxation training, assertiveness training, or combined relaxation and assertiveness training, and two additional groups served as controls. All patients enrolled in the study were seen weekly for from seven to nine weeks, during which time they all saw an allergist who was responsible for medication management and who had a nurse perform pulmonary function measurements (FEV_1—the amount of air forcefully exhaled in one second). During weekly sessions subjects in the training groups received their instruction.

Subjects who received relaxation training were taught to sequentially tense and then relax major voluntary muscle groups. Once full relaxation was attained, they were given suggestions of visual images evoking quiet, comfortable, and relaxed feelings (lying on a beach, feeling warm breezes and sunshine, and so on). The relaxation training and guided imagery sessions lasted forty minutes each.

Assertiveness training involved role playing and other exercises with the following goals: "Learning to say no to authority figures, learning to practice the expression of positive and negative feelings, learning to initiate and terminate general conversations, and learning to make a request for favors." These sessions also lasted forty minutes.

A third group received both forms of instruction—twenty minutes of assertiveness training followed by twenty minutes of relaxation training. The control groups either simply received their medication weekly or received medication and then sat quietly in a small leaderless group of peers for forty minutes.

Pulmonary function studies and weekly attack-frequency measurements at the final training session revealed that those in the relaxation group and the combined relaxation and assertiveness training group had significantly lower attack rates and improved FEV_1. The assertiveness training group and controls were unimproved. Four weeks after terminating the study, the frequency-of-attack rates were up to pretreatment levels (or higher) for all groups, but FEV_1 remained significantly improved for those who had received relaxation training alone and in combination with assertiveness training.

COMMENTARY: Relaxation training alone proved to be the most effective approach of those studied. The authors speculate that the assertiveness training was only sufficient to increase the subjects' anxiety and was not successful in helping them readjust their attitudes. The article does not mention whether or not the participants who received training practiced at home during the period of the training or continued with the exercises after the training was terminated, but it would seem likely that consistent use of the techniques (in particular, relaxation) could have led to a more sustained improvement in FEV_1 and a concomitant reduction in attack rates.

SOURCE: Hock, R. A., Rodgers, C. H., Reddi, C., and Kennard, D. W. "Medico-Psychological Interventions in Male Asthmatic Children: An Evaluation of Physiological Change." *Psychosomatic Medicine,* 1978, *40,* 210-215.

Psychotherapeutic Interventions
in the Treatment of an Asthmatic Adolescent

AUTHOR: Z. Kaminski

PRECIS: Treating severe affective and behavioral problems stemming from a dysfunctional mother-child relationship with psychotherapy on an individual, group, and family level

INTRODUCTION: At times asthma is only a secondary consideration when one is confronted with a child who manifests, in addition to his physical ailment, a severe emotional disturbance. A number of investigators have looked to the parent-child relationship in such cases in order to more fully understand the etiology of the physical disorder. Kaminski quotes from the work of several authors who have delineated several factors complicating the asthmatic's condition that relate specifically to family function. In particular, he discusses the asthmatic's conflict about crying because of a fear of maternal repudiation. Asthmatic patients' mothers are simultaneously seductive and rejecting. The case study Kaminski presents emphasizes the dysfunctional parent-child relationship that has apparently led to the development within the patient of what the author terms "a repressed cry for the mother." Information and insights encountered during the course of psychotherapy on several levels are offered.

CASE STUDY: J was a seventeen-year-old asthmatic who came to the hospital looking forlorn and depressed. He was noted to be thin and pale, had poor posture and a slow, shuffling gait, and was disheveled. His speech was childish and his affect rather flat. He stated that his hospitalization was his "last chance" to work through his problems.

In individual therapy the therapist learned that J was the second oldest of five children. An older brother had died at age two of asthma. A younger brother had mild asthma and eczema, and the two other younger siblings were well. J himself had had eczema before age two and then had developed asthma, which, although he never had to be hospitalized for it, required daily prophylactic medication. He attributed his attacks to "family rows, especially with Mom, flower pollens, swimming in chlorinated water, etc." Two years earlier he had been sent by his parents to live in the country because of his worsening condition. Since that time, though his asthma had improved somewhat, his feelings of inadequacy and depression had worsened. He found it more and more difficult to concentrate on his schoolwork and was failing every subject at school. He blamed his mother's "badgering" him to study for his lack of success—a statement the therapist noted as an exaggeration, since he had had little contact with her during the past two years. He was quite depressed living away from his family and felt the couple he was boarding with were distant and cold. In high school J's teachers felt he was remote and strange. He did not get along well with other students and was said to be a loner.

In group sessions J was noted to have difficulty with authority. He had feelings of being overpowered by adults. His usual response to most situations was anger, and his overall range of emotions was quite limited. His inability to express feelings led to his isolating himself. He would detach himself from any situation in group therapy in which a member was in obvious distress and needed comforting. Even though his mother openly made him angry, he was totally incapable of expressing such feelings to her. He suffered from a tremendous fear of failure, which had caused his progress to be slowed.

Family therapy in this case revealed a great deal that was important in understanding J's condition. Both his parents had emigrated from Western Europe shortly after World War II. His father was passive but sympathetic. The father's migratory attempts during the war were quite difficult and traumatic. Though he felt compassion toward his son, he seemed helpless in supporting him. J's mother's parents separated when she was sixteen, and she was forced to fend for herself and her mother and younger brother, even though her mother was not at all incapacitated. She harbored great anger about this situation even years later, and the therapist felt that this anger was displaced onto J, who was unconsciously identified as her inadequate mother.

Both parents felt J was very aggravating. His frequent talking about seemingly unimportant things caused both of them—and his teachers—to "switch off." He was incapable of doing anything to help around the house without becoming breathless. His mother had nothing but intense criticism for him. J was completely unable to live up to the excessive expectations she had set for him.

Finally, both parents relived the grief they had felt at the death of their first son. J had been born only two months later, and they had never let themselves attach to him too firmly for fear of losing him also. When he approached the age of two, they were again faced with the anxious feelings that they might lose him to his newly developed asthma and withdrew even more. When J was fourteen his asthma worsened and his parents, unable to deal with their ambivalence and anguish, sent him to live in the country. While their ambivalence increased, so did J's depression and feelings of abandonment.

As the therapist continued to work with J and his parents, the various factors involved started to sort themselves out and J was finally able to cry. In follow-up he was noted to be practically free of the need for prophylactic medication for his asthma, and his self-esteem and ability to feel compassion were vastly improved.

COMMENTARY: Kaminski feels that family intervention in this case was of paramount importance in uncovering the dysfunction in the parent-child relationship that was so damaging to the patient. Professionals who have worked with asthmatic children know of numerous examples in which one of the most effective ways to halt an acute asthmatic attack is to remove the child from the parents. A family-oriented psychotherapeutic approach may well be beneficial in such circumstances.

SOURCE: Kaminski, Z. "Case Report: An Asthmatic Adolescent and His 'Repressed Cry' for His Mother." *British Journal of Medical Psychology*, 1975, *48*, 185-188.

Treating Asthmatic Children
with Counterconditioning

AUTHOR: Aman U. Khan

PRECIS: Biofeedback techniques to reduce bronchoconstriction previously triggered by conditioned responses to various stimuli

INTRODUCTION: All humans may react with some degree of bronchospasm to a variety of physical and chemical irritants introduced into the respiratory tract. Asthmatics tend to respond more vigorously in these "primary hypersensitivity" reactions, which are true reflexive phenomena neurologically mediated. Bronchospastic reactions to specific allergens or to respiratory infections in asthmatics are probably primary hypersensitivity reactions as well. There are, however, a number of other stimuli that can lead to the same affects but that do not appear to follow the same pathways. Included among these are various psychogenic factors and agents that have no allergic potential. Khan feels that some asthmatics have been conditioned to react with bronchospasm when faced with these stimuli because of previous experiences with them during actual acute asthmatic attacks. In time these "secondary hypersensitivity" factors can themselves trigger asthmatic attacks. If indeed this view is correct, then children suffering from these types of secondary reactions might benefit from the effects of counterconditioning that uses biofeedback training and substitutes the reinforcement obtained for bronchodilation for the secondary gains achieved during an asthmatic attack.

METHOD: The study involved eighty asthmatic children ranging in age from eight to fifteen, and it ran over a sixteen-month period. The children were further divided in half into "reactors" and "nonreactors," depending on whether they developed any significant bronchospasm after being exposed three times to inhaled saline which they were told contained allergens that would probably cause some respiratory difficulty. Half of the reactors and half of the nonreactors were then assigned arbitrarily to either the control or the experimental group.

No conditioning was attempted for the control group, and its subjects only received periodic evaluation using measured FEV_1 (the total forced expiratory volume at the end of one second) for statistical purposes. The best of three attempts was used for the study.

The experimental group first attended five to eight sessions of fifty minutes' duration each in which they received biofeedback training to decrease airway resistance as measured by the FEV_1. The initial sessions were used to give the children a thorough explanation (using the equipment, diagrams, and models) of the method and purpose of training. After the explanations were complete, each child's FEV_1 was measured (the best of three trials) in order to have baseline readings. The FEV_1 was measured using a pulmonary function analyzer that has a numerical readout the subject can readily see. The subjects then performed three more sets of triple exhalations at three-minute intervals; they were instructed to try to decrease the amount of bronchoconstriction they had (raise the numbers on the FEV_1 readout). The goal was to decrease the baseline airway resistance by at least 2 percent at each trial (a total of 6 percent by the end of the session). By the fourth session the goal was raised to 10 percent. Verbal praise was given whenever the child succeeded in attaining the set goal. Those children who were unable to reach the goal by the fourth session were given small doses of inhaled isoproterenol, which were diminished in concentration over the next three sessions so that the eighth (last) session was conducted without it. Twenty-seven of the children were able to achieve the set goals without isoproterenol assistance, eight required it, and five were unable to reach the 10 percent reduction in airway resistance even with the medication.

The second phase of training, consisting of ten sessions, was intended to link the initial training with actual episodes of triggered bronchospasm. At the start of each session a mild degree of bronchoconstriction was induced in the subjects with one of the following methods: a suggestion to recall a previous asthmatic attack and the associated emotional stress; the inhalation of saline vapors that were said to contain allergens; listening to tape recordings of a wheezing child; voluntary hyperventilation; seeing a short film depicting separation from the mother; and as a last resort, the inhalation of a bronchoconstrictor agent (Mecholyl). Once the bronchospasm was induced, the subjects were instructed to relax and to reduce airway resistance using the same feedback (FEV_1 numerical readouts) used initially. After ten minutes a small dose of inhaled isoproterenol was given to those unable to reduce resistance. Each session ended when FEV_1 readings reached baseline figures.

At the completion of all training, statistics were then accumulated for a year on both the experimental and control subjects. The results indicated that the asthma attacks of those in the experimental group (reactors and nonreactors) and the control reactors were significantly fewer, shorter, and less severe (as measured by several indexes simultaneously). The control nonreactors showed no statistically significant improvement in any of these aspects of their affliction.

COMMENTARY: The theoretical framework for the etiologies of asthma as outlined here and by other authors is an appealing one because it gives the clinician a rationale for incorporating a number of different therapeutic methods in the treatment of asthmatic children. The particular training apparatus employed for biofeedback instruction did not have the capacity to provide continuous and instantaneous feedback, but it did have the advantage of being commonly found in many hospitals and of not requiring any extensive or expensive adaptations for use.

As a final note, it was interesting to see that even those in the control group who were reactors demonstrated improvement over the year following their inclusion in the study despite the fact no effort was made to train them. The author speculates that the attention shown them during the course of the study was sufficiently emotionally supportive to help relieve some of the anxiety that may be involved in triggering attacks based on secondary hypersensitivity reactions.

SOURCE: Khan, A. U. "Effectiveness of Biofeedback and Counterconditioning in the Treatment of Bronchial Asthma." *Journal of Psychosomatic Research*, 1977, *21*, 97-104.

Treatment of Exercise-Induced Asthma

AUTHORS: Aman U. Khan and Diane L. Olson

PRECIS: Successful deconditioning of exercise-induced asthma

INTRODUCTION: The authors discuss a number of previously published studies exploring the etiology and incidence of bronchoconstriction developing in asthmatics after significant exercise. Though a number of theories have been proposed, no clear-cut cause has been elucidated. This research sought to explore the problem from a different viewpoint. A state of "primary hypersensitivity," which is present in all asthmatics, leads to a bronchoconstrictive response to stimuli that do not cause any type of allergic reaction. The authors feel that perhaps asthmatics have been conditioned by the association between exertion and breathing difficulties to respond to exercise with bronchoconstriction. Parents' attitudes toward and concern about their asthmatic children and exercise tend to reinforce the children's beliefs and, consequently, their physiological response. If this were the case, it might be possible to decondition that response.

STUDY METHOD: Asthmatic children were divided into groups according to the degree of exercise-induced bronchoconstriction (EIB) that developed when they exercised on a treadmill until their heart rate was raised to between 160 and 170. Those who reacted with significant bronchoconstriction as measured by changes in the amount of air that was forcefully exhaled in one second (FEV_1) were further divided into two groups—experimental and control. The children who did not react to exercise with bronchoconstriction composed a third group (nonreactors).

All children in the study were seen daily, at the same time of day when possible, for seven days. The experimental reactors were treated before exercising with inhaled isoproterenol (a bronchodilator) via an intermittent positive pressure breathing (IPPB) apparatus. The initial dose of isoproterenol was 0.5 ml. in 2.5 ml. of saline. The dose was reduced by 0.1 ml. in each subsequent session. The control reactors were treated, by means of the IPPB apparatus, with room air only before they exercised. The nonreactors did not receive any pretreatment.

It was found that the isoproterenol administered via IPPB prevented EIB from developing at the initial dose, and the beneficial effect was maintained as the dose was serially withdrawn and finally eliminated. The control subjects continued to develop EIB, while the nonreactors continued to be unaffected by exercise.

At a three-month and six-month follow-up, those former reactors who had received the deconditioning with isoproterenol were found to be tolerating exercise without difficulty (with a few exceptions).

COMMENTARY: The problem of EIB is well recognized by pediatricians. Quite often they are required to fill out school health forms on which they must note that an asthmatic child cannot participate in physical education classes because of it. The deconditioning treatment offered here might well help keep that child in gym classes. Not only would this lead to improved physical fitness, but one more of the factors in a chronic illness that keep the child apart from others would be eliminated.

SOURCE: Khan, A. U., and Olson, D. L. "Deconditioning of Exercise-Induced Asthma." *Psychosomatic Medicine,* 1977, *39,* 382-392.

Training Children with Asthma to Use Inhalation Therapy Equipment

AUTHORS: Charles M. Renne and Thomas L. Creer

PRECIS: Training children to effectively employ the intermittent positive pressure breathing apparatus using an approach combining instruction, informational feedback, sequential focusing on individual responses, and reinforcement

INTRODUCTION: This study was conducted in response to the significant number of patients at the National Asthma Center in Denver, Colorado, who were not making effective use of the intermittent positive pressure breathing (IPPB) apparatus. This machine delivers liquid bronchodilator medication in an inhalable form under positive pressure to the patient's airways. It is a very useful treatment modality in asthma that can bring about rapid relief during an acute asthmatic attack and that frequently eliminates the need to use more potent medications with adverse side-effects. To be used properly, however, the machine requires a significant amount of active participation by the patient, and this is often a difficult task for children. The study showed how children with asthma who had previously been unable to use the machine properly could be trained to use it to its fullest advantage. The study also demonstrated that other professionals could be efficiently taught to conduct the training program in a satisfactory manner.

PROCEDURE: The authors identified the three principal behaviors involved in the appropriate use of the IPPB machine. The patient has to fix his or her eyes on the pressure dial on the front of the machine in order to reduce distractions and to help promote proper posture in relation to the apparatus. Second, the patient has to hold the mouthpiece properly, at a right angle with the mouth firmly around it, and must avoid breathing through the nose or allowing the cheeks to puff out. Finally the patient must employ diaphragmatic (abdominal) breathing rather than intercostal (chest expansion) breathing. These activities are important for attaining the maximum entry and penetration of the inhaled medication. Inappropriate behavior was defined as any deviation from the prescribed behaviors: that is, breaking eye contact with the dial; not holding the mouthpiece firmly at a ninety-degree angle relative to the face, flaring the nostrils, or allowing the cheeks to puff out; or any breathing in which the abdomen did not distend during inspiration or contract during expiration or breathing that was out of phase with the cycle established.

The four subjects ranged in age from seven to twelve. The training sessions were held at the same time of day for each and in the same area where the children would normally receive treatment with the IPPB machine if they actually required it. During training all the children were free of symptoms. Specific instructions were given by the trainer, as follows:

> "I am going to help you learn how to use the IPPB in a way that may help your asthma. First, sit up straight and look directly at this dial. Next, hold the mouthpiece so that it points straight out from your mouth as you look at this dial. Keep your lips held firmly around the mouthpiece and avoid puffing your cheeks or breathing through your nose when using the IPPB. Finally, you should use your stomach and abdomen to help you breathe. Push your stomach out when you breathe in and pull your stomach in when you breathe out. Now take fifteen breaths on the machine and then relax."

Fifteen breaths constituted one trial, and all instructions were given slowly and repeated for each of the target behaviors if the child's actions were inappropriate. The trainers felt that goals should be set one at a time in the order of their difficulty. Baseline measurements were obtained at first, and then all the behaviors were worked on sequentially, starting with eye fixation at the fourth trial, facial posturing at the seventh, and diaphragmatic breathing at the thirteenth. All training was completed at the end of one twenty-six-trial session. The deadlines were established by the performance of the most resistant subject.

The subjects were instructed that they could earn one ticket at the end of each trial if they did not perform inappropriately a stated number of times. These instructions were made quite specific for each of the behaviors dealt with. The standards were based on their performance during the preceding trial. The subjects were told that they could purchase a surprise gift once they had earned twenty-five tickets. The authors arranged the reward system using bonuses and other devices so that the twenty-five tickets could only be earned by mastering the apparatus. The gift was an inexpensive item the child could choose. Whenever the child earned a ticket, the author presented it with a positive comment in order to further reinforce the experience.

All the target behaviors were approached in the same basic manner. Prompting was used initially for training the children to breath diaphragmatically, because it was a difficult task for some of them. The author pushed the abdomen in during expiration while instructing the child to breathe out as fully as possible, and then told the child to push the hand away while breathing in as fully as possible. With time first the hand was removed while verbal prompting continued, and then the verbal cues were eliminated.

It was found during follow-up that the children's improved performances with the IPPB machine were maintained during actual use for acute asthmatic attacks. In one case a child seemed to deviate from the appropriate behaviors while on the machine, but the sight of the authors apparently was enough reinforcement to cause him to resume satisfactorily.

In the second part of the study, a group of nurses was successfully taught to conduct the training in only two fifty-minute instructional sessions in which they were given didactic information and practical applications.

COMMENTARY: The medical treatment team is all too often faced with the child who will not or cannot properly use the IPPB machine. The approach presented by the authors appears to have a great deal of applicability to a number of children in this situation. The procedure does not require any elaborate set-up other than the usual environment, the IPPB apparatus, the child, and the trainer. With care and attention to detail this method should help to reduce the use of more potent medications with their potential for adverse side-effects in the asthmatic child.

SOURCE: Renne, C. M., and Creer, T. L. "Training Children with Asthma to Use Inhalation Therapy Equipment." *Journal of Applied Behavior Analysis*, 1976, *9*, 1-11.

Additional Readings

Alexander, A. B. "Systematic Relaxation and Flow Rates in Asthmatic Children: Relationship to Emotional Precipitants and Anxiety." *Journal of Psychosomatic Research,* 1972, *16,* 405-410.

This study follows up a preliminary report by the author in collaboration with other investigators which demonstrated significant improvements in the peak expiratory flow rates of asthmatic children after they were trained to perform progressive relaxation. This second report validates the original findings and, in addition, shows that the degree of benefit achieved with the relaxation technique was closely correlated with the extent of the role emotional factors played in triggering the child's asthma. Thus, a "precipitant interview" designed to assess the importance of emotional stress in causing the child's condition can be a valid indicator of the usefulness of the therapeutic technique.

Knapp, T. J., and Wells, L. A. "Behavior Therapy for Asthma: A Review." *Behavior Research and Therapy,* 1978, *16,* 103-115.

This recent review article examines twenty-four published reports of the use of various types of behavior therapies for childhood asthma. In particular the authors discuss in some detail the types of treatment populations included, the basic experimental designs employed, the dependent variables selected, the specific treatment techniques used, and the ultimate findings reached. The paper concludes with a number of suggestions for further research on the subject.

Miklich, D. R. "Operant Conditioning Procedures with Systemic Desensitization in a Hyperkinetic Asthmatic Boy." *Journal of Behavior Therapy and Experimental Psychiatry,* 1973, *4,* 177-182.

A treatment regimen is described with which a six-year-old hyperactive male was helped to overcome his panic reaction during acute asthmatic attacks. The panic prevented the use of any form of medical therapy that required his cooperation, thus increasing the danger of his frequent asthma attacks. Using a token reward system, the therapist was able to shape relaxed sitting and then reinforce the calm acceptance of anxiety-provoking statements about asthma. Following treatment the child was reportedly much more cooperative during acute exacerbations of his illness.

Yorkston, N. J., McHugh, R. B., Brady, R., Serber, M., and Sergeant, H. G. S. "Verbal Desensitization in Bronchial Asthma." *Journal of Psychosomatic Research,* 1974, *18,* 371-376.

   In a controlled study, eight adults received relaxation training while six adults were verbally desensitized by a therapist who made graded statements about asthma, being sure that the patient was fully able to tolerate each one before proceeding to the next. The hierarchy started with a standard description of an asthmatic attack and progressed through the patient's own description, his or her thoughts while experiencing an attack, and a review of circumstances surrounding most attacks. The desensitization technique was found to be more effective than relaxation training in improving lung function and, during a two-year follow-up period, in reducing the need for medication to control asthma attacks.

Chronic Coughing

A cough is a sudden explosive forcing of air through the glottis. It normally is triggered by the need to expel mucus or other secretions from the respiratory tract. Occasionally a chronic cough exists without any organic basis, functioning instead as an operant behavior.

Aversion Therapy for Chronic Coughing

AUTHORS: A. Barney Alexander, Hyman Chai, Thomas L. Creer, Donald R. Miklich, Charles M. Renne, and R. Ronald de A. Cardoso

PRECIS: Electric shock aversion therapy and ancillary family treatment for chronic cough

INTRODUCTION: The authors cite studies in which different respiratory ailments were treated with various forms of behavior therapy designed to alter the behavior patterns related to the particular respiratory response. They distinguish between those kinds of therapy and a more direct approach intended to modify the specific inappropriate breathing response. In the present study they report the case of a fifteen-year-old male who suffered with a disabling chronic cough.

CASE STUDY: Marvin had been coughing excessively every day for fourteen months before his initial treatment. During that period he had been to emergency rooms eight times, had been hospitalized twenty-five times, and had missed 113 days of school. At times his coughing bouts were so severe that he would lose consciousness.

During his initial eight-month stay at the Children's Asthma Research Institute and Hospital, Marvin was free of coughing, but when he returned home, his cough began again. After discovering that a certain stimulus (beef grease) triggered his cough at home but not at the Institute, the investigators were able to elicit the cough with a saline aerosol that Marvin had been told was beef grease. Since this evidence suggested a psychological basis for his condition, they formulated a behavioral treatment plan. They interviewed the entire family and obtained information about the cough response and the family's dynamics. They found that Marvin's cough was serving several functions: he gained attention and leverage within the family, he related more with his mother, she gained feelings of self-esteem, and it enabled the entire family to avoid focusing on

other more threatening issues. During the family sessions the re-
searcher not only elicited information but counseled them to
avoid reinforcing behavior patterns in response to Marvin's
coughing.

Once the dynamics were established, behavior modification was started. Noting that the principal offending stimuli for
the cough were beef grease, shampoo, bath soap, and hair spray,
the investigators decided to undertake aversive therapy using a
painful, but harmless, electric shock (applied constant current
of 5 ma intensity for one second to the forearm). Grass silver
electrodes were taped to the skin over Beckman electrode paste.
Initially the investigators began a simple punishment procedure
whenever Marvin coughed after inhaling the odors of shampoo or
beef grease, but he became very angry and uncooperative.
Therefore they adopted a new procedure aimed at increasing
the time between the onset of the cough and the exposure to
the stimulus.

Treatment was begun with the shampoo. The open jar was
held under Marvin's nose for two seconds while he inhaled. Initially he was required to refrain from coughing for a six-second
period, the interval being timed with an electric stop clock.
Each time Marvin achieved the delay, the interval was increased
for the next trial. If he did not achieve the delay, he received a
shock. He required seventy-five trials, during which he received
twenty-four shocks, to eliminate the cough aroused by the
shampoo. Trials were held during one-hour sessions on each of
two days.

The same procedure was carried out for the other three
stimuli. At one point Marvin resisted and verbalized fears that
his family would be angry with him when they found out that
his cough was psychological and that he was crazy, but he was
given reassurance and encouragement, which apparently reinforced him sufficiently to induce a more cooperative spirit.

During several follow-up trials consisting of one-minute
exposures to the offending stimuli, Marvin did not have any
urge to cough. Eighteen months after completing the treatment he again successfully resisted coughing on exposure to
the stimuli. In addition his general hypochondriacal pattern

of behavior seemed to have been eliminated and he was functioning well.

COMMENTARY: The authors are careful to point out how this approach, involving a shaping technique that allows the patient to acquire the ability to suppress his cough, differs from a simple punishment technique. This approach was necessary as a response to the patient's initial resistance to the punishment and was a means of avoiding a true reflex cough secondary to the punishment itself. Another vital part of the treatment plan was the family counseling aimed at altering reinforcing behaviors in response to Marvin's coughing. Finally, the authors stress the importance of giving the patient more appropriate ways to gain attention.

SOURCE: Alexander, A. B., Chai, H., Creer, T. L., Miklich, D. R., Renne, C. M., and Cardoso, R. R. de A. "The Elimination of Chronic Cough by Response Suppression Shaping." *Journal of Behavior Therapy and Experimental Psychiatry,* 1973, *4,* 75-80.

Treating Chronic Coughing
with Behavior Therapy

AUTHORS: Paul R. Munford, Diane Reardon, Robert P. Liberman, and Linda Allen

PRECIS: Viewing chronic cough and mutism as operant behaviors

INTRODUCTION: Individuals who exhibit what are usually referred to as hysterical symptoms are considered by most therapists to be manifesting unconscious intrapsychic conflicts. When these behaviors are viewed as such, the therapist usually tries to define the behavior's psychodynamic significance. The authors argue that such symptoms may, in fact, cause reinforcing responses from the environment that tend to maintain the activity. They approached the treatment of an adolescent who was suffering with a chronic cough and mutism as if those behaviors were being perpetuated by the responses she was getting from her family and others.

CASE STUDY: Jennifer was a seventeen-year-old who had been coughing incessantly for four years. She had been subjected to numerous medical evaluations, including bronchoscopy (visualization of the airway with an optical rod introduced via the mouth), but no firm diagnosis or explanation had been presented. Following one such instrumentation she had lost her voice. A number of different therapeutic approaches (psychotherapy, amytal interviews, sleep therapy, hypnosis, and acupuncture) had also been tried without success.

In view of what was apparently a firm resistance to therapy, the therapist decided to hospitalize Jennifer in order to more effectively control her environment. Her therapist believed that her activities probably persisted because of the secondary gain they brought her. This theory was supported by the fact that in the hospital the frequency of her coughing varied according to the social situation she was in at the moment. While sitting alone doing a task, she coughed an average of fourteen times each minute. When she knew she was being observed through a one-way mirror, the average frequency increased to fifty-one times a minute.

To treat her coughing behavior, the therapist initiated an extinction procedure: staff members and patients were instructed to disregard the cough but to otherwise behave normally with her. At the same time a systematic desensitization process was undertaken in which she was made to interact in increasingly stressful environments—the ward, the department of psychiatry, the entire hospital, her home, and finally classes at the university. Thus Jennifer was slowly introduced into situations in which people would be less and less tolerant of her behavior patterns. With this treatment Jennifer's coughing frequency diminished considerably. After twenty weeks she coughed about twenty times each minute, and this number continued to drop until all coughing was eliminated after about one year. The total inpatient time was approximately twenty-three weeks.

Her mutism was treated by shaping her speech patterns. Since she enjoyed home visits, these were used as reinforcers—if Jennifer accomplished certain speech tasks, she was allowed a home visit. In order to maximize her chances to succeed and receive positive reinforcement, the therapist required only small increments of improvement between the rewards. In essence treatment consisted of specifying the exact activity required, giving strong verbal praise when the criteria were satisfied, and rewarding her successes with home time. If any of these components was removed from the treatment, her performance invariably suffered. Normal speech took some six weeks to be reestablished.

Important parts of the overall therapeutic program were daily individual therapy sessions for Jennifer and weekly family therapy sessions for her and her family. It was through the family sessions that her parents were aided to see their role in perpetuating Jennifer's behavior and were guided to respond more constructively. Without the family sessions the possibility of Jennifer's eventual improvement would have been reduced, because the beneficial effects of the inpatient treatment may not have been so well generalized to the outside environment.

COMMENTARY: The authors, through this case presentation, emphasize the importance of examining not only the physiological and psychological aspects of an abnormal behavior or symptom, but also the external factors that can affect, and be affected by, that behavior or symptom. When viewed in such a manner, a therapeutic approach can be designed that can take into consideration all available information and can offer the most hope of improvement for the patient.

SOURCE: Munford, P. R., Reardon, D., Liberman, R. P., and Allen, L. "Behavioral Treatment of Hysterical Coughing and Mutism: A Case Study." *Journal of Consulting and Clinical Psychology,* 1976, *44,* 1008-1014.

Additional Reading

Creer, T. L., Chai, H., and Hoffman, A. "A Single Application of an Aversive Stimulus to Eliminate Chronic Cough." *Journal of Behavior Therapy and Experimental Psychiatry*, 1977, *8*, 107-109.

The authors describe the case of a fourteen-year-old boy who developed after an upper respiratory infection a cough that persisted long after the infection was gone. Since a thorough physical evaluation did not reveal an organic etiology, the therapist tried hypnosis and behavioral therapies. When the child did not respond well to systematic desensitization or to hypnosis, aversive therapy was attempted. Following the baseline period, the boy was treated with a single mild electric shock to the forearm, after which the coughing stopped. A follow-up after two and a half years revealed no recurrence.

6

Skin Disorders

The skin is a complex organ system that serves important physical, biochemical, physiological, and psychological functions. It is susceptible to a great many traumas, abnormal conditions, and diseases and is often one of the organ systems involved in systemic illness. Its visibility, however, is what makes it such a common focus for disorders with a psychological basis.

Though a number of disorders of the skin resulting in various degrees of disfigurement create a number of psychological problems that need to be effectively dealt with while treating the underlying condition, true psychosomatic disorders of the skin—conditions in which psychological factors play a primary causative role—are rather limited. These include neurodermatitis, trichotillomania, and some cases of chronic urticaria. Since trichotillomania was treated in our previous volume as a habit disorder, we do not discuss it in this section (see C. E. Schaefer and H. L. Millman, *Therapies for Children,* San Francisco: Jossey-Bass, 1977).

Neurodermatitis is an inflammation of the skin of a nervous or emotional origin. The condition is frequently reported in children. However, the ease with which it can be confused with atopic dermatitis and psoriasis may lead to underreporting. The condition originates with an area of perceived pruritis which the child scratches. The site, usually located on an elbow, knee, or ankle, becomes mildly inflamed from the scratching and rubbing and develops even more pruritis and pain. Thus an itch-scratch-itch cycle is established which, if unchecked, leads to an area of thickened, inflamed skin that is highly pruritic.

The usual control methods include topical application of lotions and steroids intended to reduce the amount of inflammation and pruritis, as well as the use of systemic medications (antihistamines or sedatives) to help reduce the child's desire to scratch. Very frequently this approach is not sufficiently adequate to interrupt the cycle.

Behaviorists tend to view the condition in terms of a problem behavior. A thorough history and careful recording of the circumstances in which scratching occurs can often give one a good indication whether or not the behavior should be dealt with as a habit disorder or as an operant behavior that is being reinforced by external environmental factors. With this type of analysis the choice of a treatment approach will be clearer and the selection will be more likely to benefit the patient. The therapies suggested in this section can be applied to either situation and, if combined with medication, will undoubtedly improve the chances for breaking the itch-scratch-itch cycle.

The section also includes a digest of an article dealing with a patient with anxiety-provoked urticaria. This disorder is frequently associated with emotional stress, and the methods employed (systematic relaxation and desensitization) seem particularly well suited.

A subsection on the use of suggestion in treating warts is presented as well. Warts are caused by a viral infection. The theories about the etiology of common warts that have been expounded over the ages are often laughable today, but only in the past eighty years or so have we come to recognize the true cause. Coupled with the outlandish theories of their origin have been equally bizarre ideas about their treatment. It is interesting to note, however, that the cure rates obtained with simple suggestion are equal to those obtained with topical medications and surgical procedures. Though the wart's responsiveness to the power of suggestion cannot be interpreted as proof that it is in fact a psychosomatic disorder, we have added this subsection because of the appropriateness of using a form of psychotherapy in treating it. Those earlier treatment ideas which were rich in magic and ritual were no doubt as effective as our approaches are today. In fact the literature supports the view that when the therapist uses suggestion to treat children, the more magical his presentation, the more successful the therapy.

Dermatitis

Dermatitis refers to an inflammation of the skin. Neuroderma-titis is a chronic inflammation and thickening of the skin due to excessive scratching occurring in an itch-scratch-itch cycle. The initial pruritis is felt to have a psychological basis. Chronic urti-caria (hives) is also believed to be due to emotional stress in a number of instances. Both conditions benefit from some form of psychologically oriented therapy.

Elimination of Scratching
Using Maternal Reinforcement

AUTHORS: K. Eileen Allen and Florence R. Harris

PRECIS: Stopping a child's constant scratching by altering her mother's response to the problem behavior

INTRODUCTION: Many childhood behavioral problems can be successfully treated using behavior modification techniques. Unfortunately there are too few behavior therapists to directly treat all such cases. The realization that the parents' attending behaviors can affect their child's problem behavior led the authors to attempt to treat a child who chronically scratched by working with the mother to modify her response to her child's activity. Modifying adult responses was known to have altered such childhood problem behaviors as regressed crawling, socially isolating behavior, temper tantrums, and deficits in motor skills. By working with the parents the therapist also could reduce the actual number of her contacts with the patient.

CASE STUDY: Fay was a five year-old who was brought for treatment because she had been scratching her face, arm, and leg for a year. Consultations with pediatricians and psychiatrists had not resulted in any successful intervention. The child's condition had led to disfiguring sores and scabs on her face, which caused her mother to be so disgusted that she expressed a desire to place the child out of the home. In addition, the marriage was under a great deal of strain due to conflict between the parents over the best way to handle the child.

Because of time limitations the therapists enlisted the aid of the mother in conducting the treatment program. Sessions were held weekly for seven weeks. During the first session, a history and family information were obtained, and the therapists observed mother and daughter apart and interacting. They noted that the child was well developed socially, intellectually, and physically. They also noted that the mother only spoke to the child to criticize. The mother was asked to keep a record over the next week of the child's activities and her own responses to them.

The record revealed that the mother spent a great deal of time punishing and berating the child for a number of different behaviors and attitudes. In addition, although the husband punished the child severely for scratching, he enjoyed a very positive relationship with her in a number of other ways. The therapists suggested that the mother not attempt to alter her husband's behavior and that she should try to confine her directive efforts to working to control the child's scratching. She explained that a previous attempt to ignore all scratching had been unsuccessful, but when asked for details, she revealed that the child was never positively reinforced for not scratching. She was instructed to respond with approval and attention whenever Fay was doing well and not scratching but to ignore any scratching. For further reinforcement the therapists instituted a token system consisting of awarding a gold star for every twenty- to thirty-minute period Fay did not scratch. The stars were pasted in a book, and for every few that were accumulated, an additional reinforcer (a cookie, bit of candy, or the like) was added. Twice a day the stars were counted, and the mother was to express her approval and buy small gifts as further rewards.

At the third session the mother reported some improvement during the day, but the child continued to scratch at night. A stronger reinforcer was chosen—new outfits for Fay's Barbie doll. In the afternoon mother and daughter went out and bought a new outfit, which was then placed in view, but out of reach, of the child. Fay was told that if the following morning there were no fresh scratch marks, the outfit would be hers. The other reinforcement procedures continued.

The child responded well to this new reinforcer, and the mother reported all was going well. A slip did occur when the mother bought an outfit Fay did not like because she was not carrying enough money to pay for the child's choice. She was advised to be prepared in the future, and subsequently things went smoothly. An additional benefit of the program was her husband's change in attitude. He asked his wife to help him control his temper with Fay, and the therapists suggested a verbal cue for the mother to give when she noticed him about to fly into a rage ("Dear, would you please get a loaf of bread from the corner store?").

Fay's face continued to clear, and in view of the apparent success in eliminating the child's scratching, the therapists decided to start a gradual reduction of reinforcements. First the small gifts were eliminated, and then the doll outfits were gradually bought less frequently. The gold stars were to continue to be awarded because the child enjoyed filling the pages of her book with them. At all times the parents were to continue expressing strong social approval for her desirable behaviors.

A four-month follow-up after therapy was terminated revealed that the child's face was clear of sores and scabs.

COMMENTARY: In view of the fact that parents spend so much time with their young children, it makes sense to enlist them in any treatment plan, especially when it involves behavior therapy. The parents are in the best position to offer constant reinforcement, and the more effort they can make, the less time the therapist needs to spend with the patient to accomplish the treatment goals. This type of modification, as mentioned earlier, could be applicable to a host of other socially undesirable behaviors in childhood. However, it requires strongly motivated parents who are capable of being consistent with their responses.

SOURCE: Allen, K. E., and Harris, F. R. "Elimination of a Child's Excessive Scratching by Training the Mother in Reinforcement Procedures." *Behavior Research and Therapy,* 1966, *4,* 79-84.

Behavior Therapy Treatment of Urticaria

AUTHORS: Lloyd K. Daniels

PRECIS: Relaxation training and systematic desensitization for anxiety-provoked hives

INTRODUCTION: Urticaria, or hives, is a skin eruption characterized by elevated reddish or whitish patches (wheals) usually accompanied by itching. Its causes have variously been reported to include hypersensitivity to foods or drugs, various infections, and psychic stimuli. The author reports some of the work that has provided evidence that behavior therapy may be a useful treatment for people suffering from urticaria in certain situations. He goes on to describe the plan used for treating one such individual.

CASE HISTORY: A twenty-three-year-old female junior high school teacher had had an acute attack of urticaria involving her face and itching all over her body some six weeks before her initial visit. The problem occurred daily and peaked in the evenings, consequently interfering with sleep and marital relations. The hives worsened whenever she argued with her husband or had to deal with other members of his family and whenever she had difficulties in the classroom. She felt a great deal of anxiety and anger toward her father-in-law and sister-in-law in particular. Physicians had treated her with a number of medications without any real benefit.

Treatment was conducted in a number of individual sessions. The patient was first trained in deep muscle relaxation, which involves first tensing and then relaxing individual muscle groups in a sequence until relaxation can be achieved quickly without the need to go through the series of exercises. To further reduce anxiety the therapist employed a light hypnotic trance. Once the patient had mastered the relaxation technique, a hierarchy of anxiety-provoking scenes was constructed. While in the relaxed state the patient was told to visualize a neutral scene that did not evoke any particular feeling. Once this was done satisfactorily, the patient next pictured a scene that produced a small amount of stress (such as being with her father-in-law and husband at a restaurant). If anxiety was felt, the patient was told to raise a finger. Once the scene no longer elicited any tension, she moved on to the next scene, which produced slightly more anxiety. The process continued until the image causing the most tension could be calmly visualized (for instance, being alone with her father-in-law and sister-in-law and her family).

After the patient was successfully performing the initial part of the exercises, the therapist added a covert reinforcement technique: the visualization of items that evoked very positive feelings (such as ice cream, reading novels, swimming, playing cards). As the patient reached the point where she was vividly imagining an anxiety-provoking scene from the hierarchy, the therapist would say "reinforcement," the signal for her to switch mentally to a reinforcing scene. The patient received instructions to take the following steps during this part of the training:

1. Imagine the least anxiety-provoking scene until it is clear in your mind.
2. Switch to a reinforcing scene and hold it for five to ten seconds.
3. Erase the scene and relax for thirty seconds.
4. Repeat the procedure with a slightly more anxiety-provoking scene in turn.

The patient practiced each morning and evening but was instructed to rephrase the anxiety-provoking scenes in more positive ways (for example: "You are with your father-in-law and husband in a restaurant and you feel very relaxed").

To assist her in everyday situations the therapist taught her a thought-stopping process that could be used whenever she was about to be overwhelmed by stress. When such feelings were aroused, the subject subvocally said "Stop" and then "Relax," which was a cue word for achieving the relaxed state. Then she was to think a positive statement about the person or situation causing the anxiety ("He's really only trying to be helpful") and then an image from the reinforcing group.

A recurrent headache problem was also treated using the same type of behavior approach. Within two weeks of the onset of therapy the hives were no longer evident during the day, and they disappeared completely after twelve weeks. At the follow-up twenty-three months later, the patient said there had been no further problem with them; she was doing very well and seemed to be much more in control.

COMMENTARY: This form of training could be used for adolescents suffering from urticaria or other forms of neurodermatoses in view of the fact that they involve psychological as well as physiological etiologies. Though the therapy involved requires a great deal of work on the part of the patient, the rapidity of response (significant improvement within two weeks in this instance) is helpful in maintaining the patient's cooperation and active participation.

SOURCE: Daniels, L. K. "Treatment of Urticaria and Severe Headache by Behavior Therapy." *Psychosomatics,* 1973, *14,* 347-351.

Reinforced Inhibition of Scratching

AUTHOR: Robert W. Dobes

PRECIS: Treating a chronic rash due to excessive scratching with positive reinforcement methods

INTRODUCTION: It is well recognized that skin lesions variously termed atopic dermatitis, eczema, or neurodermatitis have mixed etiologies. Primary among them is the vicious cycle developed by scratching. As the patient scratches a painful or pruritic area on the skin, increased release of histamine and other active agents intensifies the skin reaction and leads to greater pain and pruritis, which in turn leads to more scratching. Successful treatment of most of these skin lesions requires the elimination of scratching.

CASE PRESENTATION: The patient was a twenty-eight-year-old woman who had been suffering from an itchy, inflamed rash on the back of her neck for fifteen years. She had undergone a number of medical treatments for her condition, including ultraviolet light and X-ray exposure and cortisone creams and injections, all without any lasting beneficial effect. The rash itself seemed to be exacerbated during times of emotional stress.

The therapist designed a simple reinforcement program in an attempt to eliminate the woman's frequent scratching, which was noted to average about seventy episodes a day during a six-day baseline measurement period. The woman kept track of the number of episodes with the aid of a golf wrist-counter and plotted each day's count on a graph that she hung in a conspicuous place—in this case, the refrigerator door. Her instructions were to try and reduce each day's score by at least two to three episodes.

Reinforcement was provided in two ways. The woman informed her friends of the project and its goal, and they were asked to aid her by checking the graph whenever they visited and encouraging her whenever they noted a decrease. If there was no improvement, they were not to comment at all, and they were never to ask the patient directly how she was progressing. In addition her husband was to take her out to dinner at the end of every week during which she had attained her weekly goal.

The patient's rash improved at a fairly constant rate, and after twenty-six days she had stopped scratching entirely for two days. After that there were a couple of setbacks related to increased stress (a visit by her mother, a personal family tragedy), but each time she was able to reinstitute the program on her own with very good results.

COMMENTARY: This is a very easy program to help eliminate one of the major etiologic factors in chronic skin rashes, but it should be kept in mind that in many such cases appropriate therapy may also include the use of topical agents and the avoidance of specific allergenic or irritating stimuli. However, a reinforcement program such as the one described would lead to a more rapid and thorough elimination of all such rashes regardless of the major underlying etiology.

SOURCE: Dobes, R. W. "Amelioration of Psychosomatic Dermatosis by Reinforced Inhibition of Scratching." *Journal of Behavior Therapy and Experimental Psychiatry*, 1977, *8*, 185-187.

Suppression of Inflammatory Scratching

AUTHORS: David L. Watson, Roland G. Tharp, and Jane Krisberg

PRECIS: Eliminating scratching through a self-designed behavior modification program

INTRODUCTION: Many inflammatory skin lesions are itchy and painful and cause the patient to scratch excessively. The scratching itself can become the greater problem because of the connotation such activity can have in a social context. In addition, the scratching can lead to a further intensification and spread of the original lesion. The authors report the case of a woman who suffered from such a condition for years and who designed a self-modification program based on a model she had learned about in a lecture course.

CASE STUDY: The twenty-one-year-old woman subject had suffered from an inflammatory rash on her legs, arms, and hands since the age of four. While medical opinion was divided about its exact diagnosis, she had been able to gain some relief with special soaps and ointments. She frequently scratched the rash, which persisted day and night, and felt that if she could stop, the rash would clear up. Accordingly, she designed the following behavioral modification program. Initially she gathered information about the frequency of scratching by recording each incident on a card over a two-week period. Nighttime scratching was assumed if her skin was more inflamed in the morning than it had been the night before. After the baseline period she began to substitute stroking for scratching whenever she felt the urge. At times she would have to scratch, but after another two weeks, stroking had become sufficient. At that point she began to substitute patting for stroking.

In order to eliminate nighttime scratching she conditioned herself to awaken whenever she scratched: "When I felt myself getting very sleepy, almost ready to fall asleep, I had to wake myself up and scratch an unaffected area of my skin. While deliberately scratching, I had to concentrate on that and stay awake." She did this each night for one to two minutes and found no new rashes the following mornings. On the seventh night she fell asleep before practicing and found evidence of scratching the next day. Over subsequent nights she successfully avoided scratching by practicing her wake-up technique.

Reinforcement was provided by positive feedback from her family and friends, and especially her boyfriend. She also awarded herself points for appropriate stroking—and then patting—behavior, which, once a sufficient number was accumulated, allowed her to bathe or study (both activities she enjoyed).

After the eighteenth day she no longer felt the desire to scratch and by the twentieth day all scratching, stroking, and patting behaviors were eliminated. Two flare-ups a number of months after terminating her program were successfully controlled using the same approach.

COMMENTARY: The shaping of activities and the use of appropriately reinforcing rewards enabled this patient to rapidly rid herself of an inflammatory rash that had plagued her for a number of years. The authors point out that her strong motivation was a very important factor leading to a successful outcome. A similarly motivated adolescent, concerned with appearance and social acceptance, would likely benefit from the same type of intervention.

SOURCE: Watson, D. L., Tharp, R. G., and Krisberg, J. "Case Study in Self-Modification: Suppression of Inflammatory Scratching While Awake and Asleep." *Journal of Behavior Therapy and Experimental Psychiatry*, 1972, *3*, 213-215.

Additional Readings

Keegan, D. L. "Chronic Urticaria: Clinical Psychophysiological and Therapeutic Aspects." *Psychosomatics,* 1976, *17,* 160-163.

Chronic urticaria is a complex condition that has a complex etiologic structure demanding a multifactorial and dynamic approach to its management. The author stresses the psychodynamic elements that can cause or exacerbate the condition and argues for a holistic treatment approach that takes into account the individual's own psychodynamics and the extent and quality of interpersonal relationships. Short-term goal-directed psychotherapy is often useful when specific psychological difficulties are encountered.

Krupp, N. E. "Self-Caused Skin Ulcers." *Psychosomatics,* 1977, *18,* 15-19.

The author, a psychiatrist, discusses twenty-six patients referred to him by dermatologists with diagnoses of self-induced skin lesions. Only three of his patients were under twenty years of age, and all suffered from separation anxiety. As he sees it, the important factor to consider when managing a patient with self-induced skin lesions is to determine the secondary gain from the problem. Only by addressing psychotherapy to the underlying psychopathology will the condition be adequately treated. In most cases the patient is unaware of the reasons for the abnormal behavior.

Williams, D. H. "Management of Atopic Dermatitis in Children —Control of the Maternal Rejection Factor." *Archives of Dermatology and Syphilology,* 1951, *63,* 545-560.

The author feels that children suffering from atopic dermatitis generally suffer also from a significant amount of maternal rejection. He bases this conclusion on a number of previous studies that delineated dysfunctional relationships between allergic children and their mothers. In this paper he presents the results of a treatment regimen that was intended to help the parent overcome her rejecting patterns of behavior toward her child. In interview sessions the mother was told of the potential harm a rejecting nature can cause and was given advice about how she could make her child feel more accepted and loved. The results revealed that those cases treated only in this manner had a better cure rate than controls treated topically without any family intervention.

Warts

Warts are caused by a virus and can be spread to other areas of the body or to other individuals. Forms of suggestion have been found to be just as successful in curing the condition as has the use of topical medications or surgical removal.

Treating Warts with Hypnotic Suggestion

AUTHOR: Richard Asher

PRECIS: A description of the author's experiences using hypnotherapy for a variety of skin disorders

INTRODUCTION: Asher describes the process of hypnosis in
some detail, calling it "suggestion in pure form." A number of
clinicians have come to realize that for any therapeutic modality to have the optimum effect, the patient must have a certain
amount of belief in its efficacy. Thus medical therapy is usually
associated with some amount of suggestion on the part of the
physician. Frequently, in fact, it is the quality of the doctor-
patient relationship, more than the procedure or medication,
that leads to improvement or cure in the patient's condition.
Hypnosis, as the ultimate suggestion therapy, therefore has a
number of clinical applications.

TREATMENT: The author ran a hypnosis clinic to which patients with a number of different types of conditions were referred by other physicians. Included among them were patients
with a variety of dermatological disorders. In particular Asher
treated a series of patients with warts.

The first induction was performed in a quiet, darkened
room where the patient lay on a comfortable couch. The patient fixed his or her eyes on a point light source (an ophthal-
moscope bulb) while hearing repeated suggestions: "You are
getting sleepy, you can't keep your eyelids open, you are going to
sleep." Once the initial induction was accomplished, the patient
was told the next time would be easier.

When treating warts the author placed the patient in a
hypnotic trance state and then touched each wart as he stated
they would soon disappear. Sessions were held weekly. In his
series seventeen individuals were able to be put under deep
hypnosis (amnesic for the time period and susceptible to post-
hypnostic suggestion), whereas eight patients only achieved
light hypnosis. The number of weekly sessions varied from four

to twenty, depending on how fast results were obtained. In the group that was deeply hypnotizable, eleven were completely cured, four were significantly improved, and two experienced no change in their condition. Of those only lightly hypnotized four were cured and four were not improved.

In a few other patients, about whom he could not tabulate data or make definite claims of efficacy, the author noted improvement or cures in such other dermatological conditions as hyperhidrosis (excessive sweating), atopic dermatitis, and alopecia (hair loss).

COMMENTARY: Asher notes some of the disadvantages of hypnotherapy: since only two in five patients are deeply hypnotizable, not everyone is a suitable candidate. Further, the therapy itself is frequently time consuming for the patient, and the physician or therapist cannot treat many patients at one time. However, inasmuch as all forms of medical therapy involve a certain amount of suggestion, it would seem beneficial in particularly resistant cases to combine other forms of medical therapy with hypnotherapy in order to maximize the effectiveness of the suggestion portion.

Finally it should be pointed out that Asher found children to be excellent subjects for hypnosis.

SOURCE: Asher, R. "Respectable Hypnosis." *British Medical Journal*, 1956, *1*, 309-313.

Important Factors in Treating Warts
with Suggestion

AUTHOR: S. Dudek

PRECIS: The role of the therapeutic relationship in the cure of warts by suggestion

INTRODUCTION: Suggestion as a treatment for common warts has been examined by a number of investigators, with promising results. But, it is difficult to decide whether it was the content of the suggestion, the relationship between the therapist and the patient, the patient's predisposition toward the therapeutic design, or a combination of these that was the most important element in the cure. Dudek's study was designed to explore the importance of the therapeutic relationship in effecting a cure for warts.

STUDY: Twenty children suffering from warts were divided into two groups. The members of each group were seen at weekly intervals, and they all received therapeutically oriented play defined as "play activity focused on some aspect of the child's life which currently he finds troublesome." This information was determined during the course of initial interviews with the parents and child. In addition, all subjects had a placebo (red ink) painted on their warts at every play session.

Children in Group A were told at the second visit (if there had been no improvement in their warts), "If the warts do not begin to disappear by the next visit, I will send you to the doctor to have them cut off." Thus these children were given conditional acceptance, which led to the establishment of generally poor rapport between the therapist and the child. Those in Group B were not given any threat and generally developed a good or very good rapport with the therapist. The definition of a successful relationship was one in which the child could communicate with the therapist about anxiety-laden matters and could play in a cathartic or symbolic way.

Cure of the warts was defined as complete remission within three months. Under that criterion, seven of the ten children in Group B (no threat) were cured, while only three of the ten children in Group A (threat) were cured. The author concludes that "adequacy of emotional rapport may be a relevant factor in effecting cure."

COMMENTARY: The children treated for their warts in this study received play therapy and suggestion (regarding the efficacy of the placebo). It was during the course of the play therapy that the relationship between therapist and child was established. Whether the therapeutic play itself was an important factor in leading to a cure or whether it was only important as a forum in which to develop the emotional relationship between therapist and child cannot be stated definitely. However, it would be hard to imagine a child who could believe in a magician he or she did not like.

SOURCE: Dudek, S. "Suggestion and Play Therapy in the Cure of Warts in Children: A Pilot Study." *Journal of Nervous and Mental Diseases*, 1967, *145*, 37-42.

Hypnotherapy for Warts

AUTHORS: Montague Ullman and Stephanie Dudek

PRECIS: Treating warts with suggestion

INTRODUCTION: The authors note that a number of studies have indicated that hypnotic suggestion can be an effective treatment for common warts of various types. One of the most frequently cited criticisms of such studies is that the reports of cure by suggestion are not valid because the suggestion may have simply coincided with the tendency of warts to undergo spontaneous resolution. In view of the continuing controversy, the authors designed their study so that a patient's condition had to be eliminated within only four weeks after initiating hypnotherapy in order to qualify as a cure.

METHOD: Two study groups were chosen. Group One consisted of fifteen subjects, all of whom were judged to be good hypnotic subjects on the basis of various criteria. Group Two was composed of forty-seven patients who had failed to meet the criteria for deep hypnosis.

All subjects were told that sleep would be induced via hypnotic induction and the state of relaxation achieved would result in a resolution of their warts. Following the induction, once the height of the hypnotic effect was reached, the subject was given the hypnotic suggestion that the warts would begin to disappear. If it was noted at the subsequent visit that there was little or no response, the suggestion was repeated.

The results obtained were quite dependent on whether or not the patient had been a good hypnotic subject. Of the fifteen who were good subjects, eight obtained a complete cure (six of them within two weeks). But only two of the forty-seven patients who were not good hypnotic subjects were considered cured within the prescribed period.

COMMENTARY: It is evident from the study that to effect a cure for warts using suggestion, the therapist has the best chance when he treats a good hypnotic subject. Excluded from this study was anyone under fourteen years of age because the authors believed children would not do well with hypnosis in a clinic setting. However, with their greater belief in magic, children who can successfully undergo hypnotic induction might well have a greater response rate than the people studied here.

SOURCE: Ullman, M., and Dudek, S. "On the Psyche and Warts. II: Hypnotic Suggestion and Warts." *Psychosomatic Medicine,* 1960, *22,* 68-76.

The Therapist's Role
in Suggestion Therapy for Warts

AUTHOR: Hermann Vollmer

PRECIS: The importance of credibility when invoking suggestion therapy for the cure of warts

INTRODUCTION: The author attempts to respond to critics of suggestion therapy by pointing out that a number of different types of medical therapies are being used for warts, and many of them have been called into question by investigators who are unable to duplicate the results of the original studies. In effect, he says, all therapies other than surgery (and the no longer used radiotherapy) for warts are forms of suggestion therapy. The physician, in choosing a particular medication or treatment, automatically suggests to the patient that this therapy will work. In his article, Vollmer presents some of the ways in which he has been able to successfully cure warts in more than one hundred children—all the ways based solely on suggestion.

TREATMENT: The child being treated with suggestion for warts must be able to comprehend the invocations and instructions. Equally important is that the child should be "impressed without being frightened."

The method Vollmer used in the majority of cases was to trace the shape of the hand with a pencil onto a sheet of paper and then mark in appropriate size and location all warts present on the hand (most of the childhood warts he saw were on the hands). The child then took the tracing home after the treatment with instructions to follow the course of them every day. The treatment consisted of painting the warts with some harmless and inactive dye while stating: "I am going to paint your warts with a blue (or red) fluid. It will not hurt, but the warts will go away. Don't wash your hands today, and don't touch the warts any more until they are gone. Now watch carefully and you will feel a very faint tingling in your warts. That is a sign that they will soon disappear." If the child admitted to feeling the "tingling," it was an indication that the physician's act was believed.

At times, generally when older and more skeptical children were being treated, a more complex routine would be used. Occasionally Vollmer would place the child under an X-ray machine and pretend to irradiate the area of the warts. Colored lights were sometimes shined on the lesions. Or routine immunizations (when needed for health maintenance) might be given special healing powers. "The creation of a certain atmosphere seems to be more important than the choice of the dye or apparatus in the treatment of warts."

COMMENTARY: Suggestion therapy of the type used by Vollmer involves a placebo in most cases (dye, unactivated X-ray machine, harmless light source, and so on). Children are far more prone to suggestion than are adults. The results claimed by the author, while not controlled or tabulated, are impressive. This form of therapy seems ideal but, as pointed out, will not be as effective if the physician is not convincing.

SOURCE: Vollmer, H. "Treatment of Warts by Suggestion." *Psychosomatic Medicine*, 1946, *8*, 138-142.

Additional Readings

Bett, W. R. "Wart, I Bid Thee Begone!" *The Practitioner,* 1951, *166,* 77-80.

An interesting historical look at the evolving theories on the causation and treatment of warts. Therapies that have been touted include one from Oscar Wilde's mother: " 'Tie up some pebbles in a bag with a piece of silver money; whoever finds the bag and keeps the money, to him the warts will go, and leave you.' " Others advocated "washing the hands by moonbeams only in a well-polished silver basin in which there was not a single drop of water." The author does not advocate any of the historical cures.

Sinclair-Gieben, A. H. C., and Chalmers, D. "Evaluation of Treatment of Warts by Hypnosis." *Lancet,* 1959, *2,* 480-482.

Fourteen patients with warts on both sides of the body were treated with a hypnotic suggestion that the warts on only one side of the body would disappear. Thus, each individual served as his or her own control. The results revealed that of the ten who were able to achieve a deep trance state, nine had unilateral clearing of their warts within three months, with no improvement noted on the contralateral side. The patients who were not good hypnotic subjects did not improve.

Surman, O. S., Gottlieb, S. K., and Hackett, T. P. "Hypnosis in the Treatment of Warts." *Archives of General Psychiatry,* 1973, *28,* 439-441.

In a repeat of the same experimental format that was used by an earlier investigator, patients with warts on both sides of the body were treated with a hypnotic suggestion that only the warts on one side of their body would clear. Of the seventeen subjects so treated, eight were excellent hypnotic subjects, while nine were unable to achieve a deep hypnotic state. The results revealed that nine subjects lost a portion or all of their warts, but only one showed a complete selective improvement. Improvement in the other individuals was noted bilaterally.

7

Urinary System
Disorders

It is well known that intense anxiety tends to increase the urge to empty the bladder. Under great stress even adults sometimes micturate without awareness. For instance, involuntary micturition is not an uncommon reaction among front-line troops in imminent danger. During wartime, too, there is a marked increase in enuresis in children. But apart from reducing voluntary control, emotional states probably also affect the chemical composition and physical nature of the urine, increasing the sugar level, influencing the presence of ketone bodies, and changing the color, volume, and specific gravity of the urine.

In children, urinary disturbances may include the inability

to urinate as well as frequent urinations and involuntary urinations. Enuresis or involuntary bedwetting is the most common and widely studied urinary disorder in childhood. In addition to causing the child intense embarrassment or guilt, urinary problems can result in child abuse incidents and situations where the child becomes a social outcast. Thus, contrary to traditional pediatric advice, it is generally not a good idea to just let children grow out of these disorders. Though 98 percent of all children cease wetting by age fifteen on their own, this spontaneous remission often occurs only after years of shame, embarrassing situations, and intense parent-child conflicts. And furthermore, some children never do outgrow bedwetting or urinary frequency.

Historically, bedwetting problems have been mentioned in various writings since Egyptian times. Over the centuries there have been as many attempts to relieve this condition as there have been explanations, some of which proved more efficacious than others. As is evident in the following digests, the behavioral approaches to treating enuresis and excessive urination have so far been the most successful.

⊚⊚⊚⊚⊚⊚⊚⊚⊚⊚⊚⊚⊚⊚⊚⊚⊚⊚⊚⊚⊚⊚⊚⊚⊚⊚⊚⊚⊚⊚⊚⊚

Enuresis

Nighttime enuresis, a common problem among children, has received considerable attention in the psychological literature. Functional nocturnal enuresis has been defined as regular bedwetting in children four years of age or older who show no sign of neurologic or urologic pathology. It is estimated that about 15 percent of all five-year-olds are nocturnally enuretic. Enuresis may be classified as primary (present since birth) or secondary (occurring after a period of toilet training).

The most popular and extensively researched treatment for enuresis is the use of a urine alarm or bell-and-pad device. This apparatus employs a sensing or detecting mechanism (urine alarm) on which the child sleeps and which is activated as urine passes onto it. The child is immediately awakened by the buzzer, ceases voiding, turns off the alarm, and then completes the act of micturition on the toilet. This treatment works in an average of five to twelve weeks, with about a 30 percent relapse rate. In recent years a number of other techniques have been developed, such as hypnosis, retention control, and dry bed training, which seem to offer effective alternatives to the urine alarm.

The following section is designed to supplement the section on enuresis in the first book in this series (C. E. Schaefer and H. L. Millman, Therapies for Children, *San Francisco: Jossey-Bass, 1977). The reader is encouraged to consult the earlier volume for other approaches to this disorder.*

⊚⊚⊚⊚⊚⊚⊚⊚⊚⊚⊚⊚⊚⊚⊚⊚⊚⊚⊚⊚⊚⊚⊚⊚⊚⊚⊚⊚⊚⊚⊚⊚

Treating Enuresis by Progressively
Earlier Waking

AUTHORS: Ratan Singh, Debora Phillips, and Steven C. Fischer

PRECIS: A new program involving waking the child two hours after she falls asleep and then progressively earlier

INTRODUCTION: Since the authors had achieved only limited control of a client's bedwetting with the Kimmel daytime retention method (see H. D. Kimmel and E. Kimmel, "An Instrumental Conditioning Method for the Treatment of Enuresis," *Journal of Behavior Therapy and Experimental Psychiatry*, 1970, *1*, 121-123), they devised a nighttime retention procedure. The thirteen-year-old girl in this case study had been completely toilet trained at age three but had resumed bedwetting again by age six. Since that time she typically had wet the bed from two to six nights a week. Four years of family therapy elsewhere had proved ineffective, since the girl seemed unconcerned about the bedwetting.

NIGHTTIME RETENTION TRAINING: A behavior analysis revealed one consistency in the girl's bedwetting: she always wet two or more hours after going to bed. Thus, she was instructed to set her alarm to go off two hours after retiring. After awakening to the alarm, she was to go to the toilet, return to bed, and not go to the bathroom again until morning (about 6 A.M.). A string of seven consecutive dry nights was the criterion for each further reduction in the time before wake-up—to ninety minutes after bedtime, to sixty minutes, forty-five minutes, and finally to thirty minutes. Then she was to go to the bathroom without the alarm every night so as to fade out its use.

In response to this procedure, the girl did not wet the bed for seven days when the alarm was set for two hours after bedtime. She wet only one to three times during the ninety-, sixty-, and forty-five-minute intervals, and not at all during the thirty-minute period. At this point training was interrupted for two months while the girl attended summer camp. She continued to set her alarm for thirty minutes at camp and had only two bed-wetting episodes.

The following changes in the training were added when the girl returned from camp. First, she agreed to wash the wet sheets, rather than have her mother do it. Second, her parents promised her a new bed if she did not have a wetting incident. After the first week of dry nights the use of the alarm was faded. Her parents praised her after each dry night, and the therapist also praised her successes when she called each week. An eight month follow-up revealed no further wetting instances.

COMMENTARY: The present procedure differs from the Kimmel method in that it directly trains the child to retain urine for progressively longer periods at night. In the Kimmel treatment, daytime retention of urine must generalize to nighttime control if bedwetting is to cease. Since this generalization does not automatically happen in all cases, nocturnal retention training may be indicated when the Kimmel method proves ineffective. The basic assumption of both daytime and nighttime retention training is that enuresis is primarily the result of the child's responding to relatively weak bladder-distension cues. In view of the limitations of the present case study design, further research is needed to explore the usefulness of nocturnal retention training.

SOURCE: Singh, R., Phillips, D., and Fischer, S. C. "The Treatment of Enuresis by Progressively Earlier Waking." *Journal of Behavior Therapy and Experimental Psychiatry*, 1976, 7, 277-278.

Applying the Kimmel Treatment Method with Older Enuretics

AUTHOR: James M. Stedman

PRECIS: Daytime retention control training with an adolescent

INTRODUCTION: The author describes the case of a thirteen-year-old girl who had been an enuretic all her life. She was currently wetting four to five times a week. The Kimmel method (see the preceding digest), which involves reinforcing the child for gradually increasing daytime retention of urine, was selected as the treatment approach. Kimmel and Kimmel report that nighttime control of the bladder usually follows in a relatively short time.

TREATMENT: Since the Kimmels typically worked with younger children, they relied on the parents to supervise the treatment program. In the present study, the author gave all monitoring responsibility to the girl herself. After explaining the rationale of the procedure to the girl, Stedman asked her to maintain a daily diary of her urinations. In the diary she recorded her awareness of bladder distension cues (at three levels—weak, middle, and strong), the frequency of urination, and the number of nighttime "accidents" during the week. The first week's record showed she tended to urinate frequently and in response to very weak bladder cues during the day.

She was then instructed to record bladder cues hourly and to discriminate between weak, middle, and strong sensations. She was to try to hold her urine for a thirty minute period beyond the onset of strong distension cues. Moreover, the girl was to continue to record all daytime urinations and nighttime "accidents." Her intake of fluids was not controlled, and she received no positive reinforcement beyond the therapist's praise.

By the fifth session, her daytime urinations had declined from an average of 4.7 per day to 3.0 per day, spaced evenly through the day in response to strong bladder cues. By the seventh week of training the frequency of bedwetting had also begun to decline, and it had stopped by the twelfth week. A follow-up indicated that she had wet the bed only four times in three months.

COMMENTARY: With certain modifications the Kimmel method was found to be effective with an older child. Noteworthy is the fact that the adolescent in this case was able to assume responsibility for her own training and did not need parental supervision. And concrete rewards were not needed to motivate the girl in this case. Further studies are needed to determine whether this adaptation of the Kimmel procedure is generally successful with older children and adolescents.

SOURCE: Stedman, J. M. "An Extension of the Kimmel Treatment Method for Enuresis to an Adolescent: A Case Report." *Journal of Behavior Therapy and Experimental Psychiatry,* 1972, *3,* 307-309.

Overlearning in the Conditioning Treatment of Enuresis

AUTHORS: George C. Young and R. T. T. Morgan

PRECIS: The use of the overlearning procedure to reduce relapse rate

INTRODUCTION: This paper reports on the use of the overlearning technique in conjunction with the bell-and-pad treatment (see the opening of this section). The data were derived from a four-year period at an outpatient clinic, during which a total of 126 children received the overlearning therapy and 218 were given the traditional bell-and-pad treatment alone. The children were followed up by letter at six-month intervals for varying lengths of time.

OVERLEARNING TREATMENT: The overlearning procedure required children on the bell-and-pad conditioning apparatus to maintain or regain their learned nocturnal bladder control for fourteen consecutive dry nights (the criterion of success) even though they drank up to two pints of liquid in the hour before bedtime. The relapse rate (the rate of recurrence of wetting in children who had become dry with the bell-and-pad) for children treated with the overlearning method was found to be 10 percent, as compared to a rate of 29 percent for those children who did not "overlearn."

COMMENTARY: A relatively high relapse rate is one of the biggest problems with the bell-and-pad conditioning method. In several studies the authors have demonstrated the effectiveness of the overlearning procedure in reducing the relapse rate to a satisfactory level. The overlearning method has proven superior to other techniques (intermittent reinforcement, CNS stimulant drugs) in counteracting the problem of relapse. It would seem, then, that the overlearning method should be incorporated as part of the standard bell-and-pad procedure.

SOURCE: Young, G. C., and Morgan, R. T. T. "Overlearning in the Conditioning Treatment of Enuresis: A Long-Term Follow-Up Study." *Behaviour Research and Therapy*, 1972, *10*, 410-419.

Additional Readings

Azrin, N. H., and Thienes, P. M. "Rapid Elimination of Enuresis by Intensive Learning Without a Conditioning Apparatus." *Behavior Therapy*, 1978, *9*, 342-354.

Recent studies have indicated that enuresis can be eliminated very rapidly with an operant approach. The authors modified the method to make it more convenient to use, especially by dropping the use of a conditioning apparatus. The new method consists of one day of intensive training involving reinforcement for inhibiting urination, practice in appropriate urination, bladder-awareness training, copious drinking, self-correction and positive practice for accidents, awakening training, and family encouragement. All fifty children, ages three to fourteen, who received this intensive treatment stopped bedwetting. Accidents were reduced to 25 percent on the first night and decreased further to 10 percent after one month and to 2 percent at one year. The average child had only four wetting incidents before achieving two weeks of dryness. Relapses were infrequent (20 percent) and always reversed by a second training session. This reduction was greater than that achieved by children in the control group, who received the standard bell-and-pad conditioning treatment. The authors conclude that this new method provides a convenient way to eliminate enuresis for almost all enuretic children over three years of age.

Baller, W. R. *Bedwetting: Origins and Treatment.* Elmsford, N.Y.: Pergamon, 1975.

This book presents a clear, concise review of the etiology, correlates, and treatments of childhood enuresis. Baller highlights the critical role played by the family in managing this disorder. Without family awareness and participation, he concludes that successful treatment is improbable.

Bollard, R. J., and Woodroffe, P. "The Effect of Parent-Administered Dry-Bed Training on Nocturnal Enuresis in Children." *Behavior Research and Therapy*, 1977, *15*, 159-165.

In this study, two major modifications were made in the dry-bed training procedure described by N. H. Azrin, T. J. Sneed, and R. M. Foxx ("Dry-Bed Training: Rapid Elimination of Childhood Enuresis," *Behavior Research and Therapy*, 1974, *12*, 147-156). The first modification was to have parents administer the intensive all-night training program rather than an outsider trainer. In fourteen children treated in this manner, nocturnal enuresis was eliminated. The median time that elapsed before the last night of wetting was only twelve days, and there were two relapses in a six-month follow-up period. The second modification involved administering the dry-bed procedure without the use of an enuresis machine. This resulted in a significantly reduced frequency of bedwetting, although noctural enuresis was not completely arrested in any of the ten children treated.

Catalina, D. "Enuresis: Parent-Mediated Modification." Paper presented at the Eastern Psychological Association Convention, New York, 1976.

The effect of parent-mediated training on children's bedwetting was explored. The procedure, similar to the bell-and-pad conditioning in which awakening follows wetting, was performed without an alarm device. Twenty families significantly reduced wetting in their children. The results are discussed in terms of the wet-awaken contingency, delay, and parental consistency.

Doleys, D. M. "Behavioral Treatments for Nocturnal Enuresis in Children: A Review of the Recent Literature." *Psychological Bulletin,* 1977, *84,* 30-54.

The treatment methods reviewed are divided into three categories: those that used the standard urine alarm or bell-and-pad; those that employed retention-control training; and those that modified the existing stimulus or consequent events but did not use the urine alarm or retention-control training as the primary mode of treatment. The author concludes that all the behavioral procedures described have some degree of effectiveness. The bell-and-pad has been the most thoroughly researched and is the only technique to have been compared with various forms of psychotherapy. The generally high relapse rate with the urine alarm has been reduced by the use of an intermittent reinforcement schedule and overlearning, although these procedures tend to lengthen treatment. The rationale underlying retention-control training seems well founded, but its clinical application has not met expectations. More well-designed and better-controlled studies are needed to determine the efficacy of this method. The dry-bed training program is probably the most promising of the more operantly oriented forms of treatment, but more replications and comparative studies involving other established procedures are needed.

Doleys, D. M., Ciminero, A. R., Tollison, J. W., Williams, C. L., and Wells, K. C. "Dry-Bed Training and Retention Control Training: A Comparison." *Behavior Therapy*, 1977, *8*, 541-548.

In this study comparing dry-bed training (DBT) and retention-control training (RCT), changes in bladder capacity as well as wets per night were recorded. The results revealed DBT to be effective in reducing enuresis, DBT to be clearly superior to RCT, and no apparent relationship between bladder capacity and changes in wetting frequency.

Finley, W. W., and Wansley, R. A. "Auditory Intensity as a Variable in the Conditioning Treatment of Enuresis Nocturna." *Behavior Research and Therapy*, 1977, *15*, 181-185.

The authors conclude that a very loud alarm bell or buzzer is definitely advantageous, especially for those children who are slow responders. More parents probably would be encouraged to continue treatment if the number of dry nights recorded during the early stage of treatment could be increased. A very loud alarm tends to achieve this goal, along with a corresponding increase in the rate of becoming dry. Relapse rates do not significantly increase or decrease with the use of a very loud alarm.

Jeru, D., Morgan, R. T. T., Turner, R. K., and Jones, A. "A Controlled Trial of the Treatment of Nocturnal Enuresis in Residential Homes for Children." *Behavior Research and Therapy*, 1977, *15*, 1-16.

The authors evaluated the practicality and efficacy of treating enuretic children in residential treatment centers by means of the bell and pad. Eighteen of the nineteen children treated achieved an initial arrest of enuresis in a mean time of 11.9 weeks. After a follow-up period of at least twenty months, seventeen of the nineteen children were found to be dry. The authors conclude that the alarm treatment is as effective and practical in children's homes as it is in the family situation.

Popler, K. "Token Reinforcement in the Treatment of Nocturnal Enuresis: A Case Study and Six-Month Follow-Up." *Journal of Behavior Therapy and Experimental Psychiatry*, 1976, 7, 83-84.

A fourteen-year-old male adolescent with primary enuresis was given token rewards for nonenuretic behavior. The boy kept records of wet and dry nights. After he had collected fifteen coupons, he could redeem them for five dollars. The coupon or token requirement was then raised to twenty and then to thirty-five. The behavior was eliminated in four months, and control was being maintained at the time of a six-month follow-up.

Young, G. C., and Turner, R. K. "CNS Stimulant Drugs and Conditioning Treatment of Nocturnal Enuresis." *Behavior Research and Therapy*, 1965, 3, 93-101.

The authors conclude that stimulant drugs facilitate the conditioning treatment of nocturnal enuresis. Methedrine was found to be marginally superior to dexedrine, and it did not produce the significant rise in relapse rate associated with the other drugs. The age and sex of the patient were found to be related to the treatment response, and early treatment, beginning at four years, seems best.

Polyuria

Polyuria is the excessive secretion and discharge of urine. The urine does not, as a rule, contain abnormal constituents. It has been suggested that "excessive" be defined as more than eight times a day during the waking hours, if urination is regularly this frequent for an extended period. As far as nocturnal urinations are concerned, even a persistent frequency greater than once a night would appear to be abnormal for older children (see A. J. Yates and A. D. Poole, "Behavioral Analysis in a Case of Excessive Frequency of Micturition," Behavior Therapy, *1972, 3, 449-453).*

The treatment of polyuria has received relatively little attention in the psychosomatic literature. It can, however, lead to intense feelings of embarrassment in a child, to a loss of self-esteem, and to a withdrawal from social relationships. Before a diagnosis of psychogenic or anxiety-related polyuria can be made, physical causes must be ruled out, such as diabetes, chronic nephritis, excessive intake of liquids, hyperthyroidism, and nephrosclerosis.

Modifying Excessive Frequency of Urination

AUTHORS: A. Desmond Poole and Aubrey J. Yates

PRECIS: Case study involving daytime retention-control training

INTRODUCTION: The subject, a twenty-four-year-old college student, stated that his constant urge to urinate was seriously interfering with his studying and social life. Although he could hold his urine for more than an hour, he would urinate every few minutes when a toilet was available, although he passed little urine on each attempt. The subject reported that he had had to urinate every hour or two since he was a boy but that the rate had increased since the death of his father several years earlier, and the urge to go had progressively become more frequent. Currently he was waking up several times a night to urinate. No organic cause of the disorder was discovered, and previous treatment with drugs had proven ineffective. He was then urinating from thirty to sixty times a day.

TREATMENT: Assuming the subject had developed the habit of urinating in response to very weak bladder-distension cues, the therapist began to train him to disregard these cues. In addition to keeping a record of the frequency of his urinations, the subject learned that between 9:00 A.M. and 8:59 P.M. each day (fixed period) he must not urinate more than a specified number of times and a specified minimum time interval must elapse between successive urinations. During the rest of each day (free period) he could urinate whenever he felt the desire to do so. Since the pretreatment time between urinations was about thirty-five minutes, the initial interval in which he was to delay urination was one hour during the fixed period. During the three weeks he was on this interval schedule, the frequency of urinations during the free period dropped from nineteen to twelve. For the next three weeks the time restriction on urinations during the fixed period was one and a half hours, and this interval was gradually raised (in half-hour increments) to four hours. A parallel decline in urination frequency occurred during the free period. After twenty-eight weeks of treatment, the frequency of the subject's urinations was within the normal range. He was then told that no further time restrictions were needed and that he could urinate whenever he felt the urge. However, he was asked to maintain a record of his urinations. A check of this record over the next three months revealed that the daily frequency of his urinations continued to be steady, that is, about seven times a day. A one-year follow-up disclosed a similar finding.

COMMENTARY: The relatively simple procedure of training the subject to refrain from urinating for progressively longer periods seemed quite effective in this case. A similar method of daytime retention-control training has been employed with enuretic children. The procedure seems to produce a greater functional bladder capacity in the subject. The advantage of this procedure is that it is simple and easy to understand and requires relatively little therapist time.

SOURCE: Poole, A. D., and Yates, A. J. "The Modification of Excessive Frequency of Urination: A Case Study." *Behavior Therapy*, 1975, *6*, 78-86.

Counterconditioning Anxiety Underlying Urinary Frequency

AUTHOR: Henk M. van der Ploeg

PRECIS: Desensitizing the anxiety of a fourteen-year-old boy with an excessive urge to urinate

INTRODUCTION: The presenting problem in this case was school phobia. The boy felt an almost constant urge to urinate in school and had started to urinate more than three times an hour. Afraid of interrupting classroom activities by frequently going to the toilet, he had not returned to school. Even at home the thought of school provoked the desire to urinate, and he was currently urinating fifteen to twenty times a day. A physical exam was negative, and acute cystitis was ruled out.

TREATMENT: A program to countercondition the school anxiety which led to the urinary frequency was set up. The therapist discovered in the initial interview that talking about the client's sailing experiences helped him reduce and inhibit the anxiety caused by the school stimuli. After briefly instructing the boy in muscle relaxation and the theory of reciprocal inhibition, the therapist presented a detailed description of an easy hour in school. After thirty seconds the therapist started discussing, for the same amount of time, a day's sailing experiences. This procedure was repeated. While talking about sailing the boy's anxiety level diminished markedly. When the easy-school-day discussion no longer aroused anxiety, the therapist proceeded to a more difficult item on the hierarchy. This procedure was continued until the boy imagined spending an entire morning at school. During these sessions the therapist also told one or two stories to distract and relax the boy. The boy had to practice repeating these stories aloud, and he was asked to continue these counterconditioning exercises between sessions.

After completing fifteen sessions in five weeks, the boy no longer exhibited anxiety when he imagined school scenes. He was then asked to go back to school; the time in school began at one hour and gradually increased until he was attending full time. The therapist used modeling and role-playing exercises to enable the boy to tell his friends and teachers about his problem and to ask to leave the classroom.

In school the boy sometimes felt the urge to go, but he could control this now by using the distracting stories and by reminding himself that he could resist the urge (since he had controlled it for several hours during therapy and at home). His teachers assisted by giving him social reinforcement for being in school. The boy soon reported no discomfort at all and never left class to urinate. His urinary frequency had returned to normal at school and at home. An eighteen-month follow-up revealed that the frequency of his urinations was still normal and he had lost no school time because of anxieties.

COMMENTARY: This case study illustrates how using competing responses can reduce intense anxiety, especially when the counterconditioning exercises are practiced at home. The treatment method in this case was very similar to the standard desensitization approach except that the therapist also used story telling to lower the anxiety. Other therapists have used reading assignments as a counterconditioning agent.

SOURCE: van der Ploeg, H. M. "Treatment of Frequency of Urination by Stories Competing with Anxiety." *Journal of Behavior Therapy and Experimental Psychiatry,* 1975, *6,* 165-166.

Treating Excessive Frequency of Urination by Desensitization

AUTHOR: Davis W. Taylor

PRECIS: Successful treatment of a fifteen-year-old female with desensitization procedures

INTRODUCTION: Assuming that anxiety is a major cause of too frequent urination, it follows that desensitizing the child to this anxiety should be a particularly effective form of treatment. The subject in this case study complained of excessive frequency of urination while in school or engaged in school-related activities. The difficulty had been intermittently present since the age of six but had become much more pronounced during the current school year. The urgency would begin while the girl was waiting for the school bus and would intensify when she arrived at school. She would often have to leave a class several times during the period. Embarrassed by this difficulty, the girl was trying to avoid school and was withdrawing from extracurricular activities and social relations. Physical and urological exams were negative, and chemotherapy with tranquilizers had proven ineffective. On the Fear Survey Schedule the girl revealed strong fears of riding in buses, public speaking, feeling different from others, and being scrutinized.

TREATMENT: The girl first learned muscle relaxation in three weekly sessions and was told to practice relaxation three times a week at home. Then the following three hierarchies of feared activities were constructed: (1) riding in a school bus; (2) being in school buildings and classrooms; and (3) actively participating in classroom activities. The weakest item in the hierarchy of being in school was "You are riding in the school bus and can see your school," and the strongest was "You are sitting in the classroom and the class is in progress. The teacher is talking, asking questions." It required five one-hour sessions to desensitize the girl to the three hierarchies in succession. Since she still was uncertain about her ability to conquer her fears in real life, she was seen for two "overlearning" sessions. During these sessions she was given continuous exposures (of three and ten minute durations, respectively) to imagining the sequential activities of a typical school day, riding the school bus, and answering questions in class. All the therapy sessions were initiated and completed during her three-month summer vacation.

When she returned to school in the fall, she reported by phone that she experienced no urinary urgency. She requested some additional sessions to discuss some problems with family relationships. After five more sessions all therapy contact was terminated. A follow-up four months later disclosed that the frequency of urination was normal and her social relationships were satisfactory.

COMMENTARY: Noteworthy was the observation that when an item from a hierarchy was presented, the girl reported a sensation of urinary urgency rather than the usual report of anxiety. Like most anxiety responses, the sensation of urgency diminished in intensity with later presentations of the item. Because of the case study design the author could not evaluate the relative contribution of the overlearning procedure. But he speculates that the overlearning modification might help certain refractory cases of polyuria.

SOURCE: Taylor, D. W. "Treatment of Excessive Frequency of Urination by Desensitization." *Journal of Behavior Therapy and Experimental Psychiatry*, 1972, *3*, 311-313.

Additional Readings

Geist, R. W., and Antolak, S. J. "Interstitial Cystitis in Children." *Journal of Urology,* 1970, *104,* 922-925.

Diurnal frequency of urination, the *sine qua non* of interstitial cystitis in children, was the chief complaint in most of the cases studied by these authors. Those children whose diurnal frequency was associated with a small bladder usually responded to antispasmodics and not to distension of the bladder with water, whereas those with interstitial cystitis did not respond to antispasmodics but did to distension. The remarkably high incidence of psychological problems evident in children with interstitial cystitis suggested that the dynamics underlying this disorder were psychosomatic in origin. The authors recommend that a diagnosis of interstitial cystitis be made for children with urinary frequency and urgency if the following conditions are met: (1) the urine is sterile and there is no history of infection; (2) typical petachiae are seen after distension of the bladder; (3) no other pathology is found; and (4) dramatic relief of symptoms occurs after diagnostic distension with only seventy cm. of water.

8

Conversion Reactions

A conversion reaction is a partial or total loss of a sensory, motor, or autonomic function that is due to psychological (not organic) factors. The word *conversion* is used synonymously with *hysteria*. Emotionally stressful situations usually trigger the loss. Typical symptoms are impaired gait, paralysis of limbs, and visual difficulties. The condition usually provides significant secondary gains, since children with conversion reactions often are removed from stressful situations and permitted to avoid activities at which they have frequently failed. Paralysis and anesthesias take the form that the child believes would occur, and the neurologic and

muscular groups that would be affected by organic causes
are not involved. Many theorists believe that the symptoms are
symbolic expressions of psychological conflicts. Rather than experience anxiety, the child converts these emotional conflicts
into physical symptoms. An attempt to avoid seeing painful situations may lead to hysterical impairment of vision, for example. Or paralysis may be a way of avoiding performance or
symbolically getting even with adults by losing a function.
Many patients show a lack of concern (*la belle indifférence*)
regarding their symptoms; others appear quite agitated about
them. Whatever the degree of concern, the practitioner must
rule out both conscious malingering and organic factors. But
while he is trying to do so, he must also avoid painful, hazardous, and possibly unnecessary medical tests, because these often
have the effect of reinforcing psychogenically caused physical
symptoms. The keys to success in these cases are stopping the
medical tests and treating the psychological causes while providing physical rehabilitation. And once the conversion symptoms
have been eliminated, one need not fear symptom substitution,
according to most studies.

No statistic is available on the incidence of conversion
reactions in children. However, it is clear from the literature and
from the frequency of hospital admissions that conversion reactions are a serious and relatively frequent occurrence in children. Suggestive techniques combined with reducing stress have
been effectively used by pediatricians.

In this last section of the book, we present works on conversion reactions in general or on symptoms that do not fall in
any other psychosomatic category (such as migraine headaches,
tics, seizures, abdominal pain, and vomiting). Although some
types of seizure are viewed as conversion reactions, for instance,
we have included treatment of that symptom in the section on
seizures, rather than here.

Hysterical Disorders of Motor Function

AUTHORS: Victor Dubowitz and Lionel Hersov

PRECIS: A discussion of the minimum assessment of organic disease, the use of immediate physical rehabilitation, and the treatment of psychological stress

INTRODUCTION: Dubowitz and Hersov discuss the need to recognize hysterical disorders and efficiently rule out organic disease, without performing large batteries of unnecessary, painful, and often hazardous tests that may exacerbate symptoms. The authors recommend the use of a team composed of a physician, psychiatrist, physiotherapist, psychologist, and social worker. They also review various definitions of hysteria. The term *conversion hysteria* denotes neurological symptoms caused by the conversion of anxiety into somatic problems. There can also be an hysterical prolongation of an originally organically caused symptom. Dubowitz and Hersov find the concept of a "sick role" helpful in understanding how the positive aspects of being sick outweigh the negative aspects for the child. The "hysterical" sickness can be prolonged by treatment that confirms the sick role and cured by making the advantages of health more pronounced.

TREATMENT: One case they describe concerns a twelve-year-old boy who was unable to stand or walk because of pain and excruciating tenderness in his calves and a consequent resistance to having his feet flexed. No muscle group was overtly weak, and all tendon reflexes were normal. The diagnosis was past myositis followed by hysterical paralysis. He was an excellent student with no psychological problems other than being unhappy with boarding school and wanting to live at home. A muscle biopsy that was performed to assess the possibility of active myositis showed complete normality. When the therapist reassured parents and child, the paralysis disappeared in two and a half months.

Another case also involved a boy who was unable to stand.

At first fallen arches were diagnosed, X rays taken, and plastic arch supports prescribed. When the pain worsened, the ten-year-old was put in traction for two weeks, but with no benefit. Various blood studies were all negative. After leaving the hospital, he developed weakness in his arms and double vision. Further blood studies, a lumbar puncture, and a myelogram were normal. A muscle biopsy resulted in a diagnosis of polymyositis and a treatment with prednisolone, which also did not work. Eventually the authors decided that hysterical paralysis had followed an illness which had been exacerbated by intensive tests and prolonged hospitalization. Rapid and sustained improvement resulted from stopping the diagnostic tests and instituting physical rehabilitation. Psychological intervention took the form of reassuring the father about the boy's health. The authors also note that the father became more supportive of his wife and the boy, who had been suffering from stress caused by a recent move.

Three other cases having the same elements of prolonged medical treatment are reported in detail. In each case physical rehabilitation and psychological intervention were successful. A ten-year-old boy would not walk and had a variety of other symptoms. The diagnosis was hysterical paralysis following a pyrexial illness of unknown nature. All medical treatment was stopped, and the parents and child were assured that the weakness followed a febrile illness and that he would get well. The mother was a key element in rewarding and praising his progress toward physical recovery. A twelve-year-old girl showed a similar pattern in recovering from a gait disturbance related to a rheumatoidlike illness. Active rehabilitation, reassurance, and encouragement were also successful with a thirteen-year-old girl with gait problems and pain following a myositic or traumatic illness. The girl's anxiety and depression appeared to result from the death of her father.

In all five cases, the nonorganic nature of the gait disorder was evident from the bizarreness of the gait and the lack of objective muscle weakness. Three cases illustrate a useful diagnostic indicator of hysterical paralysis: the child is unable to raise his foot, which seems to be glued to the floor, and the effort to raise it is always accompanied by exaggerated movements and contortions of the other limbs. None of the five cases showed *la belle indifférence*—a lack of concern on the patient's part about his illness.

COMMENTARY: Dubowitz and Hersov make a significant contribution by describing the treatment methods they developed and by reviewing the literature concerning the inappropriate medical treatment of hysterical disorders. They report good success with a bicycle and treadmill in the physiotherapy program. A token economy is also mentioned as a possible form of treatment. They stress that the patient and parents must give up the "sick role" and that treatment must be instituted rapidly and not after prolonged medical treatment. Clearly, rapid intervention is indicated once the hysterical symptoms are recognized. But better yet is the prevention of such symptoms; this can be achieved by a physician who is sensitive to the need to discourage the development of a "sick role" in children who are recovering from acute illnesses while experiencing psychological stress.

SOURCE: Dubowitz, V., and Hersov, L. "Management of Children with Nonorganic (Hysterical) Disorders of Motor Function." *Developmental Medicine and Child Neurology*, 1976, *18*, 358-368.

Brief Intervention for Children with Conversion Reactions

AUTHORS: David Faigenbaum and Steven Spector

PRECIS: Reducing or eliminating physical symptoms by reducing emotional stress

INTRODUCTION: In one year at a children's hospital, the percentage of total psychological referrals was tabulated by members of the psychiatry and psychology staff. Twenty-four percent were considered conversion reactions (males 24/119 = 20 percent, females 32/113 = 28 percent). Even though this definition includes a broad range of symptoms, Faigenbaum and Spector feel that the condition is more common than previously thought. The psychology and pediatric departments worked closely in diagnosing these children. The cooperation not only between these departments but among parents, medical staff members, and patients played an integral part in therapy. The children usually presented as either indifferent to their symptoms or acutely anxious. Their parents sought a physical diagnosis, and their wish to find a physical cause made it more difficult for the staff to take a positive attitude in dealing with these children (the staff also feared a malpractice suit). The authors believe the staff's difficulties may have reinforced these patients' fears about their illness and caused them to become more frightened and confused. The children's anxieties were usually compounded by the fact that by the time of referral they had been seen at a number of hospitals, none of which had been able to render a medical diagnosis. At this hospital, the parents were given the option of sharing in the diagnostic procedure before a psychological consultation was sought. This participation enabled them to prepare for intervention for their child and helped with the therapy.

TREATMENT: The approach employed was to remove the symptom, regardless of its psychological origins. Symptoms included paralysis, blindness, back pain, dizziness, and narcolepsy. Since conversion reactions stem from many problems and the child might be acting "a sick role," the procedures used had to be fully accepted by the child's parents. They had to be aware that the treatment might be authoritarian and action-oriented. They also had to realize that the illness was not life threatening, that it was real to the child, and that there were no physical findings to explain the disease. The parents saw that reacting to the child's symptoms, and not to the cause, often added to the child's problems. By ignoring the symptoms and realizing there was no harm to the child, the parents played an active role in the child's therapy. To allow the child to perceive his illness differently, the therapist prescribed self-help, ambulatory activities (no wheelchairs), street clothes during the day, and meals in the dining room. The therapist also interviewed the patient when the child was out of bed, reassured him that there was no serious illness and that he was not "crazy," and ignored his symptoms and did not ask about them. When the parents soon understood how they were being manipulated, they often became angry with themselves. At this point the need for further outpatient psychotherapy was stressed.

COMMENTARY: This article illustrates the need for cooperation between pediatricians and psychologists in treating the conversion reactions of childhood. Once this "alliance" is established, parents and hospital personnel can focus on the child's needs. The removal of the symptoms that have served as an excuse to avoid underlying emotional problems will enable the child to function again. Continuing outpatient therapy may be indicated either for the family or for the child alone.

All too often pediatricians are reluctant to seek psychological help for their patients. We have found this to be the case on most pediatric wards. Handling children with possible conversion reactions as outpatients (while giving appropriate diagnostic tests) and making an early referral to a psychologist may be the preferred method of treatment.

SOURCE: Faigenbaum, D., and Spector, S. "Brief Intervention Techniques Applied to Children with Conversion Reactions." Paper presented at the American Psychological Association convention, San Francisco, 1977.

Visual Conversion Reactions in Children

AUTHORS: Richard T. Rada, Alex E. Krill, George G. Meyer, and Dorothy Armstrong

PRECIS: A discussion of diagnostic indicators, the importance of ophthalmologic and psychiatric follow-up, and treatment suggestions by ophthalmologists

INTRODUCTION: After studying hysterical blindness, the authors report that only 35 percent of the twenty children examined were diagnosed as having a hysterical personality. They concluded that the eyes become the target organ for expressing a variety of emotional conflicts and stress in visual conversion reactions. Since coexisting or incipient organic visual or neurological disease is possible, ophthalmic follow-up is necessary.

TREATMENT: Twenty children between the ages of seven and eighteen were seen in a university outpatient ophthalmology department and then referred to the outpatient psychiatry department. Follow-ups by the ophthalmology department occurred between three and six months after treatment and then at yearly intervals. Visual examinations included the usual ocular examination, a measurement of the central visual field at one and two meters, and a test of adaptation to the dark. (Abnormalities characteristic of hysterical amblyopia can be detected by these tests.) Psychiatric reevaluations lasted from one to one and a half hours. Often these interviews explored current conflicts and stresses. A main focus was the patient's relationships with peers, school, and siblings. In both follow-up and other psychiatric interviews, the therapeutic techniques included giving psychological support, offering specific suggestions to the patient and his family, and making interpretations of the family's dynamics.

Several cases, both improved and unimproved, are described. Typical of the six children who improved both psychiatrically and ophthalmologically was a ten-year-old girl. She had blurred vision and a loss of vision when reading closely. But watching television or engaging in sports or other activities presented no visual problems for her. Her major psychological difficulties derived from the death of her grandmother, a rivalry with the older sister, and not having a father (he died when she was very young). An analysis of the family dynamics showed that the mother's suppressed grief had prevented proper mourning and that the independent, confident older sister was an avid reader. In treatment the girl received approval from the mother for her sports interest and thereby avoided competition with the sister. The visual symptoms disappeared, and no further eye problems developed. In other cases, two girls (both having hysterical personalities) were able to discuss their specific family and personal problems during the initial psychiatric evaluation. Their visual impairment disappeared immediately, but follow-up revealed continued psychological problems. The authors report in several instances that symptoms reappeared under stress. The two children who were completely unimproved had parents who were uncooperative and who resisted accepting the idea that psychological problems were causing the visual impairment. Three cases illustrated how coexisting or incipient organic eye disease may be involved. A twelve-year-old boy with definite macular changes (central scotoma) is an example. Two characteristics of his condition were useful in increasing the suspicion of organicity: visual symptoms began while he engaged in a favorite activity (baseball), and visual problems did not interfere with academic progress in his favorite subject, German.

Stress was clearly related to the occurrence or termination of visual symptoms in these cases. When many patients realized that blurred vision indicated social and emotional stress, they learned to examine those precipitating causes. The therapist did not prescribe plain eyeglasses, because these reinforced the idea of organic disease and probably increased secondary gain.

COMMENTARY: Since a hysterical personality was not seen in the majority of these children with psychosomatic visual problems, the authors prefer the term *conversion reaction* to *hysterical amblyopia*. They believe that sophisticated ophthalmologists can handle conversion reactions by reassuring the child and parents and discussing sources of conflict. Screening for tubular central visual fields is seen as a method for identifying children currently psychologically stressed. Organic eye disease is suggested when symptoms occur during a favorite activity rather than during academic tasks. Very striking is the possible quick and efficient cessation of symptoms when stress is diminished by changing the environment or by focusing discussion on the underlying psychological or social conflicts.

SOURCE: Rada, R. T., Krill, A. E., Meyer, G. G., and Armstrong, D. "Visual Conversion Reaction in Children." *Psychosomatics,* 1973, *14,* 271-276.

Conversion Hysteria in Childhood

AUTHORS: Alayne Yates and Margaret Steward

PRECIS: An analysis of some behavioral and psychological diagnostic indicators and the role of family dynamics, accompanied by a description of specific treatment techniques used with a twelve-year-old boy with multiple conversion symptoms

INTRODUCTION: Yates and Steward briefly discuss hysteria in children. Tics, abdominal spasms, and sensory disturbances are frequently reported, and physicians continue to see cases with conversion symptoms. The twelve-year-old the authors report on had hit his helmeted head forcibly on the ground during a football game. Headaches, vomiting, irritability, insomnia, and other aches and pains ensued. The symptoms subsided with rest and intravenous fluids in the hospital. But one week after discharge he complained of leg pain and weakness and had to crawl. He also became uncoordinated, frequently fell, and had brief periods of amnesia. During two more hospitalizations he was tentatively diagnosed as having a brain tumor and a psychiatric consultant found no emotional basis for his condition. When he was hospitalized the fourth time, the doctors thought he might have multiple sclerosis, muscular dystrophy, collagen disease, or a psychiatric disorder. The authors note that his family had earlier adopted the mother's fundamentalist faith, and consequently all followed many prescribed rules such as not using cigarettes, alcohol, or certain foods and not watching television and movies.

DIAGNOSIS AND TREATMENT: He was thin, tense, fragile, and most cooperative; all examination and laboratory findings were normal except for symmetrical weakness of all extremities. While walking, he stumbled and reeled, appearing to be drunk. However, he easily climbed into bed. During psychological testing, he discussed his problems with an indifferent, unconcerned attitude. Intellectual functioning and perceptual-motor skills were above average. There were no indications of organic deficit or psychosis. He refused to answer a question on the intelligence test ("What would you do if a child smaller than you started to fight with you?"), saying that no child would do that. When asked if his little sister might fight with him, he absolutely denied it and asked for a pan to vomit in. His figure drawings were poor and had a ghostly, asexual quality, suggesting the use of denial. His responses to pictures on the Tasks of Emotional Development test very frequently concerned an adolescent boy who had a severe disease, such as leukemia, mononucleosis, vomiting, rheumatic fever, or "multiple skeerosis." Projective testing suggested poor impulse control and the need for authority to control his impulses (especially aggression). He felt dominated by rules and regulations, yet felt little ability to control himself. His desexualizing of males and females was seen as a defense against feeling feminine, and the failure to repress this led to conversion symptoms. In the hospital he was a model patient, showing no concern about the future or painful diagnostic procedures. He never became angry about late meals or other negative events. When comments were made about his improvement (like playing well in a game of catch), his symptoms immediately worsened.

Discussions and psychological interpretations with the boy and his parents together resulted in an improved gait. The father felt that outpatient psychiatric treatment was advisable, but the mother decided against it. Thereafter the symptoms were not as dramatic, but disturbing throat noises in class led to his remaining at home with his mother.

The authors consider the diagnosis of conversion hysteria to be difficult, even when emotional causation is considered at an early point. Multiple symptoms can lead to expensive, unnecessary hospitalizations and to risky medical diagnostic procedures. In this case, hysteria should have been considered earlier, in view of the generalized inhibition of anger, delayed development of sexual interests, unusual degree of compliance, general unconcern, and insignificance of the original injury. Psychological testing and observation confirmed the diagnosis of conversion hysteria, which was discussed with the family. The value of the illness to the family was not fully assessed, and the mother strongly resisted treatment. As noted, throat noises replaced the symptom of paralysis.

COMMENTARY: Yates and Steward see their case study as confirming the view that mothers of hysterical children are overprotective and fathers distant or ineffectual. Parents subtly encourage the development of symptoms. The authors provide a valuable reminder that conversion reactions must be considered immediately, before unnecessary and risky diagnostic procedures are employed (often causing secondary gain). The need for appropriate treatment of the family is clear. Parents must be counseled in terms of their contributions to the cause and maintenance of conversion symptoms. In this case individual therapy for the child was not followed through because of the mother's resistance. We believe it is essential to explain that certain parental attitudes are destructive to the child. Many parents may become amenable to treatment and change their rigid attitudes if they become aware of their detrimental effect on the child's psychological and social development.

SOURCE: Yates, A., and Steward, M. "Conversion Hysteria in Childhood: A Case Report and a Reminder." *Clinical Pediatrics,* 1976, *15,* 379-382.

Additional Readings

Brodskey, L. "Anger Provocation as a Crisis Intervention Technique." *Hospital and Community Psychiatry,* 1977, *28,* 533-536.

Brodskey describes how patients are encouraged to express repressed anger to a therapist, who allows himself to be the target in crisis and emergency situations. The author successfully used this technique with a patient with conversion hysteria. Anger provocation is recommended for cases where repression of anger causes incapacitating symptoms but not for situations where anger is the cause of disorganization.

Creer, T. L., Weinberg, E., and Molk, L. "Managing a Hospital Behavior Problem: Malingering." *Behavior Therapy and Experimental Psychiatry,* 1974, *5,* 259-262.

A ten-year-old asthmatic boy was treated for "malingering"—exaggerating symptoms in order to be hospitalized or to prolong hospitalization. Since reinforcement encourages malingering, whereas time-out in a dull environment reduces or eliminates malingering, he was removed from positive reinforcements. When hospitalized, he was given a single room, allowed no visitors other than the attending staff, given only school books, and expected to eat all meals alone in his room. Gains were maintained by simultaneously shaping appropriate classroom behavior and training the parents how and when to use the time-out procedure.

Ericksen, R. A., and Huber, H. "Elimination of Hysterical Torticollis Through the Use of a Metronome in an Operant Conditioning Paradigm." *Behavior Therapy,* 1975, *6,* 405-406.

Drugs and milieu therapy had been ineffective in relieving an adult male's tonic head position to the left, which he could not change. The condition caused pain and embarrassment. The authors, knowing that a metronome had been used by other therapists to reduce stuttering (which, like torticollis, is a spasmodic disorder of the voluntary muscles), told him to make small head movements in time with the beat of a metronome. A target on a wall was gradually moved so that he had to turn his head more and more in order to see the target. In eight sessions, he achieved complete voluntary control of his neck muscles.

Fitzgerald, B. A., and Wells, C. E. "Hallucinations as a Conversion Reaction." *Diseases of the Nervous System,* 1977, *38,* 381-383.

An adult female had visual hallucinations, which were viewed as a conversion reaction. Treatment consisted of medications, supportive psychotherapy, and bolstering the environmental supports. Conversion symptoms permit expression of a forbidden wish, self-punishment for having the wish, removal from disturbing life situations, and a new way of relating (a sick role). Fitzgerald and Wells state that hallucinations are rarely recognized as being conversion reactions, since hallucinations are often regarded as evidence of psychotic thinking.

Kallman, W. M., Hersen, M., and O'Toole, D. H. "The Use of Social Reinforcement in a Case of Conversion Reaction." *Behavior Therapy,* 1975, *6,* 411-413.

An adult male who could not walk was diagnosed as having a hysterical neurosis of the conversion type (astasia-abasia). In the hospital, standing was reinforced by social praise from a young female research assistant. Three times a day she visited the patient for ten minutes, commenting, "You're standing very well today," "I'm very proud of you," and the like. Continuous progress was made with reinforcing of walking, the use of a walker, and then walking unaided. During a second hospitalization a simple procedure with his family was used involving instructions and modeling to ensure transfer of the gains made. The family was told to ignore his complaints and to praise all positive efforts, including normal walking.

Ohno, Y., Mineyasu, S., Takeya, T., Akagi, M., Tanaka, Y., and Idemi, Y. "The Treatment of Hysterical Blindness by Behavior Therapy." *Psychosomatics,* 1974, *15,* 79-82.

Three adults with hysterical blindness were treated with operant conditioning, suggestion, and systematic desensitization. The authors state that if the original anxiety-provoking situation still exists in the patient's life, anxiety should be decreased by assertive and autogenic training, abreaction, and environmental manipulation. One man was shown slides, including slides of nude girls as reinforcers. Vision improved only slightly. But when an electric shock was administered for wrong responses to visually presented arithmetic problems, rapid success was achieved. A young woman was successfully treated with one hundred milligrams a day of Chlorpromazine, which lowered her anxiety. The suggestion was given to her that intravenous injections of ten milligrams of Diazepam would improve her vision, and improvement soon resulted. Additionally, environmental manipulation—having her change her profession—was successfully employed.

Rada, R. T., Meyer, G. G., and Kellner, R. "Visual Conversion Reaction in Children and Adults." *Journal of Nervous and Mental Disorders,* 1978, *166,* 580-587.

The authors provide some clinical findings on children and adults with visual dysfunction without organic cause, and they suggest treatments as well. They make useful and practical distinctions among visual conversion, malingering, and organic disease. Hysterical blindness was very rare in the children they saw, who (more than the adults) were often confused about feelings of being threatened by others. Two children are discussed in detail. In their cases, a concerned and understanding opthalmologist provided reassurance and talked about family conflicts. This approach is successful with many cases in which a child's visual dysfunction had begun only recently. Other treatment methods offered include operant conditioning, contingency management, and direct suggestion (while hypnotized).

Williams, D. T., and Singh, M. "Hypnosis as a Facilitating Therapeutic Adjunct in Child Psychiatry." *Journal of Child Psychiatry,* 1976, *15,* 326-342.

Hypnosis was successfully employed with a number of children having diverse problems. Notable were several children with conversion reactions, including very poor vision, possession by a spirit, an inability to walk, and impaired gait. In all cases, practical and successful hypnotic exercises were designed and taught. While in a trance, the children repeated helpful phrases. For poor vision, a child repeated statements concerning over-coming scared feelings and being able to see and engage in enjoyable activities. The common element was the repeating of phrases that suggested overcoming the problem and losing the symptoms. The statements were designed to promote self-confidence and self-control.

Author Index

343

Subject Index

A

Abandonment, and ulcerative colitis, 46, 51

Abdominal pain, recurrent: among children, 104-112; described, 104-105; and operant conditioning, 109-110; and parents, 107, 109-110; and personality, 111; and physiological changes, 111; and reinforcement, 109-110; and school, 111; secondary gains from, 105; standard treatment for, 106-108; stress factors and, 107-108, 111, 112; therapies for, 104-112

Acting out, and asthma, 249-252

Adolescents: anorexia nervosa among, 144-147, 150, 152-162, 164-165, 168, 171; asthma among, 253-257; chronic coughing among, 270-276; dermatitis among, 286, 290; enuresis among, 306-309, 315; hypertension among, 26, 29, 31, 33, 36, 38; migraine headache among, 17, 20; obesity among, 141-142; polyuria among, 319-322; seizures among, 213, 219, 222-223, 225-226, 227, 230, 233; tension headache among, 180, 181-183; tics among, 192-196, 199-200,

349